W9-AYZ-330

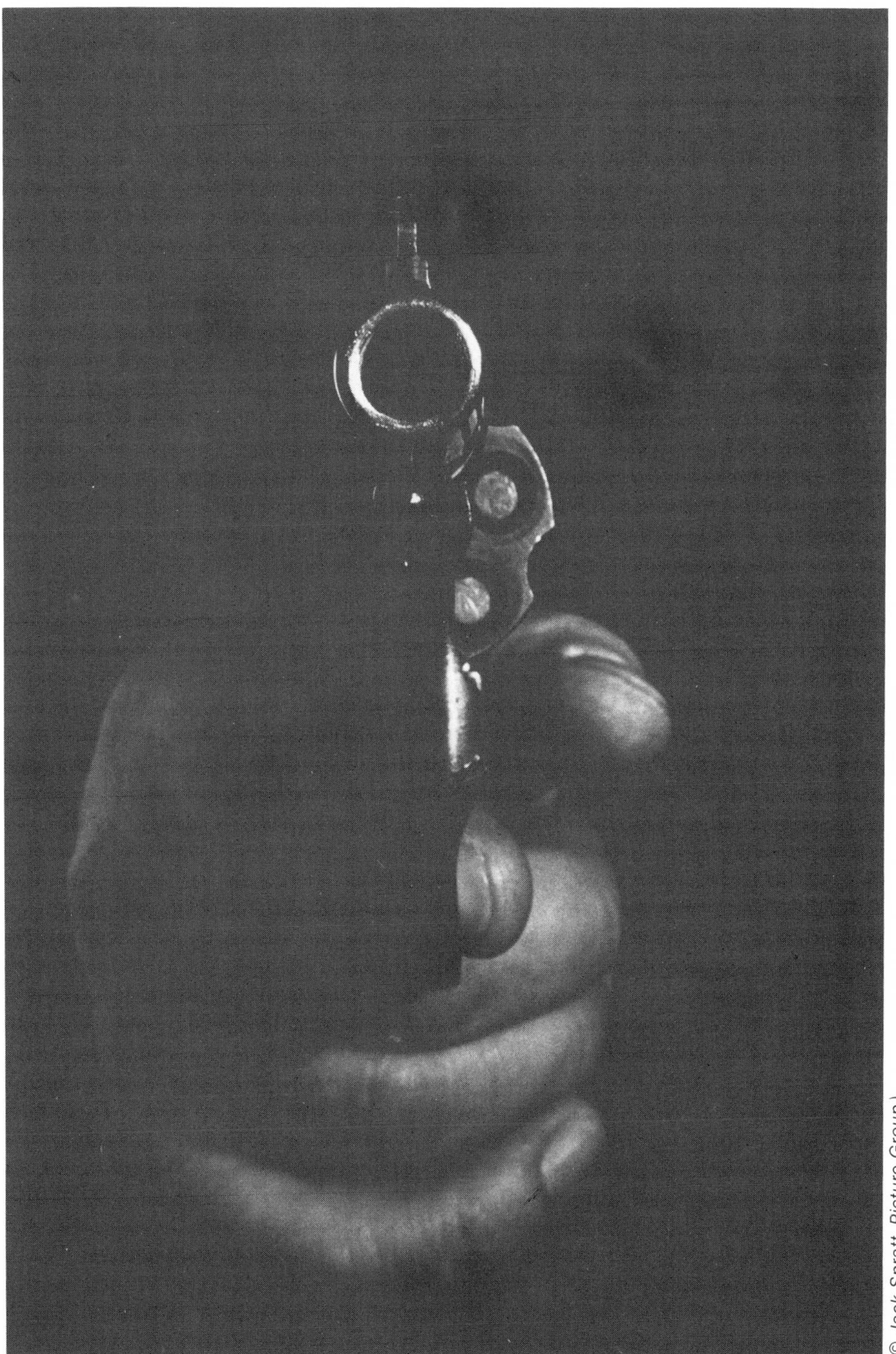

(© Jack Spratt, Picture Group.)

INTRODUCTION TO

CRIMINAL EVIDENCE

JULIAN R. HANLEY

County Judge, Retired
Wyoming County, New York

WAYNE W. SCHMIDT

Operating Director of
Americans for Effective Law Enforcement, Inc.

Former Director of the Legal Center,
International Association of Chiefs of Police

McCutchan Publishing Corporation
2526 Grove Street
Berkeley, California 94704

ISBN 0-8211-0764-X
Library of Congress Catalog Card Number 81-83252

Printed in the United States of America.

To Betty
—J.R.H.

To Jody
—W.W.S.

Preface

Law enforcement personnel of today must have a basic understanding of the current laws of criminal evidence in order to operate successfully. Problems like these face law enforcement officers every day: Can the hidden gun from a suspect's automobile be used as evidence against him? Can his subsequent confession be used as well? Evidence that satisfies the police investigator may never be allowed in court. This book will give the law enforcement officer and the student of law enforcement the rules of evidence that direct the enforcement of criminal law in its important stages of investigation and trial.

The field of criminal evidence continually changes because of new statutes and court decisions. Monday's Supreme Court ruling may affect today's burglary investigation. The investigative law enforcement officer's success in gathering evidence that is admissible in court depends on a thorough knowledge of court decisions and the rules of evidence.

The authors draw from their diverse experiences as lawyer, legal writer, appellate advocate, county prosecutor, and judge of a court of record hearing all types of criminal cases to present exact answers to criminal evidence problems. Their discussion of these problems is presented in a clear and comprehensive manner.

It is hoped that this book will help both the student of law enforcement and law enforcement personnel to better understand a critical law enforcement area—criminal evidence.

Contents

chapter **5**

Arrest and Search Warrants 77

chapter **6**

Interrogations, Confessions, and Nontestimonial Evidence 93

chapter **7**

Discovery 115

chapter 1

(© John Hanlon, Picture Group.)

BREAK IN—WHAT KINDS OF EVIDENCE WILL BE FOUND?

Introduction to Evidence

(1.1) *SCOPE OF TEXT*

Once a person is suspected of having committed a crime, how is he arrested, tried, and convicted? We are not concerned here with the court procedure from arrest to conviction, but with the legal proof that is required along the way. The only evidence that can be used is *legal* evidence, that is, proof that is allowed in court. This book is, therefore, devoted to a discussion of legal evidence.

The standards of evidence are not the same in all stages of criminal procedure. These may vary in some respects according to whether you are involved in a preliminary hearing or an actual trial. Therefore, anyone interested in the field of law enforcement must have an understanding of the rules of criminal evidence and the normal processing of a criminal case.

Legal criminal process begins with an arrest, but what proof is needed in order to make an arrest in the first place? Suppose you are a patrolman on the street. A tipster whispers to you from a dark alley that there is a heroin sale taking place in a nearby apartment. Is this sufficient evidence to justify your pounding up the stairs, breaking down the door, and arresting the supposed drug dealers? Or perhaps you stop a car for a traffic violation, and the occupants arouse your suspicion. Do you need a search warrant to open the trunk of the car? If so, what proof must you supply to a judge in order for him to issue a search warrant? In both cases, you must know the law of criminal evidence in order to answer these questions.

After the arrest, there are a number of preliminary steps that usually take place before there is a trial. The defendant must be arraigned in court with the charges explained to him, and his entry of a plea, either guilty or not guilty, must be made. There will be some type of hearing to determine probable cause to hold him. There also may be grand jury proceedings, evidence suppression hearings, and dismissal motions.

The trial begins with the questioning and selection of jurors; some are excused, some retained until a jury is finally chosen and sworn in. Next come opening statements by the attorneys, followed by the prosecution's presentation of its evidence. After the state has rested its case, the defendant puts in any evidence he may have. When all the proof is in, both counsel make closing arguments to the jury. The judge then instructs the jury on the law. The jury retires, deliberates, and then brings in its verdict.

Through all of these steps, from arrest to verdict, questions, objections, and court rulings may be made on the validity of the evidence that is offered. If the defendant is found guilty, he may appeal to a higher court. The only way this conviction will stand in the appellate court is if there was sufficient evidence against the defendant.

Evidence is anything offered to prove the truth or falsity of a fact in issue. What concerns us, concerns every court. What evidence is legal and what is not?

Arrest is one thing, conviction another. The police may have much information about a suspect—a tip from an informer, an intercepted phone call, or physical evidence from the scene of the crime. These, however, may not be admissible in court. The accused cannot be convicted by *any* proof, only by *legal* proof, that is, evidence that can be used in court.

What are the court rules that admit one kind of evidence in a criminal case but disallow another? It is not as difficult to decide this as some lawyers and judges would have you believe. The rules of criminal evidence are, in fact, exact, and it takes judgment and knowledge to apply them to any particular case. Anyone involved in law enforcement must include a knowledge of these rules among his basic working tools.

Impression of a sneaker found near scene of a safe burglary.

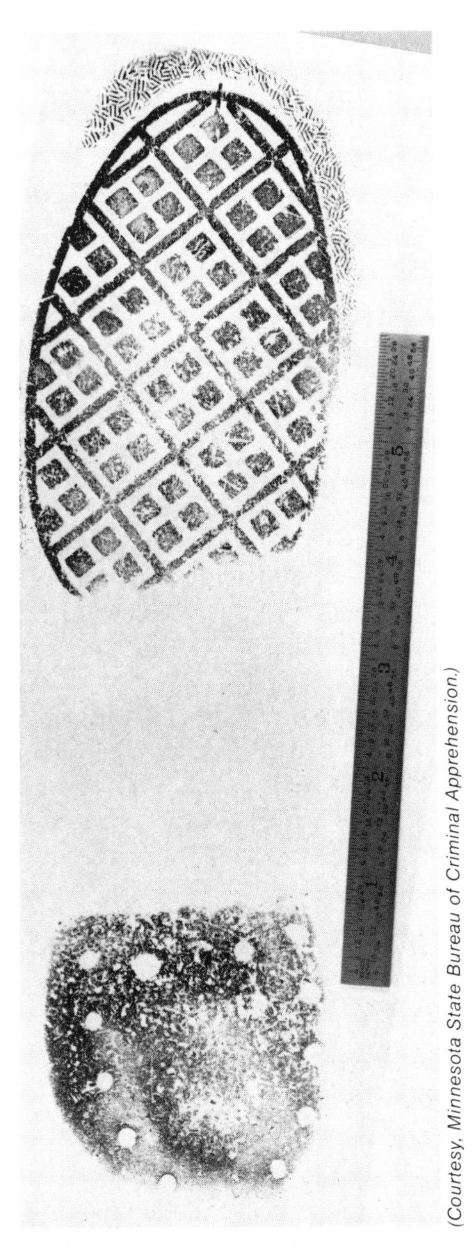

Inked impression of a sneaker owned by a suspect in a safe burglary case.

(Courtesy, Minnesota State Bureau of Criminal Apprehension.)

CIRCUMSTANTIAL EVIDENCE

(1.2) *DEFINITIONS*

"Evidence" is anything offered in court to prove the truth or falsity of a fact in issue. "Testimony" is the spoken evidence given by a witness in court. "Real evidence" refers to a tangible object or to exhibits offered in evidence, such as a murder weapon, burglar's tools, or illegal drugs involved in a crime. "Demonstrative evidence" is in the form of a model, an illustration, a chart, or an experiment offered as proof.

There are two general classes of evidence—direct and circumstantial. "Direct evidence" comes from any of the five senses of a witness and is, *in itself*, proof or disproof of a fact in issue. For example, if a witness saw and identified the murderer or heard the shooting, he would be giving direct evidence, that is, something he observed that directly proves the crime.

"Circumstantial evidence" is indirect proof showing surrounding circumstances *from which the main fact is inferred*. Typical circumstantial evidence would be a detective's description of the track of something having been dragged across the lawn at the scene of the murder or bloodstains found in the trunk of a car belonging to the husband of the victim.

"Admissibility of evidence" concerns the question of whether evidence will be allowed to be used in court. "Weight of evidence" refers to its believability. Though evidence may be technically legal and, thus, admissible in court, the question remains as to whether or not it should be given any real value or "weight."

(1.3) *DEVELOPMENT OF THE RULES OF EVIDENCE*

Every society evolves its own court system to resolve individual disputes or to settle the claim that one of the rules of the group has been broken. We classify the first (disputes between individuals) as a civil action. This type of suit usually concerns property or money. The second (violating the rules of the group) is a criminal case.

We have come a long way from settling matters by trial by combat or trial by ordeal. Neither have the English-speaking peoples adopted trial by inquisition, in which the accused himself must supply much of the proof by answering questions. In the United States we employ the adversary trial system. This plan is based on the idea that the truth will more nearly come out if it is tested by the giving of testimony in open court under the questioning and cross-questioning of opposing lawyers.

In order that everyone who is accused of a crime might receive the same treatment, the courts of England, on which our system is based, gradually developed rules defining what matters would be allowed as proof in criminal cases and how trials should proceed. Without such rules, one person's case might be tried in one way and another person's differently. Without such court-approved consistency, we could never hope to approach a system of equal justice.

The gradual development of our law of evidence traces back to early English court decisions. Even today judges will occasionally use an old English case as a guide in deciding a question of evidence. Through the years they have had to decide what proof would be received in individual court cases and what would be rejected. Many of these judicial decisions are written down and then collectively printed in book-form court reports. The federal government and every state publish their own court reports throughout the year. These reports are available to bench, bar, and public as guides to past judicial rulings.

The law ever seeks stability. Thus each court tries to follow the precedent of earlier cases within its jurisdiction that have been decided on the same issue. This adherence to legal precedent is known by the Latin phrase "stare decisis."

Another basis for legal stability is the fact that the lower courts are bound by the decisions of the higher, appellate courts in their state. If, for example, the highest court in California rules that bookmaker slips can be used as evidence in a gambling case, then every lower court in that state must do the same thing.

The body of law found in court decisions is generally referred to as being part of the "common law," as opposed to the statutes enacted by legislatures. Legislative bodies do pass laws concerning evidence, and we must often consult both sources to determine what constitutes legal evidence in our area.

Thus, the rules of evidence, whether common law or statutory, are not the same in every state: nor are they identical with those in the federal courts. The similarities, though, are much greater than the differences. In general, all American courts follow the same basic rules of criminal evidence. A detective from Chicago testifying in a murder case in Ohio would find himself very much at home.

Though we depend heavily on legal precedent, our law is not stagnant. With the passage of time, the courts themselves gradually modify, change, and sometimes overrule prior decisions. In the past fifteen years, for example, largely because of federal court decisions, there have been more changes in the American law of criminal evidence than in twice the number of years preceding. Times change, and so do the courts. For example, rules governing the use of letters and documents as evidence in court have evolved to include the use of tape recordings, moving pictures, and closed-circuit television. Just over the judicial horizon is coming the use of lie detectors and voiceprint analyzers.

We are protected by the law's slowness, but nurtured as well by its change. To know the law of evidence requires the learning of its rules of yesterday, but prudence dictates that we also anticipate its changes of tomorrow.

(1.4) *ENACTMENT OF EVIDENTIARY CODES*

Some foreign countries are code states and do not have a common-law system. From the time of Hammurabi to that of Napoleon, governments have attempted to put all their law into statute form. The strength of the system of legal codes is that all the law is in one place, the statutes. The weakness of it is its rigidity, because human affairs are never constant.

As stated, the United States combines the two systems, mixing the rigidity of the statutes with the flexibility of the common-law court decisions.

All states and the national government have statutes on the law of evidence. Some states, among them California (California Evidence Code), have complete evidentiary codes. The Congress of the United States by Public Law 93-595 (Federal Rules of Evidence, effective July 1, 1975) has also enacted a complete evidentiary code. It covers a broad spectrum from defining what evidence is relevant to the use of document and expert testimony and the method of hearing witnesses. (*See* Appendix.)

Laws affecting the use of evidence are also often found in many individual state statutes that are not included in an evidentiary code as such. They may range from a motor vehicle statute governing the use of blood-alcohol tests in traffic arrests to the use of official laboratory reports before grand juries and the use of police and business records in criminal trials.

All of the above brings us back to the same point. In order to be certain of any specific rule of criminal evidence, you must consult your area's evidentiary code, if there is one, its statutes and its court decisions on the subject.

(1.5) *BURDEN OF PROOF IN GENERAL*

There is a common saying among prosecutors that it is easy to indict but hard to convict. This is true. Before the indictment and arrest of a suspect the advantage is with the state, with its paid professional staff of investigators, its laboratory technicians, and its police and prosecutors—all supported by public funds. Once the suspect is arrested, he becomes the defendant; then the advantage is with him. His greatest advantage is that the prosecution has the entire burden of proving his guilt. The prosecution must, in fact, not only prove the defendant's guilt, but must prove it beyond a reasonable doubt. It is not necessary for the defendant to prove a thing. Unless he chooses to do so, he need not even take the stand to testify and to answer the accusation against him.

Many thoughtful people question the wisdom of this system because it so favors the defendant, but the majority feel that it is preferable to have a guilty person go free than to have an innocent person be convicted.

The roots of the idea that the prosecutor must prove everything go back to the days of the king's hangmen, the rack, and the torture chamber. Confessions were extorted by literally stretching men's bones, and the axman's block was almost a relief. Hence, the Fifth Amendment to the Constitution, which manifests our suspicion of tyrannical oppression, provides that no man may be compelled to testify against himself. Thus, the People must not only prove guilt beyond a reasonable doubt, but they must do it without taking any testimony from the defendant. In fact, the right against self-incrimination is so carefully guarded that it "forbids either comment by the prosecution on the accused's silence or instructions by the court that such silence is evidence of guilt," as was stated in *Griffin* v.*California*, 380 U.S. 609 (1965).

Certain information may, however, be obtained from a nontestifying defendant: a handwriting sample, a mental examination, or observation of the defendant in court (*21 Am Jur 2d,* Secs. 360–365).

An additional factor, adding still more to the prosecution's burden of proof, is the presumption of the defendant's innocence. From the moment he steps into the courtroom, the jury must presume he is innocent. This presumption stays with him throughout the entire trial until, and if, it is overcome by the People's proof of guilt beyond a reasonable doubt. The presumption of innocence applies to every element of the crime with which the defendant is charged. This practice is not intended to shield the guilty but rather to prevent the conviction of the innocent.

Reynolds v. *U.S.*, 238 F. 2d 460 (1956), stated: "The presumption of innocence is predicated not upon any express provision of the federal constitution, but upon ancient concepts antedating the development of the common law." Legal historians trace the idea to Deuteronomy and the laws of Sparta and Athens. In *Coffin* v. *U.S.*, 156 U.S. 432 (1894), it is said to be not so much a rule of law as a substantial right of a citizen.

In summary, the burden of criminal proof is completely on the People; the defendant is protected by the Fifth Amendment, and the trial commences with the presumption that he is innocent. The prosecution's burden, and, by extension, law enforcement's, is a heavy burden of proof indeed, and this burden never shifts.

(1.6) *PRIMA FACIE CASE*

When the prosecution rests, the defense counsel usually moves for a dismissal of the charge on the ground that the People have failed to prove a "prima facie" case. Sometimes this motion is granted.

Prima facie literally means "first view." Prima facie in a criminal case is evidence that on its surface is sufficient to prove the charge. It is not necessary that the proof be conclusive. The defense may always rebut it by contradictory or explanatory evidence, if it has any.

The prosecution has the burden of producing enough evidence that, at first view, standing alone, is sufficient beyond a reasonable doubt. For example, in a rape case, the victim might only be able to give a general description of the accused. The state then offers the testimony of a witness who saw the suspect leave the building where the rape took place, or it may have proof that a sample of the victim's hair was found on the defendant's clothing. Although the defendant may have an alibi or other defense, the state at this point has proved a prima facie case.

(1.7) *CORPUS DELICTI*

The prosecution must always prove the "corpus delicti," the fact that a crime has been committed. A jury cannot deliberate as to who committed it unless the state first proves that there has been a criminal act (*People* v. *Beltowski*, 162 P. 2d 59 [1945]; *People* v. *Battle*, 10 Cal. Rptr. 627). The jimmied store door and the blown safe inside is the corpus delicti of a burglary, that is, proof that there was a criminal act of breaking in to steal. The half-burned house with evidence of the

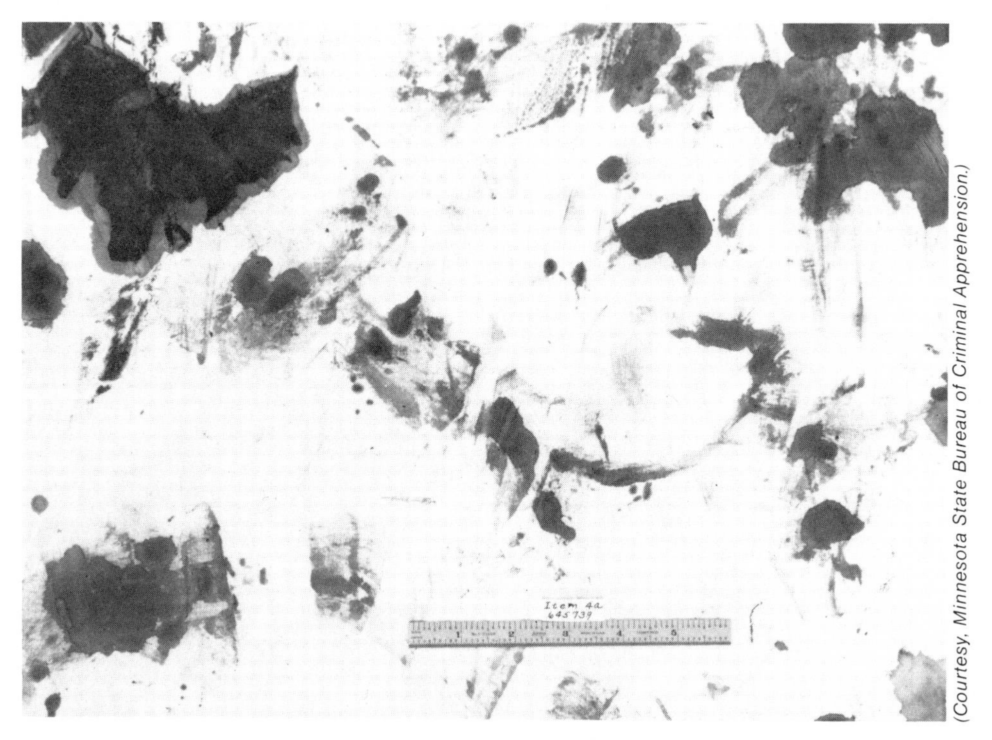

(Courtesy, Minnesota State Bureau of Criminal Apprehension.)

Portion of bedsheet found beneath homicide victim.

PROOF OF CORPUS DELICTI

gasoline used by the arsonist to start the fire would be the corpus delicti of arson.

Because the phrase "corpus delicti" literally means "body of the crime," people often mistakenly think it only refers to the body in a homicide. A popular misconception has grown up that the police cannot prove a murder unless they find the body. This is not so. Producing the corpse only proves a death, not a crime. Murder has been proven many times by circumstantial evidence of the crime even though the body was lost forever.

In the days of sailing ships, an English murder case (*Rex* v. *Hindmarsh,* 2 Leach C.C. 569) established a rule that is still followed today. There was an indictment for two counts of murder, one for killing by beating and the other for killing by drowning. The alleged crime occurred at sea. A witness testified that he was awakened at midnight by a violent noise, that on reaching the deck he saw the accused murderer pick the captain up and throw him overboard, and that the captain was not heard from again. Another witness stated that he had earlier heard the prisoner threaten to kill the captain. Near where the captain had been seen a large piece of wood was found, and the deck and part of the accused's clothing were stained with blood. The defense counsel called for an acquittal because the body was never found, arguing that the captain might have been picked up at sea by a passing ship. The court found sufficient proof of corpus delicti, however, and sent the case to the jury. The jury found the defendant guilty, and he was executed.

Years ago an English judge, in discussing the proof required for the corpus delicti, supposed a situation in which a man was seen to enter the London docks quite sober, only to come out later quite drunk, staggering from the door of a wine cellar where millions of gallons of wine were stored. "I think," said the judge, "that this would be reasonable evidence that the man had stolen some of the wine, though no proof be given that any particular vat had been broached."

Larceny can be proved without recovering the stolen jewels, kidnapping without finding the victim, England's great train robbery without the million pounds—just as long as the prosecution can prove by other evidence that a crime was committed, that is, the corpus delicti.

And so, today as yesterday, evidence proving the corpus delicti is always a part of the prosecution's burden of proof.

(1.8) *SHIFTING OF THE BURDEN OF PROOF*

Appellate courts everywhere have wrestled with the legal theory of whether or not the burden of proof ever shifts from the prosecution to the defense. What happens when the defendant offers to explain the crime in some way, such as presenting an alibi? Does the defendant also have to give proof beyond a reasonable doubt and assume all the other responsibilities that are normally those of the prosecution? Though the legal theory of shifting the burden of proof is mainly a problem to be discussed by court and counsel, men's necks have, nonetheless, often been stretched over legal points finer than this one.

The generally accepted answer to the question above is that the accused is not required to explain anything, although he may do so if he wishes. After the state has made a prima facie case of guilt, the task of showing any contrary evidence is up to the defendant. The accused must come forward with any defense he may have. Thus it is said that he has the "burden of explanation" (*State* v. *Buckley,* 133 A. 433 [1926]).

Evidence offered to explain or excuse the charge that is peculiar to the defendant's own knowledge or that is more readily available to him is always his responsibility to initiate. From that point on, courts have split on who has the burden of proof. Some authorities have ruled that when such a positive defense is raised by the defendant, the burden immediately shifts to the People, who are then required to prove the negative beyond a reasonable doubt (*People* v. *Kelly*, 302 N.Y. 512 [1951]; *People* v. *Sandgren*, 302 N.Y. 331, 334 [1951]).

A variation of this is found in N.Y. Penal Law, Sec. 2500 (2), which holds that when the defendant has offered such a defense, he must prove it by a preponderance of the evidence. The constitutionality of this contention has been questioned in some cases, among them *Stump* v. *Bennett*, 398 F. 2d III (1968), cert. den. 393 U.S. 1001; *People* v. *Balogun*, 372 N.Y. 2d 384 (Misc. 1975).

The most generally accepted rule is that once the defendant introduces this type of explanatory evidence, the burden of proof rests with the prosecution, but the jury must consider all the evidence and find guilt only if it is convinced beyond a reasonable doubt (*People* v. *Egnor,* 175 N.Y. 419 [1903]).

Another problem of burden of proof arises when the criminal charge rests on a negative. Some examples of this are a charge of operating a business without a permit or a criminal charge of carrying a pistol without a license. The state does not have to prove an absence of a permit or a license in these cases because knowledge concerning the charges rests solely within the defendant. If the defendant has such a permit or license, he can easily offer it in evidence (*29 Am Jur 2d*, Sec. 153, but see *Johnson* v. *Wright*, 509 F. 2d 828 [5th Cir. 1975]). The state is only required to prove a negative matter if it is something not peculiarly known to the accused.

(1.9) *AFFIRMATIVE DEFENSES*

In criminal cases there are a variety of explanatory defenses that the law labels "affirmative defenses." When one of these is used, the defense in effect may be saying "Yes, I do not deny the crime occurred, but I am not guilty because . . . ." The burden of proving such matters and the way they affect the state's case may vary with the nature of the defense.

a. Alibi

An alibi is evidence that the defendant was at another place at the time the crime was committed. Case law has often quibbled and squirmed about the question of whether an alibi is an affirmative defense and how much evidence is required to sustain it. Many jurisdictions now require the defense to give the state pretrial notice that an alibi defense is going to be used and may require notice of the names of the alibi witnesses and counteralibi witnesses on the other side.

The settled rule now is that the accused must take the initiative to prove alibi, but he is not held to any definite measure of proof. The ultimate burden of proving guilt still stays with the prosecution.

b. Capacity and Insanity

The law assumes that everyone has ordinary intelligence and is, therefore, capable of committing criminal acts. Though there was an old common-law provision that infants under seven were incapable of committing a crime and that those between seven and fourteen were presumed to be incapable, this has largely become obsolete as each state has enacted its own laws defining juvenile delinquents.

Since normality is presumed, the state does not have to prove it and, therefore, does not have to prove criminal capacity in general. This is simply a practical matter. If the prosecution had to prove every defendant was normal, conviction would be impossible. Hence, this is the basis for the assumption that every person has ordinary intelligence and the capacity to commit criminal acts, with the exception of certain matters involving infants that have been referred to previously.

By the same reasoning, the law also presumes that everyone is sane. In most jurisdictions insanity is considered an affirmative defense to be proven by the accused. The measure of proof required of the defendant to prove insanity can be set by statute (*People* v. *Brown,* 37 A.D. 2d 685 [1971]). Requiring the defense to prove insanity by measurable proof is constitutional because it does not actually shift the burden of proving one of the elements of the crime, there being a presumption of sanity (*Leland* v. *Oregon*, 343 U.S. 790 [1952]).

c. Statute of Limitations

In the absence of a law setting a time limit on bringing criminal charges, prosecution could be started at any time. Most jurisdictions, however, have statutes of limitations listing the time various criminal prosecutions must begin. In general, all misdemeanors and most felonies have time limits; murder usually does not.

The prosecution has the burden of showing that the crime was committed within the proper time. Some statutes state that the time limit is suspended when the defendant is out of the state. If so, the defendant must prove he was not absent all of the time, as this would be something that would be peculiarly within his knowledge.

d. Duress

Sometimes the accused claims that he was coerced or forced to commit a crime. This is the affirmative defense of duress. Suppose, for example, a banker was taken at gunpoint from his home, with his wife held there as a hostage, was driven to his bank, and was directed to remove $200,000.00 from the vault. He would have a good defense of duress were he charged with grand larceny.

Since the affirmative defense of duress does not remove any element of proof from the prosecution, the defendant has the burden of proving it. As with the proof of insanity, the measure of the defendant's proof of duress may also be set by the jurisdiction, such as in N.Y. Penal Law, Sec. 25 (2), 40.00.

e. Entrapment

Entrapment is inducing a person to commit a crime that he would not otherwise have committed. It is recognized everywhere as an affirmative defense. Entrapment, like duress, does not negate any essential element of the state's proof. It is an affirmative defense, and statutes may define the amount of proof required.

People v. *Laietta*, 30 N.Y. 2d 68, (1972), cert. den. 407 U.S. 923, illustrates the burden of proof required in an entrapment case. Laietta was charged with attempting to extort money from a businessman named Friedman. The police "wired" Friedman and tape recorded Laietta threatening him by saying "We're not threatening you [but] look, you are going to get hurt if you don't pay. This idiot called some Ginzo in—Italian families are closely knit." Laietta claimed entrapment saying that Friedman was actually an agent of the police and had induced him to commit the crime.

A New York statute made entrapment a defense to be proven by a preponderance of the evidence. The trial was held on this theory, and Laietta was convicted. The appellate courts sustained the conviction, holding that entrapment was an affirmative defense, and the defendant could be required to prove it, since this did not in any way lessen the People's burden of proving its own case beyond a reasonable doubt.

The well-known FBI Abscam bribery investigation of various congressmen involved undercover FBI men whose bribe offers to various officials were recorded on videotape and resulted in bribery prosecutions. The defendants all claimed entrapment. There were differing rulings on this subject at the trial level, and the whole matter is yet to be resolved by appeals to the Supreme Court of the United States. (*U.S.* v. *Jannotti*, 501 F. Supp. 1182 [U.S.D.C.-E. Pa. 11/26/80].)

f. Miscellaneous Defenses

There are other affirmative defenses that the defendant must raise and prove if he is going to use them. Among them are a claim of double jeopardy (being tried more than once for the same crime); immunity from prosecution granted by a prior court in return for testimony incriminating another defendant; consent of the victim; and self-defense.

In many cases, statutes (for example, N.Y. Penal Law, Secs. 150.05–150.10, 190.15, 155.15) define other affirmative defenses, such as the claim in an arson case that a fire was set for a legal purpose; in the defense in a bad check case that the loss was paid back in a specified time; or in a larceny case that the property was appropriated under a good faith claim of right. This type of defense also does not shift the burden of proof in any way, and the People must still prove a prima facie case beyond a reasonable doubt.

(1.10) *THE BURDEN OF GOING FORWARD*

When courts are concerned with the technical problems involved in the burden of proof, they are careful to distinguish between the burden of going forward—introducing the proof of the explanatory defense—and the burden of proving such a defense.

In all cases of positive defense, where the crime is not denied but the defendant offers proof to explain or justify himself, the courts are unanimous in saying that such a defendant has "the burden of going forward." That is, the defendant, not the state, first has to introduce the evidence of avoidance of guilt. If it is an accepted affirmative defense, the defendant may be required to prove it by a preponderance of the evidence. The courts insist, however, that in the end the burden of the proof of guilt, regardless of the type of positive defense, never shifts from the state. The state must still prove guilt beyond a reasonable doubt.

(1.11) *PROOF BEYOND A REASONABLE DOUBT*

In a civil case, such as a suit for money or property, all that is required of the plaintiff is that he prove his case by a "fair preponderance of the evidence," enough simply to tip the scales of justice. But in a criminal trial, as we have emphasized, much more evidence is needed, since proof of guilt must be beyond a reasonable doubt.

This ancient precept of English justice, which applies to everyone accused of a criminal act, means exactly what it says: a doubt based on reason and arising out of all the evidence or the lack of it. A reasonable doubt is not just any doubt that a person might have. It is a doubt to which one can assign a reason. The prosecution is not, of course, required to prove guilt to a mathematical certainty. If that were so, it would be useless to prosecute anyone. It is possible, however, to prove guilt to a reasonable certainty, and the People are held to that standard only. This, then, is the measure of evidence that law enforcement personnel must gather and produce in legal form in order to convict a suspect—proof beyond a reasonable doubt.

(1.12) *STIPULATIONS*

An entirely different way of admitting proof is by stipulation, that is, agreement of the attorneys. Opposing lawyers sometimes agree to let certain evidence by used. Evidentiary matters can then be settled by a stipulation in open court by both the prosecution and the defense. They may stipulate, for example, that a certain state of facts exists or that if a named witness were called he would testify in a certain manner. A counsel will occasionally stipulate that something be introduced as evidence that the court would ordinarily reject; polygraph test results are sometimes used in this way. Usually, however, stipulations as to evidence are employed by counsel for noncontroversial matters, and they are made to expedite the trial of cases.

(1.13) *SUMMARY*

Much that the police gather as "evidence" cannot legally be used in court. It is necessary, therefore, that every law enforcement officer have a basic knowledge of the law of criminal evidence.

Evidence is any matter offered in court to prove the truth or falsity of a fact in issue. There are two general classes of evidence—direct and circumstantial. Direct evidence is proof from a witness's five senses that in itself is proof of the fact in issue. Circumstantial evidence is indirect proof from which one can logically infer the ultimate facts in issue.

There are two sources of the law of evidence. One is the common law, which is based on past court decisions. The other is found in individual statutes or in evidentiary codes. Both must be consulted in order to learn the laws in any one jurisdiction. Though the law of evidence varies from state to state, the basic rules are the same in all of our courts.

The defendant in every criminal case is presumed to be innocent. Because the accused is protected by the Fifth Amendment, he cannot be made to testify, and he is not required to prove anything. The prosecution must overcome this presumption of innocence by proving the guilt of the defendant beyond reasonable doubt.

The state initially attempts to prove a prima facie case, that is, proof of guilt "at first view." It has the burden in every criminal trial of proving the corpus delicti—the fact that a crime was committed. If some affirmative defense is to be used, such as insanity, alibi, or duress, the accused must introduce this proof. Even if the accused employs an affirmative defense, however, it is generally accepted that the state must still prove guilt beyond a reasonable doubt. This burden, in fact, never shifts.

chapter 2

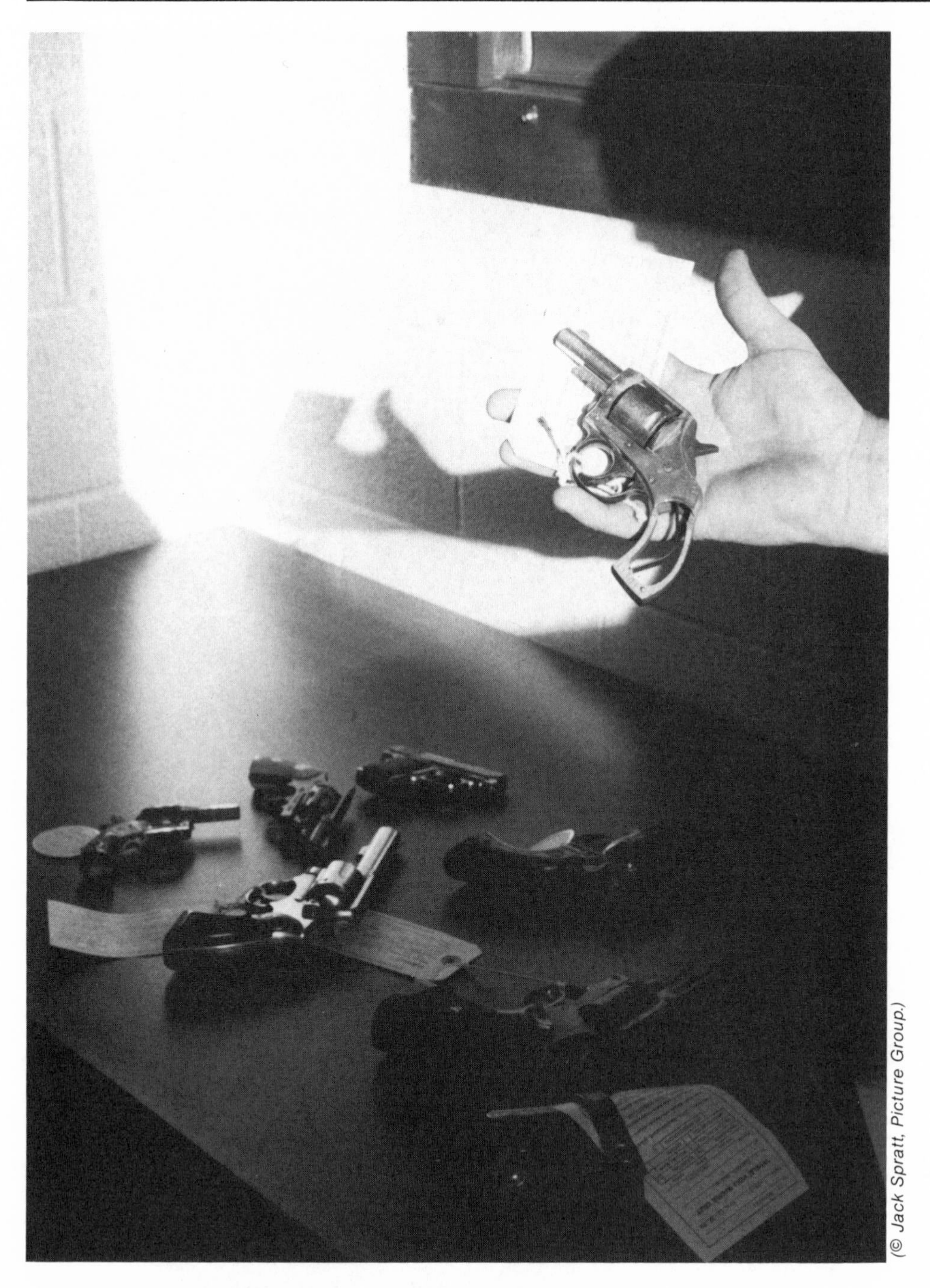

(© Jack Spratt, Picture Group.)

CONFISCATED WEAPONS—BUT ARE THEY ADMISSIBLE?

Admissibility of Evidence

(2.1) *GENERAL RULES*

Evidence has no practical value unless it can be used in court. First, it must be "relevant" to the issues, and then it must pass a variety of other tests in order to be admitted in evidence.

(2.2) *RELEVANCE AND MATERIALITY*

Many a legal hair has been split by judges, attorneys, and authors in an attempt to decide whether an item of evidence was "relevant" or "material." The difference can be disregarded. The test is, does the evidence tend to prove guilt or innocence of the accused? If it does, it passes the first test of admissibility—materiality. There is no legal definition of what relevant evidence is. It rests on common sense. When proof is offered and an objection raised, the trial judge must decide its relevancy.

(2.3) *EXCLUSION OF RELEVANT EVIDENCE*

Relevant evidence may be excluded, however, for other reasons. The judge may keep out proof that he feels might lead to prejudice, hostility, or undue surprise. Uncommonly gory police photographs are often not admitted as evidence because they might influence the jury excessively. Otherwise relevant evidence will sometimes be kept out simply because it is cumulative. If a matter has been proven once, it need not be proven a second, third, or fourth time.

Generally, no evidence will be excluded unless one side makes an objection. Opposing counsel must take the initiative in excluding evidence. If he makes no objection, he waives the rule and any evidence may be used.

There are a variety of rules that may bar evidence that is otherwise material. This means that the law of evidence is largely a study of these rules of exclusion.

(2.4) *EVIDENCE OF OTHER CRIMES*

At this point we are not dealing with the use of evidence of other crimes to discredit a witness or as rebuttal evidence. What happens when the prosecution offers proof of other crimes committed by the defendant as direct proof of guilt in the present situation? Great caution must be exercised when this type of evidence is allowed, since the commission of one crime is not proof that an individual would commit a second. Thus, evidence of other crimes is objectionable, not because it has no probative value, but because it has too much. "The natural tendency of the tribunal . . . is to give excessive weight to the vicious record of crime thus exhibited and either to allow it to bear too stongly on the present charge or to take the proof of it as justifying a condemnation, irrespective of the guilt of the present charge" (*Wigmore on Evidence,* v. 2, Sec. 193). Even a habitual criminal may well be innocent of the crime with which he is charged (*State* v. *Rand*, 238 Iowa 250 [1947]).

In non-English-speaking countries, the entire past criminal record of the accused is an important part of the prosecutor's case. So it was in England before 1680. Eventually the English changed this and barred the use of such proof by the crown. In 1692 there was an English murder case known as Harrison's Trial, *12 How. St. Tr.* 833, in which a witness for the crown was asked about a felony committed by the accused three years before. The judge stopped the testimony, saying: "Hold, hold. What are you doing now? Are you going to arraign his whole life? How can he defense himself against charges of which he has no notice? And how many issues are to be raised to perplex me and the jury? Away! Away! That ought not to be: that is nothing to the matter."

Like so much of the law of evidence, this rule of exclusion is subject to several exceptions. Three hundred years after the judge's cry of

"Away! Away!" in Harrison's trial, New York's highest court had to deal with the same problem. In so doing, it enumerated and explained the exceptions that do allow the state to include additional crimes as part of its case.

The case in New York was concerned with a society murder that was a sensation in its day. On December 24, 1898, Henry Cornish received a package in the mail containing a blue bottle labeled "Bromo Seltzer®." Thinking it a Christmas gift, he passed it on to one of the women of the household. A day or two later he saw another one of the women (Mrs. Adams) in the kitchen with her head resting on her hands, suffering from a headache. At his suggestion she took some of the medicine from the blue bottle to alleviate the pain. When she complained about the taste, Cornish took some of the medicine, saying "Why that stuff is all right." Mrs. Adams started for the kitchen and collapsed. Her face turned blue, and she was dead before the doctor arrived. Meanwhile, Cornish had become ill and, after visiting the police, left for the Knickerbocker Athletic Club, "the journey being marked by frequent interruptions necessitated by the condition of his stomach and bowels."

The "Bromo Seltzer" was found to contain cyanide of mercury. Molineaux, an athletic director of the Knickerbocker Athletic Club, had had a dispute with Cornish, had sent him the bottle of poison, and was thus tried for Mrs. Adams's murder. The prosecutor was not content simply to prove the murder at hand, although he had ample evidence, including proof of Molineaux's handwriting on the package. The state proved, in addition, all the details of a prior murder, claiming that Molineaux had once poisoned a man named Barnet by mailing him a packet of "Kutnow" powder containing cyanide of mercury. It seems that Molineaux was jealous of Barnet's attentions to the woman with whom the defendant was in love.

The court explained the rule on this type of additional criminal proof: "Evidence of other crimes is competent to prove this specific crime charged when it tends to establish (1) motive (2) intent (3) the absence of mistake or accident (4) a common scheme or plan . . . (5) the identity [of the accused] . . . ." The court thus reversed Molineaux's first-degree murder conviction, pointing out that proof of the Barnet murder did not come within any of the exceptions that would allow evidence of one crime to prove another (*People* v. *Molineaux,* 168 N.Y. 264 [1901]).

Though the Molineaux trial occurred many years ago, its rule still applies today. The five exceptions allowing evidence of additional crimes as proof of the crime charged are detailed below.

a. Motive

When motive is an issue, evidence of other of the defendant's acts is admissible, if the acts are not too remote. Proof that a police officer charged with bribery had previously received hush money from other houses of prostitution has been allowed. In cases of adultery, statutory rape, or incest, sexual acts subsequent to the act charged are relevant to show a lascivious disposition on the part of the accused. In cases involving assault, previous similar acts of the defendant against the victim are allowed as proof of motive. In cases concerned with gambling, previous possession of betting slips or proof of prior gambling convictions is allowable. Examples of actual cases include *People* v. *Duffy,* 212 N.Y. 57 (1914); *People* v. *Thompson,* 212 N.Y. 249 (1914); *People* v. *Thau*, 219 N.Y. 39 (1916); *People* v. *Goldstein*, 295 N.Y. 61 (1945); *People* v. *Formato,* 286 A.D. 357, affd. 309 N.Y. 979 (1956).

b. Intent

Motive and intent are often thought of as being the same, but there is a clear legal distinction between them. Motive is the moving power, the reason for doing something. Intent is the mental purpose to do a specific thing to bring about such a result. The jealous husband may well have had a good reason (motive) to kill his wife's lover but probably did not have the intent to kill him, since he stated: "I only meant to scare him away. The gun went off by accident."

Sometimes guilty knowledge as bearing on intent may be proven separately, often by evidence of other crimes. For example, in a homicide case, the state would be allowed to prove that the defendant stole a pistol the day before the killing and used it in the crime (*Stone* v. *State*, 210 Miss. 218 [1950]). Other illustrations might include proof of previous occasions of passing counterfeit money to show this was an intentional act in the present case; earlier receipt of stolen property as evidence of a similar present offense; prior offenses of forgery as proof of possessing forged checks; former fraudulent thefts to demonstrate larceny by false pretenses.

c. Absence of Mistake

Where guilty knowledge is an issue, evidence of other offenses by the accused can properly be used to show that his act was not done by mistake. Illustrations used previously allowing evidence of other crimes to prove intent apply equally here.

d. Common Scheme or Plan

Evidence of other crimes is admissible when it is closely connected with the crime charged and tends to prove a common scheme. It is relevant, however, only if it is offered as circumstantial proof of the present charge. Often one crime may be closely connected with another so that proof of crimes A and B can be introduced as good evidence of crime C. Proof of a series of treatments might be offered to show one event of practicing medicine without a license. Mail fraud or embezzlement cases might involve evidence of a series of these acts to establish the one being charged.

e. Identity

Frequently evidence of other crimes is used to prove the defendant's identity. This can only be done, however, where identity is an issue in the case. There must be a connection between the two offenses to show that whoever committed the first crime also committed the second (*People* v. *Mazza,* 135 C.A. 2d 587 [1955]). This connection can usually be made where an unusual method (modus operandi) was used. If the same method was employed in both crimes, proof of the earlier one would be allowed as tending to identify the accused as the guilty party in the present offense.

In a federal fraud case, one Fernandez was charged with defrauding a bank with a supposed timber sale that was part of a swindle. The bank received telephone calls about the timber deal from a man calling himself Belcher and from a timber cruiser supposedly named Rotschy. The government claimed that Fernandez made all these calls. A bookkeeper who had formerly worked for Fernandez was allowed to testify that on various occasions, not connected with this case, Fernandez made other telephone calls in which he misrepresented himself. One of the counts of the indictment in the crime being charged against Fernandez involved a forged deed. The bookkeeper told how Fernandez had used the duplicating machine and cellophane tape to add unauthorized signatures to other papers.

The court approved the use of all of this testimony as showing a particular modus operandi. It ruled that this was circumstantial proof that Fernandez was the guilty person in this case, even though the testimony involved proof of other crimes (*Fernandez* v. *U.S.,* 329 F. 2d 899 [1964], cert. den., 379 U.S. 832).

f. Use of Confessions Involving Other Crimes

An entirely different problem arises when the accused makes a confession in which he also admits to other crimes. The police are not going to stop his recital since it could be very useful. But what happens at the trial when the prosecutor attempts to offer this confession in evidence?

If possible the confession will be redacted (a legal term for edited) to remove any mention of other crimes. Should a confession containing references of other crimes be admitted in evidence over objection without being redacted, any conviction is apt to be set aside on appeal.

A murder case in Washington, D.C., involved just such a situation. Davis was found murdered in the hallway of a tourist home, having been shot in the chest. A witness had seen a man wearing dark trousers and a blue jacket with gold buttons near the premises. A detective noticed the similarity of dress on a man named Wiggins, who had been arrested later on another charge. He interrogated Wiggins at the station house, later in an unmarked police car, and in various locations around the city, asking him about the Davis murder. When they were riding in the police car, Wiggins began to talk. At the murder trial the officer testified about this conversation:

> "I don't know what you are going to think, but I killed Frank, and I don't know what you are going to think, but I killed Davis." He continued to talk and he told me there was a contract out for Davis' life and that he took it . . . that killing Davis didn't bother him but the fact that . . . he was looking at Davis face to face when he shot him bothered him . . . the contract was worth fifteen hundred dollars. He got five hundred dollars and was supposed to get the other one thousand. He mentioned that this wasn't the first time he had killed someone. He had killed three other people. He looked at me and said "You want to know their names don't you?" and I said "No." Then he stated "Well I'm not crazy. I kill only on contract."

The appeals court, noting the prejudicial effect of allowing proof of the other killings, pointed out that this material could have been excised without impairing the confession. Wiggins's murder conviction was reversed, and the case was sent back for retrial (*U.S.* v. *Wiggins,* 509 F. 2d 454 [1975]).

The law enforcement officer should always keep the Wiggins case in mind. If a suspect's confession includes references to other crimes he has committed, be sure that if the confession is put in writing, the additional crimes are included in one paragraph. That portion can then be omitted when the defendant comes to trial.

g. Confessions of Codefendants

There is an additional problem involving the use of confessions. When there are codefendants, the confession of one may implicate the other. But confessions can only be used to incriminate the person who has made the confession and not his accomplice.

If A and B are tried jointly, and the prosecution uses A's confession, which implicates both, B has no chance to defend himself against the accusation unless A testifies. If A does take the stand, then B's lawyer can cross-examine him concerning the matter that was in the confession. There is, however, no guarantee in most cases that A will testify in his own behalf. Therefore, unless the references to B can be omitted from A's confession, there will have to be separate trials for each defendant in order that the court can be certain that A's confession will be used only against A. At B's trial, A's confession could not, of course, be used (*Bruton* v. *U.S.*, 391 U.S. 123 [1968]).

(2.5) *WEIGHT OF EVIDENCE*

During the course of a trial an objection may be made regarding the "weight of evidence," as opposed to its admissibility. For example, in a case of drunk driving, the defense might object to the acceptability of the blood-alcohol test as evidence because the blood sample was kept in the arresting officer's home overnight. The defense might claim that the sample was contaminated. A judge could well admit the test results in evidence for whatever they might be worth, holding that the irregular custody did not preclude the legal admissibility but could only affect the "weight of the evidence," that is, its accuracy and believability.

Though courts and attorneys sometimes confuse the two terms, as long as evidence is legally admissible, it should be allowed for whatever value or weight the jury might assign to it.

(2.6) *CIRCUMSTANTIAL EVIDENCE*

Circumstantial evidence is indirect proof of a fact. For example, the defendant's fingerprints found on the murder weapon would be circumstantial evidence that he had used it. Bloodstains from the trunk of a murder suspect's car and the sudden wealth of a bank officer suspected of a computer theft are other examples of circumstantial evidence. None of these is direct proof of a crime, but each provides strong circumstantial proof of guilt.

There is a popular misconception that circumstantial evidence should not be believed. All courts, in fact, carefully circumscribe its use. First of all, it cannot be too remote, and it must be logical and not mere conjecture. Circumstantial evidence cannot be used to draw "an inference from an inference," and it must be "clear and convincing." Accepted with these limitations, circumstantial evidence is often the most convincing type of proof there is.

We commonly use circumstantial evidence in our daily lives. Suppose, for example, Mother goes into the kitchen and finds Junior with crumbs on his face and the lid off the cookie jar. Junior, perceiving the danger, says, "I didn't do anything!" Whom is she going to believe—Junior or the circumstantial evidence? The evidence in our cookie case can be classified like that of any crime. If the mother were called on to testify, her recitation about the cookie crumbs would be direct evidence that her son had a dirty face, but it would be circumstantial evidence that he had taken the cookies from the jar and had eaten them.

Usually the only way to demonstrate a state of mind, intent, motive, or malice is by circumstantial evidence. Intoxication normally falls into this category since the proof may largely be a description of the individual's unsteady walk, slurred speech, or erratic driving.

It is plain, then, that both kinds of evidence—direct and circumstantial—are acceptable in court. There is no reason for anyone to refuse to accept circumstantial evidence in a criminal case as long as there are proper instructions from the court concerning its use.

(2.7) *GENERAL PRESUMPTIONS*

What if the prosecutor had to prove that the judge was qualified and was legally elected or appointed, that the criminal statute involved had been properly passed by the legislature and signed by the governor, and that every defendant was sane? If the state were required to do all this, it might never get around to proving the crime itself. But all this and much more are eliminated by a variety of presumptions applicable to criminal cases. Some are presumptions of law and others of fact, but both materially affect the burden of proof.

Legal scholars argue whether something from which a jury can draw a conclusion is a "presumption" or an "inference." Though the modern trend is to use the latter term, the legal result is largely the same regardless of which is used.

Some presumptions are said to be "conclusive" and others "rebuttable." Strictly speaking, there cannot be a "conclusive presumption" in the sense that an opponent is precluded from showing any evidence to rebut it. A conclusive presumption is usually a rule of law. Examples might include the presumption that a child under a stated age cannot commit a felony or that a boy under fourteen is incapable of rape (*Wigmore on Evidence*, v. 9, Sec. 2492; *Farnsworth* v. *Hazlett*, 197 Iowa 1367 [1924]). It must be remembered that in the jurisdictions that have these rules, they are actually laws. You cannot rebut them, and you must accept them.

Several classes of genuine presumptions are recognized everywhere. They are discussed below.

a. Presumptions of Fact and Law

These presumptions are generally regarded as being the same as an inference. To be legally valid, however, there must be a reasonable connection between the fact proven and the ultimate conclusion inferred from it. The inference must flow naturally and logically from it. Otherwise the presumption will be ruled unconstitutional because it lacks due process of law. There have been a number of court decisions on this precise point.

One of the earliest landmark cases in the U.S. was *Yee Hem* v. *U.S.*, 268 U.S. 178 (1925). The federal law stated that illegal possession of opium gave rise to the presumption that it had been unlawfully imported. The court held that the statutory presumption was logical and therefore valid on the ground that it was highly improbable that there could be a legitimate possession of opium outside the medical field. Thus, any possessor must know that the opium was illegally imported.

In 1969 the same court had to deal with a federal marijuana charge against Timothy Leary (*Timothy Leary* v. *U.S.*, 395 U.S. 6 [1969]). Customs agents found marijuana in Leary's car when he tried to cross from Mexico on the international bridge. The drug was on the person of his teenage daughter. A federal statute authorized a jury to infer from a defendant's possession of marijuana that it was illegally imported. The courts struck down this statute as unconstitutional, saying that since marijuana is grown in this country, there is no logical basis for stating that because a person has it he must "know" that it was imported.

The Supreme Court met the problem again in a case involving heroin and cocaine (*Turner* v. *U.S.*, 396 U.S. 398 [1970]). Turner and two other men were stopped by federal agents in New Jersey just as their car emerged from the Lincoln Tunnel. The agents saw Turner throw a package on top of a wall. It proved to be a foil-wrapped package of 1.468 gram mixture of cocaine. Under the car seat they discovered a tinfoil package of heroin. At the trial the government introduced both packages in evidence but gave no other proof of where they came from.

A similar federal statute was involved. It stated that the possession of heroin and cocaine created a presumption that the possessor knew that the drugs were illegally imported. The court upheld the presumption concerning heroin, since it is not produced in this country, but struck down the law making the same presumption regarding cocaine. Because cocaine is manufactured here, a possessor cannot "know" that the drug was illegally imported.

The courts must also deal with problems concerning presumption in areas other than drugs. An example was a federal statute involving the possession of a gun or ammunition by any person who had been convicted of a crime of violence or who was a fugitive from justice. It stated that if such an individual were found in possession of a gun or ammunition, he could be presumed to have transported it in violation of the federal law governing interstate shipment of firearms. The decision was that there was no reasonable inference between such possession and illegal interstate transportation of guns. The statutory presumption was thus held to be unconstitutional (*Tot* v. *U.S.,* 319 U.S. 463 [1943]).

The state of Washington passed what might be considered a very convenient statute. It stated that, if a defendant charged with a violent crime is armed with an unlicensed weapon, it is prima facie proof of his intent to commit such a crime of violence. A defendant named Odom left the state employment office, returned with a .44 caliber magnum (unlicensed), and shot the supervisor twice, leaving him permanently paralyzed. The appellate court, in reversing Odom's conviction, pointed out that a presumption created by statute must follow beyond a reasonable doubt from the first fact. You cannot conclude that because a man has an unlicensed weapon he intends to do violence with it. The statute therefore lacked constitutional due process of law (*State* v. *Odom,* Wash. 519 P. 2d 152 [1974]).

b. Presumption of Innocence

The presumption of innocence (discussed in chapter 1) is perhaps the best-known presumption in English criminal law. Here, the jury must assume that the accused is innocent from the moment he enters the courtroom. This presumption stays with him through the entire trial and remains until, and only if, the prosecution overcomes the presumption by proof of guilt beyond a reasonable doubt. This presumption is surely the strongest we have that favors the defendant.

c. Presumption of Intent

Intent is a material element that the prosecution must prove in the majority of criminal cases. Did the youth really intend to steal the car, or did he simply take a joyride? When the janitor picked up the wallet from the washstand shelf in the airport men's room, did he intend to steal it, or are we to believe his story that he was going to turn it in at the airline desk? Intent is a mental operation. One cannot open a person's head, look inside, and determine his intentions. The law must, therefore, give the prosecution some practical assistance if it is ever going to get a conviction.

The law provides this assistance in the form of a well-recognized presumption: a person is presumed to intend the logical consequences of his act. His intent may be inferred from what he does. If a man points a gun he knows to be loaded at you and pulls the trigger, the law presumes that he intended to shoot you. Either by statute or by general rule, every person is presumed to intend the natural and probable consequences of his voluntary acts (*31-A, C.J.S.,* "Evidence," Sec. 15, p. 243). This presumption is rebuttable (*Sandstrom* v. *Montana,* 442 U.S. 510 [1979]).

d. Knowledge of the Law

A general belief exists that everyone "is presumed to know the law." A more accurate way of putting it is that an accused may not claim ignorance of the law as a defense in order to escape punishment.

A common illustration of this concerns possession of a gun. A man from a state where a license is not required may drive into one where it is. He has a pistol on the seat of his car, which is perfectly legal in his home state but is a serious crime in the new state. Even though he was completely ignorant of the requirement of a special license, this is no defense.

e. Failure to Testify

There is no presumption against an accused who fails to take the stand in his own defense. He is protected by the Fifth Amendment, and the Constitution "forbids either comment by the prosecution on the accused's silence or instructions by the court that such silence is evidence of guilt" (*Griffin* v.*California,* 380 U.S. 609 [1965]). On the contrary, where the defendant does take the stand (except in some limited situations such as pretrial hearings), he waives this constitutional privilege and may be completely cross-examined on any pertinent matter, the same as any other witness.

f. Nonproduction of Evidence

It may be inferred from the unexplained failure of a defendant to call an available witness who has a particular knowledge or to produce evidence within his control that the evidence would be unfavorable to the accused. There are, however, at least three conditions under which this inference will not be made: if the witness is equally available to both sides; if the witness has been subpoenaed, but fails to appear; or if the witness is hostile.

Even when the above conditions are met, the courts are cautious in allowing the inference and may give a narrow interpretation as to whether the witness is "available" or "under the control" of the party or whether he actually has a "particular knowledge" of the facts.

g. Character or Reputation

In criminal cases "character evidence" is a recognized and often effective defense. The most widely accepted view, however, is that there is no presumption one way or another as to whether the accused is of good or bad character (*Greer* v.*U.S.,* 245 U.S. 559 [1918]).

Some jurisdictions do maintain that there is a presumption of good character. Whether the court rules that there is or is not such a presumption, the practical result at the trial is the same. First of all, the phrase *character evidence* is a misnomer. The prosecution cannot prove that the accused is a nasty character by demonstrating that he pulled wings off butterflies when he was a child and now runs nefarious errands for the Mafia. Neither can the defense show what a good character he is by having his minister testify that he goes to church every Sunday, gives generously to the United Fund, and is fond of dogs and little children.

Character evidence is, actually, the rankest kind of hearsay. It reflects the reputation one has in his community, and it depends on the reputation for truthfulness of the person who is testifying.

Should the defense offer evidence of good character, the state may, in rebuttal, offer evidence of bad character if it has any (*People* v. *Lingley*, 207 N.Y. 396 [1913]).

(2.8) *OFFICIAL PRESUMPTIONS*

There are many official presumptions. They presume that official acts were performed properly, and they are rebuttable.

a. Legality of Proceedings

It is presumed that all past legal proceedings have been legally and properly carried out. The rule applies to courts, commissions, and all other legal bodies (60 A.L.R. 2d 780; *Permian Basin Area Rate Cases*, 390 U.S. 747 [1968]).

A court hearing a criminal case is presumed to have been regularly constituted and to have jurisdiction over the defendant concerning the crime for which he is being tried. It is also presumed that the court's records and its warrants are correct (*People* v. *Wissenfeld,* 169 C.A. 2d 59 [1959]).

An even wider application is involved where the accused claims a conviction or court judgment was unconstitutional under either the state or federal Constitution. Here, too, it is presumed that the judicial proceeding was constitutional. The objector has the burden of overcoming this presumption.

b. Acts of Officers and Officials

Similarly the acts of officers and officials in the performance of their duties are presumed to have been done legally and within the realm of their authority (*Vitelli* v. *U.S.,* 250 U.S. 355 [1919]). Unless there is proof to the contrary, the acts of officers making court-authorized searches and seizures or in executing warrants are presumably legal. The same is true of arrests.

This presumption of official legality applies to all officers and agents of the government. Included among them are the governor who forwards extradition papers, the postman who mails the requisition, the sheriff who serves the governor's warrant, the district attorney who conducts the hearing, and the officers who return the wanted man to the state demanding him.

c. Legislative Acts

All laws, ordinances, and other legislative acts are presumed to have been validly adopted. Were this not so, the prosecution would have the ridiculous burden of proving the validity of every law involved in every criminal case, from the murder statute down to the evidentiary code. Thus, all federal, state, and local laws are presumed to be valid and binding.

d. Foreign Laws

In some criminal cases, the law of a sister state or a foreign nation is involved. Proof can always be presented by testimony from a legal expert knowledgeable in the field or by the introduction of reference material. If such proof is absent, the court may presume that the foreign law involved is the same as that of the local jurisdiction. In some situations, however, the court may take official notice of what the foreign law may be.

(2.9) *PRESUMPTIONS CONCERNING PARTICULAR ACTS*

Many acts are presumed without proof being given.

a. Use of the Mails

In the ordinary course of postal service, any letter that has been properly addressed and mailed is presumed to have been received (California Evidence Code, Sec. 641; *People* v. *Rosenbloom*, 119 C.A. 759 [1931]). This practical rule is universally adopted, not because the courts have some unwarranted confidence in the U.S. mail, but because the sender is not in a position to prove that the letter was received. The recipient must overcome the presumption of delivery, if he can.

b. Identity

Identity will ordinarily be presumed from the same name. The more unusual the name, the stronger the inference of identity (*Wigmore on Evidence,* v. 2, Sec. 411). Thus, a record of conviction in the same name will be sufficient in some jurisdictions to establish the defendant's criminal history. In other courts it is taken as prima facie proof but not enough standing alone to establish the record.

c. Continuing Fact or Condition

It is often difficult to prove the exact conditions that existed at the time of the actual crime. Police photographs may show road conditions days after the event. A rape or assault victim may not be examined by a physician until the day after the crime. A sanity test is often much delayed, but the mental condition at the time of the crime may be a vital issue. Sometimes, the only evidence will be of a condition before or after the event.

In this situation, the law of evidence comes up with a presumption: Once a fact is proven, the condition continues until proven otherwise. A few states restrict the use of the rule when it is applied to criminal cases (*Sokolic* v. *State*, 228 Ga. 788 [1972]). As a general rule, however, evidence of a condition before or after the event is accepted on the commonsense ground that it was the same at the time of the crime.

The use of such evidence is largely left to the discretion of the trial judge. Its admissibility and, of course, its weight will be affected by how closely it is connected in time with the crime itself.

d. Sobriety, Normality, and Sanity

The law presumes that individuals are normal, that is, that they are sober, competent, and sane, The presumption may be rebutted by evidence to the contrary. If a sex offender claims he is mentally retarded, he must produce evidence of low intelligence. If insanity is a defense, the accused must offer proof of his insanity. The definition of criminal insanity does vary from state to state.

The usual rule is that if the accused was aware of his act and knew it was wrong, he is criminally responsible regardless of any label of mental illness that the medical profession may attach to him. The psychiatric definition of insanity is much broader than the legal one, and efforts are continually made to widen the definition of "legal insanity."

Since the defendant's mental and physical condition is something peculiarly within his own knowledge, it is only fair that he be required initially to offer proof of any abnormal condition when this is pertinent.

e. Suicide

Suicide is a most abnormal event, and so there is a legal presumption against it (*Byers* v. *Pacific Mutual*, 133 C.A. 632 [1933]). Should suicide be a defense in a murder case, for example, the defendant, to overcome this presumption against suicide, must do so by offering what evidence he can to show that the victim did in fact kill himself.

f. Legitimacy

This is one of the strongest presumptions known to the law. The husband is presumed to be the father of any child born in wedlock. It occasionally is involved in criminal matters where the relationship is material. Family offenses or incest are examples that come to mind.

This presumption of legitimacy sometimes produces harsh results, but it is necessary. Otherwise, a husband could escape responsibility for his children simply by denying parentage.

(2.10) *PRESUMPTIONS INDICATING GUILT*

If the evidence plausibly points toward guilt, it may be accepted. Such proof is, strictly speaking, not a presumption. It is circumstantial evidence from which an inference of guilt may be drawn (*People* v. *Stewart,* 74 Ill. App. 407 [1966]).

a. Flight or Concealment

Suppose, for example, there is a bank robbery, and the police catch a suspect running down the street away from the bank. One might consider his flight strong evidence of guilt. Or suppose the police find a man hiding in a closet in an apartment where drugs have recently been purchased. Again, one could assume from the suspect's concealment that an inference could be made concerning evidence of guilt.

Though all courts desire to protect the accused from false charges, they differ somewhat on the value to be given evidence of flight or concealment before an arrest. Most courts, however, hold that neither raises a presumption or inference of guilt (*Starr* v. *U.S.*, 164 U.S. 627 [1897]; *People* v. *Davis*, 29 Ill. 2d 127 [1963]).

Courts will accept proof of flight or concealment, such as that of a suspect fleeing the city soon after a crime has been committed and then hiding out. These actions will be taken as some proof of guilt, although other reasons may be introduced to explain them (*People* v. *Hoyt,* 20 C. 2d 306 [1942]).

Proof of flight or concealment may be shown, but it is up to the jury to determine what value it has, without benefit of any presumption or inference. Juries have more common sense than they are often given credit for, and they are quite likely to take either of these actions as a strong indication of guilt.

b. False Statements

The prosecution can occasionally prove that the accused gave false statements, either in oral or written form. They may have evidence at other times that the defendant obtained false statements from third parties to support his defense. In either case an inference of guilt results.

c. Malice

In some cases actual malice is an element. The only possible way to prove this is by evidence of the facts and circumstances. The very nature of the crime itself may create a presumption that it was done maliciously, that is, with a deliberate attempt to harm or destroy. Assault with a deadly weapon is often cited as an example of this.

d. Possession of Fruits of Crime

The possession of the fruits of crime is by itself proof from which an inference of guilt may be drawn. Though the possession of stolen goods soon after a crime has been committed is not conclusive proof, that fact alone gives rise to a strong inference of guilt (*Wilson* v. *U.S.,* 162 U.S. 613 [1896]; *People* v. *Volpe,* 20 N.Y. 2d 9 [1967]). Once the crime has been proven, the unexplained or falsely explained possession of stolen property, such as from burglary, robbery, or larceny, is generally said to give rise to a presumption of guilt (*People* v. *Russell,* 34 C.A. 2d 665 [1939]; *People* v. *Kulig*, 373 Ill. 102 [1939]).

e. Possession and Ownership

Some presumptions regarding possession and ownership are widely accepted in civil law and occasionally come into play in criminal cases. The general rule is that whatever is found in a person's possession is presumed to be his. Also, if a person exercises acts of ownership over property, there is a similar presumption that it is his.

f. Statutory Presumptions

The state and federal governments all have various statutes containing presumptions that arise from certain situations. Illustrations of this type were discussed in the cases listed earlier under "General Presumptions." Some examples are statutes that presume that a pawnbroker has knowingly accepted stolen goods if he had made no reasonable inquiry as to the legal ownership; that the presence of a weapon in an automobile is the possession of everyone in the car; and that the presence of illegal drugs in a car or in a room in clear view is evidence of possession by all the occupants (N.Y. Penal Law, Secs. 165.55, 220.25; *Ulster County* v. *Allen*, 25 Cr. L. 3113 [1979]).

(2.11) *JUDICIAL NOTICE*

There are some things that a court will accept as true without any proof. The judge does this by taking "judicial notice" of them without any introduction of evidence. Though this is an inherent power in all courts, in some jurisdictions its use may be somewhat restricted by statute (for example, California Evidence Code, Sec. 453). In addition, different judges have different ideas on the subject. Thus the wise police officer will find out in advance what the judge's attitude is on taking judicial notice. He will then know, for example, whether the court will take judicial notice that La Salle Street runs into Green Street or whether he will be required to testify to this fact.

It must be remembered that a judge can take judicial notice of matters of general knowledge, not of something that he may be acquainted with. He may, for instance, be personally aware of the fact that there is a stoplight in front of a certain station house but cannot, without proof, take judicial notice of it at a trial (California Evidence Code, Sec. 450).

a. Judicial Notice of Facts

Facts that are so universally known that they cannot reasonably be the subject of dispute will generally be recognized by judicial notice. When this is the case, it is not necessary to introduce an almanac or an encyclopedia in evidence. Matters of common knowledge, natural phenomena, history, language, and geography fall within this category. No one, for example, has to offer proof that water freezes or objects fall.

Scientific phenomena are often recognized by judicial notice. In recent years, for instance, courts have taken judicial notice of the validity and accuracy of radar. It is only necessary to prove the accuracy of the particular apparatus used in the case (*People* v. *MacLaird*, 264 C.A. 2d 972 [1968]).

Matters of geography are commonly accepted in this way. As an illustration, one court took judicial notice that the tide affects the San Joaquin River past the port of Stockton (*Colberg* v. *California*, 67 C. 2d 408 [1967]).

In the realm of language, even "street talk" has been judicially noticed. Thus, in a drug case in California, the court took judicial notice that the term "reds" means capsules of Seconal® (*People* v. *Hubard*, 9 C.A. 3d 827 [1970]).

One judge aptly stated the rule concerning the judicial notice of facts in *AhKow* v. *Nunan,* 5 Sawy. 552: "We cannot shut our eyes to matters of public notoriety and general cognizance. When we take our seats on the bench, we are not struck with blindness and forbidden to know as judges what we all see as men."

b. Judicial Notice of Laws

Without exception, every court takes judicial notice of treaties between the United States and foreign countries, including official interpretation of these treaties. Courts even take judicial notice of the absence of treaties such as those concerned with extradition.

They also take judicial notice of the laws within their jurisdiction, even if the attorneys forget to mention one. Courts above the municipal level are sometimes fussy about taking judicial notice of municipal ordinances. They may require proof of their existence, but will allow the presumption that they were validly enacted. In addition, official regulations, such as sanitary codes and rules governing income tax, are judicially recognized since they have the force of law.

Courts generally do not take judicial notice of foreign laws since these are beyond their field of knowledge. A number of states, however, judicially recognize the laws of sister states.

In regard to judicial records, a court always takes judicial notice of its proceedings, but not of other courts. Official records of the latter must be introduced in evidence.

(2.12) *SUMMARY*

Evidence is of no value unless it can be used in court. To be admissible, it must be relevant, and even then it must pass a variety of other tests.

Evidence of other crimes committed by the accused may be offered by the prosecution. Courts restrict its use, however, because of possible undue prejudice toward the defendant. Such proof is limited to proving motive, intent, identity, absence of mistake, or a common scheme or plan.

Motive and *intent* are terms that are easily confused. Motive is the reason for the crime. Intent is the conscious purpose to commit a criminal act.

Confessions containing reference to other crimes raise difficulties in the trial. Often the only way such a confession can be admitted in evidence is if the recitals of other crimes can be removed.

There are a number of legal presumptions or inferences. Some of the well-recognized ones are the presumption of innocence; the presumption that a person intends the normal consequences of his actions; and the negative presumption against a litigant resulting from the nonproduction of evidence that is within his control.

In order for a presumption to be constitutionally valid, there must be a logical connection between the initial fact proven and the conclusion drawn therefrom.

There exist several official presumptions: that past legal proceedings are valid; that officials have acted legally in performing their duties; that laws were properly adopted.

Some presumptions apply to particular situations—that mail has been received; that a proven fact has continued to exist; that persons with the same name are the same. Sanity, normality, and sobriety are presumed. There is a strong presumption against suicide. Finally, the husband is the presumed father of children born in wedlock.

There are presumptions of guilt. The giving of false statements or possession of the fruits of crime are examples. Flight or concealment, while not labeled a presumption of guilt by many courts, is accepted as circumstantial evidence against the accused.

Courts will often take judicial notice of generally known facts of geography, history, or science, thus bypassing the necessity of proof. Judicial notice will also be taken of the laws of the forum or of a court's own proceedings.

chapter 3

(© John Hanlon, Picture Group.)

FIRST TIME IN

Detention and Arrest in General

(3.1) *DETENTION IN GENERAL*

The right of the people to be secure . . . against unreasonable searches . . . shall not be violated, and no Warrants shall issue, but upon probable cause . . .

4th Amendment, United States Constitution.

The Fourth Amendment to the United States Constitution is the root from which court rulings have grown that bar the use of evidence coming from any illegal actions on the part of the police. Since warrants of any kind must be based on "probable cause," all arrests as well as searches require probable cause in order to be valid. If a detention, arrest, interrogation, or search is done unconstitutionally, the trial court may refuse to accept any evidence discovered from this illegal action, and the state will then be forced either to drop the case or proceed with the prosecution without this proof. The suppression of evidence by the courts is referred to as the "Exclusionary Rule" or "Fruit of the Poisoned Tree." (For a fuller explanation *see* sec. 4.2.)

Any understanding of criminal evidence must depend first on a thorough knowledge of the legality of police detentions, searches, interrogations, and arrests.

a. Detentions

"Detention" is a temporary police restraint of a suspect without a formal arrest. The most common form of temporary detention is a "stop and frisk."

For many years conscientious police officers have stopped suspicious individuals to ask them questions about their conduct. These stops are frequently accompanied by frisks, a limited form of searching the person's outer clothing. In 1968 the Supreme Court, in an eight-to-one decision, upheld the right of police officers to detain suspicious individuals temporarily and to frisk those who appear to be dangerous. The landmark case was *Terry* v. *Ohio,* 392 U.S. 1 (1968).

Terry was one of three men who was pacing back and forth in front of a jewelry store in downtown Cleveland. Police Detective McFadden, who was highly experienced in foot patrol surveillances, believed they were casing the store in contemplation of an armed robbery. He confronted the men and asked them their names, but their reply was not understandable. He grabbed Terry, turned him around, patted his overcoat, and removed a pistol he found there. A companion had a bulge in his coat that also turned out to be a weapon. Terry was convicted of carrying a concealed weapon, and he appealed.

The Supreme Court agreed that McFadden's actions amounted to a "search" but ruled that it was legal. The court felt it could not "blind" itself to the increasing dangers to police officers from armed assault. For the first time the court set out a sliding scale: The greater (or lesser) the physical intrusion, the greater (or lesser) the amount of proof required to sustain police action under the Fourth Amendment.

The decision acknowledged the duty of police to investigate suspicious conduct, to question the suspect, and to "pat down" for a weapon. Weapons so confiscated would be admissible in evidence against the accused.

(3.2) *EVIDENTIARY FACTS JUSTIFYING STOPS*

Police officers have a sworn duty to investigate crimes that have been committed or are in the process of being committed and to prevent those that are about to be committed.

The *Terry* case involved a crime that was about to take place—a robbery. The officer did not have "probable cause" for an arrest. As a peace officer, though, it was his duty to prevent an impending crime. The law gives him the constitutional power of temporary detention and questioning.

What factors are legally sufficient to give reasonable cause for a police stop? Suspicious behavior, such as sneaking down an alley, hiding in bushes, carrying a bag and flashlight might be everyday examples. An officer's past experience and training is also an element to be weighed in judging if he had reasonable cause for a stop. The validity of any stop must almost be decided on an individual case-by-case basis, depending on the facts involved.

(3.3) *EVIDENTIARY FACTS JUSTIFYING FRISKS*

The power to stop is not the power to frisk. Police cannot make a search for a weapon in every case. The officer must *reasonably suspect* that the suspect is armed and dangerous in order to frisk him. Similarly, an officer who has the right to conduct a pat-down of a suspect's clothing may also check his car for weapons. This does not include a locked glove compartment or trunk. (*Adams* v. *Williams,* 407 U.S. 143 [1972]; *State* v. *Pace*, 26 Cr. L. 2289 [N.J. Super. Ct. 1979].)

A frisk is usually restricted to outer clothing, but a coat may be unbuttoned. Pockets may not be reached into unless the officer first feels a bulge. Women are not exempt, but discretion should be used if done by male officers. Handbags may be squeezed and opened if firm.

If an arrest follows, the officer must carefully document his activities step by step in his report. Otherwise, the search may be found to be illegal.

Stop and frisk is a search governed by the Fourth Amendment. The standard is less rigid, being a "reasonable suspicion" rather than probable cause. Since the suspect is not under arrest at the time, "reasonable" rather than deadly force is all that can be used to detain him.

Detainees are not required to identify themselves, although some states, such as California, require that identification be given if stopped under suspicious circumstances.

Courts scrutinize this type of situation very closely. In *Brown* v. *Texas*, 443 U.S. 47 (1979), the police stopped two men in an El Paso alley after midnight in a high crime area. They asked one, a man named Brown, to identify himself. When he refused, he was arrested and later convicted under a Texas law that made it a crime not to identify yourself to the officer "who has lawfully stopped . . . and requested the information." The United States Supreme Court reversed Brown's conviction, pointing out that a stop is a "seizure" of his person and, while not requiring "probable cause," it does require "reasonable suspicion." Further, the court found that simply being in a "high crime" area at night did not give rise to reasonable suspicion. The stop being illegal, Brown could not be punished for refusing to identify himself. (*See also People* v. *Bower,* 156 Cal. Rptr. 856, 597 P. 2d 115 [1979].)

(3.4) *COLLATERAL EVIDENCE FOUND*

The reason for allowing a "stop and frisk" is to protect the police and public from assaults with weapons. What happens in a properly conducted frisk if other evidence is found? Narcotics are often discovered this way. If the frisk was properly a search for hard objects and the object turns out to be narcotics or paraphernalia, the confiscation will be upheld. Soft objects, such as cellophane packets and the like, would be suppressed.

In a California case, *People* v. *Leib*, 548 P. 2d 1105 (Cal. 1976), the police were executing a search warrant when the defendant walked into the premises and said, "I'm here for my stuff." A stop and frisk turned up a pill bottle on his person. The court held that the bottle did not resemble a weapon and the presence of the bottle did not justify a search of his person. The evidence was suppressed.

It is important to differentiate between evidence found in a "stop and frisk" situation and evidence found when there has been an actual arrest. (*See* sec. 4.5.) After an arrest, police have a much wider latitude to search the suspect and the immediate area.

(3.5) *ELEMENTS OF AN ARREST*

A person is arrested when he is taken into custody to answer a charge in court. It is sometimes argued that a suspect is "arrested" when his freedom is significantly restrained.

There are four parts to an arrest: authority, intent, custody, and knowledge.

Authority requires that the officer must have a right or claim of right to make the arrest, not a temporary stop or the issuance of a citation. For the second element, intent, there must be a bona fide intention to take the person in custody for his appearance in court.

Custody means an actual or constructive restraint of the suspect. Physical contact or handcuffing is not required if the person arrested submits to the arresting officer.

The suspect must know that he is being arrested. Usually, it is enough to tell him he is being arrested. The act of handcuffing him or using other physical restraint by a uniformed officer will have the same effect.

(3.6) *PROBABLE CAUSE*

All arrests, whether by state, local, or federal officers, must be based on the constitutional Fourth Amendment requirement of "probable cause." This is because the Fourth Amendment has been made applicable to the states through the Fourteenth Amendment's requirement that everyone is entitled to "due process" in the courts.

To put the matter simply, an officer must know of sufficient facts and circumstances to form the belief that, first, a crime *probably* was committed and that, second, the arrestee *probably* committed the offense.

Then the court must agree that a person of reasonable caution would also have concluded that probable cause in the constitutional sense did exist. There is no precise definition of "probable cause"; each case depends on reason and its own factual situation.

In common-law states, an officer can make a misdemeanor arrest without a warrant if the crime takes place in his "presence"; that is, he either saw the offense or became aware of it through any of his senses such as sound (a shot), smell (marijuana), or taste (liquor). In these common-law states, if the misdemeanor did not take place in his presence, the officer must get an arrest warrant in order to make a legal arrest. In case of warrantless felony arrest, an officer may act on "information and belief." Many states have abolished this distinction by statute and permit warrantless arrests for either misdemeanors or felonies if done on information and belief.

The courts have now added restrictions to police actions in felony arrests even where there is "probable cause" if they enter a private home to make the arrest. In *Payton* v. *N.Y.*, 445 U.S. 573 (1980), the police had probable cause to believe that Payton had committed a homicide. They went to his apartment and, when there was no response to their knock, broke in and found a shell casing in plain view.

In a companion decision, *Riddick* v. *N.Y.*, the police had probable cause to believe that Riddick was guilty of armed robbery. They went to his house and saw him inside when his young son opened the door. The officers went in without a warrant and arrested him. The court reversed the convictions of the lower court in both the *Riddick* and *Peyton* cases, holding that a nonconsensual entry into a suspect's home to make a routine felony arrest without a warrant violates the Fourth Amendment right to privacy.

(© Andrew Dickerman, Picture Group.)

A QUICK ARREST—WAS THERE PROBABLE CAUSE?

Several state decisions have followed this same rule, requiring warrants to make felony arrests in private residences of the suspect, but they have also added a requirement that there be exigent circumstances for such entries. (*State* v. *Love*, 598 P. 2d 976 [Ariz. 1979]; *State* v. *Olson*, 598 P. 2d 670 [Or. 1979]; *State* v. *Allison,* 257 S.E. 2d 417 [N.C. 1979]). In view of these court decisions, the best police procedure is to obtain an arrest warrant whenever possible, since there is no way of knowing where the suspect will actually be when the arrest takes place.

"Probable Cause" is a question of probabilities. Officers need not be legal specialists, and courts ordinarily will not require precise legal analysis from them. Each arrest will be judged on the facts and circumstances known to the officer at the time a warrantless arrest is made or when an affidavit for an arrest is written. Some of the factors that may lead an officer to conclude that he has probable cause for an arrest are the same as those that would justify a stop. (*See* sec. 3.2, above.) The amount of proof needed to justify an arrest is, of course, necessarily higher than that required to justify a temporary detention.

In determining the existence of probable cause, an officer can use evidence that is legally inadmissible at the trial of the accused but is admissible at the suppression hearing. Common among this type of evidence are statements obtained from a confidential informant that implicate the accused. Other factors of restricted admissibility include flight, furtive movements, evasive answers, records of arrest or of conviction, lack of identification, known criminal associations, and otherwise "suspicious" conduct.

The degree of proof from the beginning of a police investigation to the final conviction of the suspect can be shown on a scale from zero to one hundred. A slight degree of proof would be evident when it appears that an officer has a "mere hunch" (MH) that a suspect is guilty. This occurs when the officer knows that something is "wrong." It is sometimes called "police intuition."

At the next level is the standard required to justify a valid stop and frisk, a "reasonable suspicion" (RS). This is based on facts but is less than probable cause. Probable Cause (PC) is the amount of proof necessary to justify a warrantless arrest (or search) and to obtain an arrest warrant (or a search warrant). It is still not enough for a conviction, however, since proof in criminal cases must be beyond a reasonable doubt (BRD).

Even though officers have probable cause at the time of an arrest, they may not have enough evidence for a final conviction but get it through their efforts in the post-arrest period. It may be that physical evidence is found at the time an officer makes a search incident to a custodial arrest. The subject might respond to lawful questioning and confess. A witness may identify the suspect after his apprehension. In such cases, the amount of proof escalates from probable cause to proof beyond a reasonable doubt.

A number of factors can invalidate an otherwise lawful arrest. For instance, an officer cannot obtain the necessary probable cause by illegally secreting himself on someone's property or by making a forcible entrance. If an officer is lawfully on the premises for another reason, anything seen may be used to support probable cause. Thus, an officer responds to a fire alarm and sees smoke inside a building. He makes a forcible entry to determine if anyone needs aid. When he gets inside, he observes a burglar on the premises. He would be justified in apprehending the burglar. Alternatively, if he had observed illicit activity on the premises, such as contraband in plain sight, he could later charge the owner or occupant with illegal possession.

(3.7) *COLLECTIVE INFORMATION AND RADIO BROADCASTS*

Officers can rely on information that they give each other. Several police may take part in an investigation, and any one of them, after conferring with the others, may swear out an arrest warrant.

Suspects are often arrested based on "all-points bulletin" (APB) or "be on look out" (BOLO) messages. If the evidence supporting the broadcast amounts to probable cause, the arrest is valid. The following example demonstrates the point. A radio bulletin alerts city officers to be on the lookout for Smith, who is wanted for the burglary of a TV repair shop. A full description of Smith's station wagon is included by the sheriff of a nearby county where the alleged crime took place. Officer Jones, on seeing the vehicle, pulls it over and asks the driver for his license. In the back of the wagon Officer Jones sees six TV sets.

In this example, we simply do not have enough information to know whether the local sheriff had probable cause to order the arrest of Smith. A warrant, based on an affidavit indicating the existence of probable cause, was not obtained. A warrant issued on a conclusory affidavit would have the same effect. Officer Jones did, however, sufficiently corroborate the information he received, which would lead a reasonable man to conclude that Smith had, indeed, taken the TV sets in the reported burglary.

Often several officers take part in an arrest. One man may ask others to assist him. The legality of the arrest depends on the information known to the requesting officer. Also, police may assist each other in pursuing a fleeing suspect without first being told the details underlying the chase.

(3.8) *FEDERAL OFFENSES AND IMMUNITY*

State and local officers are sworn to uphold the Constitution and the laws of the United States. They frequently make arrests for offenses that are both state and federal in nature, such as bank robbery, possession of narcotics, interstate theft, and certain crimes concerned with weapons. Either the federal or state government may decide to prosecute the crime involved. If a county prosecutor refuses to charge the suspect, the U.S. attorney can act instead, and vice versa.

Some offenses are solely federal in nature. Many involve the postal service, the Internal Revenue Service, or crimes committed on federal reservations. Pursuant to 18 U.S. Code, Sec. 3041, a state or local officer may swear out a warrant in either state or federal court for individuals suspected of federal offenses. While a state court judge cannot try the offense charged, he can order the defendant held for trial or discharge him from custody. A state or local officer may arrest, without warrant, a person who commits a purely federal offense if a warrantless arrest is permitted by state law.

Certain classes of persons are, by federal law, immune from arrest. Ambassadors, foreign ministers, their families, members of their official households, civil and military attachés, their personal servants and personal secretaries have full diplomatic immunity. Delegates to the United Nations, the Organization of American States, and the North Atlantic Treaty Organization also have official immunity. Foreign nationals and U.S. citizens employed as clerical staff, as well as all ranks of consuls, do not have diplomatic immunity except when they are on official foreign business. To ascertain whether a person has full or partial immunity, the chief of protocol of the U.S. Department of State should be contacted.

Law enforcement officers should, as a matter of courtesy among friendly nations, notify the closest embassy, consulate, or legation of the arrest of any foreign national. The imprisonment or assault of a foreign ambassador or minister is a federal crime punishable by up to ten years of imprisonment in accord with 18 U.S. Code 112.

The Constitution prohibits the arrest of all United States senators and representatives, except for treason, felonies, and breach of the peace, during their attendance at a session of Congress and while they are traveling to and from such sessions. Thus, they are immune from arrests for misdemeanors and traffic violations during the entire time Congress is in session, not just during their working hours.

Many state senators and representatives have immunity from state misdemeanors and traffic offenses, similar to members of the U.S. Congress. Members of the state militia who are on duty, judges, lawyers, and jurors attending court, and other classes of persons may be given limited immunity under state law.

(3.9) *PARTICULAR TYPES OF ARRESTS*

Not every arrest is for a criminal offense. Persons may be arrested on civil process, issued by a court of competent jurisdiction. For example, bench warrants may be issued for comtempt of court, as when a witness fails to appear on a subpoena that has been served in a civil case.

Citizens are authorized to make arrests in criminal cases, without warrant, when the offense is committed in their presence. This power does not normally extend to offenses concerned with municipal ordinances but is reserved for felonies and breach of the peace. Citizens may also be "deputized" to assist officers in making an arrest. This is not a new procedure. The *posse comitatus* is of ancient origin, and no one who has seen a Western can fail to have witnessed posses in action. The common law recognizes that it is the duty of all male adults to come to the aid of officers who request it; recent statutes have included women when the rule has been codified. As a matter of fact, in some cases it is a criminal offense to refuse to assist law enforcement officers in the execution of their office.

Under statutes existing in most states, merchants are given powers of arrest or detention with respect to shoplifting offenses. They may, if they have sufficient information and belief, detain and sometimes arrest suspected shoplifters. Under such laws, police officers need not view misdemeanors committed only in the presence of shopkeepers and security personnel hired by the store.

An individual who is on parole does not enjoy the civil rights of an ordinary citizen. He may be apprehended without warrant for parole violations. He may be searched by a parole officer whenever the officer believes it is reasonably necessary, and this can be done without a warrant. The parole officer may make such a search without probable cause and without first placing the parolee under arrest.

Probationers also may be searched by their probation officer. (*Latta* v. *Fitzharris,* 521 F. 2d 246 [9th Cir. 1975], cert. den., 404 U.S. 1025; *Smith* v. *State,* 383 So. 2d 991 [5th DCA 1980]; *Grubbs* v. *State,* 373 So. 2d 905 [1979]).

Bondsmen, under common law, have an absolute right to retake those for whom they have posted bond should those individuals attempt to skip town or otherwise impair the conditions of their appearance in court. They may cross state lines and, without warrant or other legal process, capture and return the accused to the jail from which he was released on bond.

Police officers may arrest and detain a person who is wanted, on warrant or bulletin, to answer for the commission of an offense in another state. This power is granted by the United States Constitution, which requires that each state give "full faith and credit" to the legal processes of sister states. Except in exigent circumstances, however, resident police officers should not apprehend suspects on a bulletin alone, unless the request indicates a warrant has been issued. In situations where the suspect is fleeing, an officer can, of course, detain him until a warrant has been obtained. Officers may promptly pursue a fleeing suspect across state lines to make the apprehension, but the offender may not be returned to the state in which he is supposed to have committed the crime without due process of law. Nearly all states have adopted the Uniform Fresh Pursuit Act and the Uniform Extradition Act. These statutes give an accused the right to a hearing before the governor of the state to which he has fled before he can be returned to the state that issued the warrant.

(3.10) *USE OF FORCE*

Police officers may use reasonable and necessary force to apprehend a criminal suspect. They are not required to retreat from an assault, as an ordinary citizen is in most cases. They are not required to time an arrest so that it can be effected with the least amount of resistance. They are not bound to use psychology or to wait for hours or days before flushing out an armed suspect who offers resistance. What is good police policy and what is good law may surely differ. Thus, an officer may be fired for escalating or not defusing a situation, but ordinarily he cannot be sued or prosecuted for immediately apprehending a suspect who is resisting arrest.

If the offense is a misdemeanor, an arresting officer may not use deadly force to apprehend a fleeing suspect. In every state an officer may—as a last resort—use deadly force to apprehend a suspect who is believed to have committed a dangerous felony. In most states this applies to all grades of felonies. It makes no difference that the offense is minor. To state the matter simply, the law will not permit felons to flee from justice.

What constitutes a "last resort" is open to question. An officer does not have to assume that the suspect will probably be captured by other officers or that he may give himself up. If it can be shown, however, that the chase was too short or that the officer was too lazy to give chase, a jury will probably conclude that the officer was not justified in killing the suspect.

Regardless of whether the offense is serious or whether the suspect's arrest is attempted or not, a police officer may use deadly force to defend himself against the use of deadly force. This principle does not escalate in degrees. An attacker with a knife, with a broken beer bottle, with a fireplace poker, or with an automobile that he is using as a weapon may be shot dead with an elephant gun. Even though there may be twenty-five armed officers against one armed suspect, any officer may return the fire as though the suspect were taking aim against him individually.

Most cases where excessive force has been alleged do not involve the use of deadly force. An officer is not only privileged to use a reasonable and necessary amount of force to make an apprehension, he is obligated to use more force than the person resisting arrest. Here, then, the law will examine the degree of responsive force. There are no ready answers, and the progression is not necessarily from pebbles to boulders or from table lamps to chairs.

Entry of dwellings and other premises by force in order to effect an arrest is limited to two situations. The first occurs when officers are in hot pursuit or the criminal acts are of a continuous nature. The second takes place when officers who are armed with an arrest or search warrant have first requested consensual entry, which is refused. (This aspect of law is more fully discussed in chapter 5.)

Handcuffs may be used to restrain or transport arrested persons who are suspected of felonies, breach of the peace, or minor offenses when it is thought that they might escape or assault the arresting officers.

(3.11) *FALSE ARREST*

Civil damage suits can be brought against police officers and the governmental agency employing them for false arrest, imprisonment, or malicious prosecution. Both compensatory and punitive damages may be recovered, with the amount almost at the discretion of the jury. "Probable cause" and "good faith" on the part of the officer are often difficult questions to be resolved in these cases.

(3.12) *ENTRAPMENT*

Inducing a person to commit a crime that he otherwise would not have done is called *entrapment*. This is now recognized as a legal defense in most jurisdictions. Normally, it comes about when an undercover officer becomes involved in criminal activities under his investigation. (*See* sec. 1.9[e].)

The 1979 Abscam bribery charges involving several members of Congress is an example of a situation where entrapment is alleged. Unless the prosecution has some evidence of a predisposition to crime, the accused has a valid argument for entrapment.

It is not wrong for a police officer to give a suspect marked money or to pose as an addict or hoodlum. However, there often is a fine line between legitimate undercover police work and actual entrapment involving an otherwise unsuspecting person.

Though entrapment as a defense must be raised by the defendant, in some cases the judge will rule as a matter of law that officers encouraged the defendant's participation in the offense. Generally, though, this will be a question for the jury because of variances in testimony between the officer and the defendant.

(3.13) *SUMMARY*

Not every time a police officer deprives a citizen of his freedom is there an arrest in the legal sense. The Supreme Court has made clear that a temporary detention, although it constitutes a seizure within the meaning of the Fourth Amendment, is not an arrest. Police officers may stop citizens, forcibly if necessary, to conduct a preliminary investigation in order to determine whether a crime has taken place, is in progress, or is about to take place.

To justify a stop, a police officer must be able to articulate facts that would lead a prudent person to believe that the officer reasonably suspects a person of criminal activity. This detention is incident to his power to investigate. Moreover, if the officer reasonably suspects that the person with whom he is dealing might be armed, a limited search can be conducted. This search, called a frisk, is restricted to a pat-down of the suspect's outer clothing for weapons. If the frisk is properly conducted and is not a generalized search of the person, evidence fortuitously found is admissible in a criminal trial.

To consummate an arrest, an officer must have the authority to make an arrest and the intention to arrest the suspect. There must be some restraint of the suspect, either physical or mental, and the suspect must understand that he has been arrested. The Fourth Amendment requires that police officers have probable cause before a lawful arrest can be made. This means that an officer must reasonably believe that a crime has been committed and that the suspect is the perpetrator.

The law recognizes that police officers have unique experience and specialized training that make them more proficient in their field than the normal citizen. They may use this combination of education and experience to determine whether there are sufficient grounds to justify a stop or an arrest. They must, however, be able to fully recount the underlying facts and circumstances in court, or the detention or arrest will be found unlawful.

chapter 4

(© George Cohen, Picture Group.)

SEARCH INCIDENT TO AN ARREST

Search and Seizure Generally

(4.1) *THE FOURTH AND FOURTEENTH AMENDMENTS*

Two phases of the Fourth Amendment to the U.S. Constitution contain the real substance of its protections. The first is the prohibition against "unreasonable" searches. The second is the requirement of "probable cause." In regard to the first prohibition, the amendment states that the people have the right to be secure in their persons, houses, papers, and effects from unreasonable searches and seizures. Thus, the amendment protects people, not corporations, animals, or inanimate objects. Although it specifies "houses," the word has been interpreted to include barns, warehouses, offices, and other structures. No mention was made of boats, which, of course, existed in the eighteenth century, or of automobiles, trucks, and aircraft, which did not. Nevertheless, the protections of the Fourth Amendment have been extended, by interpretation, to these forms of personal property. The essence of the amendment is that people are protected from unreasonable searches, regardless of what is searched.

Only a few types of searches can be considered unreasonable. If a search is reasonable, other things being equal, the search is constitutional. It is sometimes claimed that a warrantless search is unreasonable and therefore illegal because there was ample time to procure a warrant. That is not, however, the proper test. The real question is whether it was reasonable to require a warrant under the circumstances of the case.

The second major prohibition of the amendment states that no warrants shall be issued except on "probable cause." This requirement has also been extended to warrantless searches, warrantless arrests, and arrest warrants, as discussed in chapter 3. The specific requirements to be met in determining the existence of probable cause are discussed in chapter 5 under the heading "Probable Cause."

The Fourth Amendment also requires that warrants be based on an oath or affirmation, which particularly describes the place to be searched and the persons or things to be seized. For a discussion of these matters, *see* chapter 5 under the heading "Grounds for Issuance."

The Fourteenth Amendment is important in constitutional history because it was originally thought that the first eight amendments only applied to congressional enactments and to federal officers. But the "due process clause" of this amendment makes it clear that these amendments also apply to state enactments and to locally constituted law enforcement officers.

(4.2) *THE EXCLUSIONARY RULE*

One of the most important of evidence rules is the "exclusionary rule," a court-ordered rule that rejects any proof that was obtained in an "illegal" manner. In earlier times, it made no legal difference to courts how evidence was obtained. But in 1914, the United States Supreme Court changed that. In *Weeks* v. *U.S.*, 232 U.S. 383 (1914), the court decided that evidence gathered by officers should be excluded from a federal criminal trial if it had been obtained in violation of the Fourth Amendment.

Following this, many states adopted a similar rule for state criminal trials, also barring the use of "illegally" obtained evidence. For over thirty years after 1914, nearly half of the states did not follow this rule; some applied it only to *state* searches and still admitted evidence illegally seized by federal agents. So, too, federal courts admitted evidence if it was illegally seized by state agents. The "illegal evidence" was thus "served up" on a "silver platter."

In 1961 the Supreme Court in *Mapp* v. *Ohio,* 367 U.S. 643, applied the exclusionary rule to all state courts. The *Mapp* case involved the seizure of obscene material from the defendant by an illegal search. She was convicted, but the Supreme Court rejected the conviction by holding that the evidence was gained illegally by the Ohio police and that the state was bound by the requirements of the Fourth and Fourteenth Amendments.

This decision has been called "The Criminal Law Revolution," for not only was the federal exclusionary rule made to apply universally via the "due process" Fourteenth Amendment, but this, and later Supreme Court decisions, left that court as the final arbiter of *all* state criminal procedure.

The exclusion of tainted evidence is not automatic. The defendant must raise the issue by making a "motion to suppress." Normally, the motion is made before the actual trial begins. In some cases the motion can be made to suppress evidence that might be used before a Grand Jury to obtain an indictment. If the accused fails to raise the motion before a trial, he may still be able to object to the admissibility of the evidence at the time of trial. Most courts will deny his right to raise the issue for the first time on an appeal.

In addition to evidence directly acquired illegally, any "derivative evidence" that is a product of this may be rejected under the "Fruit of the Poisoned Tree" doctrine. However, evidence that is suppressed is not necessarily returned to the accused. Examples of this are items such as contraband, stolen goods, or forfeited property.

One long-standing exception to the exclusionary rule is the "inevitable discovery" rule. If the state can show that the illegal evidence would inevitably have been discovered anyway by legal means, the proof can be used at trial. (*Silverthorne Lumber Company* v. *U.S.*, 251 U.S. 385, [1920]; *Lockridge* v. *Superior Court*, 3 Cal. 3d 166 [1970]; *Houlihan* v. *State*, 51 S.W. 2d 719 [Tex. Crim. 1977]).

Currently the United States Supreme Court decisions appear to be weakening the exclusionary rule without actually overturning it. One of these cases, *U.S.* v. *Havens,* 64 L. Ed. 2d 559 (1980), involved illegally seized T-shirts taken in a drug case. At the trial, the defendant on cross-examination denied that he had had the T-shirts. In rebuttal, the government introduced the shirts in evidence. The court affirmed the conviction by approving the use of illegal evidence for impeachment on cross-examination.

In *U.S.* v. *Paynor*, 27 Cr. L. 3220 (1980), federal agents used an attractive woman decoy to keep a Bahamian banker in a downstairs room of the hotel while agents broke into his hotel room, opened his briefcase with the help of a locksmith, and photographed deposit lists. The government used the data from these lists to convict a depositor named Paynor of criminal tax evasion. The court approved, saying that the illegally obtained evidence could be used against Paynor because he was not the one illegally searched.

Some objections to the rule are: It handicaps all police officers; it violates the purpose of a trial, the search for truth; it encourages perjury by police; extra delays are added to the process of punishment; there is an added expense to society; and, finally, the rule does not "punish" police, it rewards criminals. Alternatives to the rule could be mandatory civil liability for improper police conduct, contempt of court procedure against offending officers, or an effective system of police discipline. All of these would serve to curb police misconduct without freeing guilty suspects.

(4.3) *SEARCHES, DISTINGUISHED FROM PLAIN VIEW*

Courts hold that a "search" is seeking something that is not in plain sight. If the officer *has the right to be in position where the object is in plain view*, it is subject to seizure and may be admitted in evidence. (*Harris* v. *U.S.*, 390 U.S. 234 [1968]).

The plain view rule frequently arises in the course of police duties. Every time a police officer talks with a pedestrian, stops a motorist, or questions a suspicious person, the rule applies. For example, a patrol officer stops a motorist for speeding. While writing a notice for the motorist to appear in court, the officer observes the barrel of a gun protruding from under a newspaper on the seat of the car. Noticing the barrel is not a search, and the officer has probable cause to remove the newspaper and seize the weapon.

Observations within the rule are not limited to sightings with an unaided eye. Flashlights and vehicular spotlights may be used at night or in dark places. Thus, a foot patrolman, walking down the sidewalk at night, might routinely shine his flashlight into parked cars. If he observes narcotics paraphernalia on the backseat of an unoccupied sedan, he would have probable cause to seize the vehicle and arrest the driver on his return.

a. Open Fields

Under the "open fields doctrine" police may enter outdoor private fields without a warrant and any evidence seen may be legally taken as in the case of "plain view" seizures. The legal theory is that owners cannot expect privacy for objects that can be seen in open fields, as opposed to property inside buildings. Even the presence of a fence is not determinative. Is the fence designed to keep animals in or people out? Unless the fence is obviously designed to keep out intruders and that fact is clearly indicated, occupants of the land do not have a constitutionally protected right to be free from police invasion of property.

The question for courts to decide in these cases is whether this is an open area where the defendant had a reasonable expectation of privacy. (*Katz* v. *U.S.*, 389 U.S. 347 [1967]). Recent case law has applied this doctrine by holding that the proper measure is the "privacy" test for each case, rather than allowing a general "open fields" rule. (*U.S.* v. *DeBacker*, 27 Cr. L. 2479 [U.S. D.C.N.Mich. 1980]; *Florida* v. *Brady*, 379 So. 2d 1294 [1980]; *Burkholder* v. *Superior Court,* 26 Cr. L. 2025 [Calif. Ct. App. 1979]).

b. Curtilage

"Curtilage" is the immediate area surrounding a home and all attached structures. The law holds this to be a private zone immune to all but a valid search warrant. Police observation into the area may be disputed in some cases. Curtilage cannot be precisely defined, and each case depends on its own circumstances. For example, a son told police that his father had murdered a girl and buried her in a goose house that was four hundred feet from their home. The police without a warrant went in and dug up the body. The court approved, saying at four hundred feet this was not part of the curtilage. (*Saiken* v. *Bensinger*, 546 F. 2d 1292, cert. den. 431 U.S. 930 [7th Cir. 1976]. For general curtilage definitions *see U.S.* v. *Williams,* 581 F. 2d 451 [5th Cir. 1978]).

The use of telescopes and binoculars, by themselves, does not render an observation unlawful. Police officers can, therefore, position themselves in a location where it is lawful for them to be and observe suspicious activities using magnifying lenses, except in Hawaii.

Police officers are not free, however, to accomplish illegal searches with the use of mechanical devices and stand on technical concepts of trespass. For example, an officer cannot stand outside the bedroom window of a suspect and peer inside, because this is a violation of curtilage. He could stand across the street on a sidewalk and look through an open window, as could any citizen. He could not climb to the roof of a nearby office structure and, with the aid of binoculars, look down into an apartment bedroom, if the only other way to look through the window was by standing just outside the window, within the curtilage. There is no "expectation of privacy" that a neighbor will not look out his window, but there is a reasonable expectation that one will not be spied upon from a nearby roof.

Thus, officers, by sitting in a parked car on the street, would be able to look into the front window of a home and see illegal activity because the occupants had carelessly left the drapes open. Anything they would see with the aid of binoculars is lawful because anyone parked on the street could see the same activities. There is no "search," and the events observed fall within the plain view rule.

c. Semiprivate Places

Defining a "public place" is legally difficult. Observations of criminal actions in a public place are admissible. Public rest rooms, for example, are indeed public, but the closed toilet area is semiprivate, and observations therein are invalid without a search warrant. So, too, if an officer is in a private place without consent or without a warrant, his observations are not admissible against the accused.

Not every place is clearly public or private. Many are semiprivate. If, for example, a police officer walks through a department store during business hours, he is in a public place. When the officer enters an unlocked rest room, he is still in a public place. But if he enters a commode stall, stands on the plumbing, and looks over into another stall, he is conducting a search of a semiprivate area. If, therefore, an officer observes an addict taking a fix under these conditions, the observations will be excluded at the trial.

d. Execution of Search Warrants

The plain view exception often takes effect during the course of searches conducted pursuant to a warrant. Thus, a warrant might command an officer to search for stolen goods. In the course of the search, he finds narcotics. The contraband, although not named in the warrant, is admissible. Officers executing a search warrant are in a place where they lawfully have a right to be. Anything they see of an evidentiary nature, therefore, can later be related in the courtroom. Police do not have to close their eyes to contraband, weapons, instrumentalities of a crime, or fruits of other crimes. The same rule holds true for plain view evidence found when executing arrest warrants.

e. Inventories

Pursuant to departmental regulations or standing custom, officers usually check the contents of impounded vehicles. The routine taking of an inventory is not a search as defined by the Fourth Amendment. It is conducted for the purpose of safeguarding any valuables found in the vehicle, and it protects the officers from false claims of theft or from liability from mysterious disappearance. Police officers would be derelict in their duties if they failed to remove weapons or valuable property from vehicles that are impounded, stored in an unprotected lot, or left parked beside a roadway.

Except in California, any items found in the course of conducting a vehicle inventory are admissible in court (*South Dakota* v. *Opperman,* 96 S. Ct. 3092 [1976]). This is because an inventory is not a search, and items found inadvertently come within the plain view exception.

The courts in California have rejected this philosophy and so exclude items found during the course of an inventory (*Mozetti* v. *Superior Court*, 4 Cal. 3d 699, 484 P. 2d 84 [1971]).

Caution should be used in opening luggage in the car (*People* v. *Bayless,* 28 Cr.L. 2194 [Ill. Sup. Ct. 1980]). The better procedure is to obtain a search warrant before opening any luggage found during the inventory of an automobile's contents.

(4.4) *ABANDONED PROPERTY RULE*

Abandoned property is always open to police use as evidence. Objects may be thrown away. "Dropsie cases," where subjects drop narcotics in the street, fall within this category. Property permanently left behind in motel rooms or found in abandoned buildings or refuse cans is also considered abandoned.

A bizarre case of this nature was *Venner* v. *State,* 354 A. 2d 483 (Md. App. 1976), where a drug suspect had been hospitalized for a drug overdose. A nurse took drug-filled balloons from his bedpan excrement. The court admitted this in evidence, saying it was abandoned property since the defendant had exercised no further dominion over his excrement.

(4.5) *SEARCHES INCIDENT TO ARREST*

One of the most important exceptions to the requirement that officers have probable cause to search suspects is the incident-to-a-legal-arrest exception. In the past, police officers would search an entire house or automobile when they placed an occupant under arrest. No further showing of cause was necessary.

In one of the most revolutionary cases decided by the Supreme Court under Chief Justice Earl Warren, the scope of searches incident to a legal arrest was dramatically curtailed. In *Chimel* v. *California,* 395 U.S. 752 (1969), the court announced that, thereafter, officers could only search the arrestee and the area immediately around him. The court said:

> It is reasonable for the arresting officer to search the person arrested in order to remove any weapons that [might be used] to resist arrest or effect his escape. Otherwise, the officer's safety might well be endangered, and the arrest itself frustrated. In addition, it is entirely reasonable for the arresting officer to search for and seize any evidence on the arrestee's person in order to prevent its concealment or destruction. And the area into which an arrestee might reach in order to grab a weapon or evidentiary items must, of course, be guided by a like rule. A gun on a table or in a drawer in front of the one who is arrested can be as dangerous to the arresting officer as one concealed in the clothing of the person arrested. There is ample justification, therefore, for a search of the arrestee's person and the area "within his immediate control"—construing that phrase to mean the area from within which he might gain possession of a weapon or destructible evidence.
>
> There is no comparable justification, however, for routinely searching rooms other than in which an arrest occurs,—or, for that matter, for searching through all the desk drawers or other closed or concealed areas in that room itself. Such searches, in the absence of well-recognized exceptions, may be made only under the authority of a search warrant.

The *Chimel* rule initially gave rise to the "arm's reach" doctrine. Most courts have more liberally construed the case and have adopted variants of the "lunge" doctrine. In its simplest analysis, the case restricts searches to those areas of a room where the arrestee can reach or jump over to.

Chimel also applies to arrests made when the suspect is apprehended in a motor vehicle. Officers may search the seat tops, under the front seats, the floorboard, above the visor, and an unlocked glove compartment. They may not extend the search to the trunk, a locked glove compartment, or under the hood.

A more serious question arises over whether an otherwise acceptable search can be continued after the suspect has been restrained or removed from the area where he was arrested. If the search of the room or the car is contemporaneous with the arrest, the search is proper. If the suspect has been placed in a transport vehicle or has been physically removed from the premises, the searching process must be discontinued. Inquisitive officers might think it wise to permit an arrestee freedom to move around unrestrained as long as possible. Not only is this dangerous to the officers, but the courts would find it a sham to avoid the restrictive consequences of the *Chimel* ruling.

No justification need be shown for a search of the clothing and accessories of the arrestee. They may be thoroughly searched if the search is conducted contemporaneous with the arrest and transport of the accused. Courts have disagreed over whether an officer can search a suitcase that an accused is carrying *at the time of the arrest*. Such inspections can often be justified on the theory that its contents are being inventoried, particularly when the accused was apprehended on the street or in a car (*U.S.* v. *Garcia,* 605 F. 2d 349 [7th Cir. 1979]).

Two qualifications of the *Chimel* ruling must be made. First, officers may, in many cases, walk into adjacent rooms, open closets, or peek under beds. This is to ensure that cohorts of the arrestee are not hiding in wait. These individuals might assault the arresting officers and prevent the arrest. Even stronger justification arises when accomplices in the crime are still at large, and their whereabouts are unknown. Second, under the plain view exception, officers need not ignore contraband, weapons, and evidence observed in open places while they are apprehending the accused and ensuring themselves against attack by concealed cohorts.

Finally, it must be noted that, long before the *Chimel* case was decided, courts condemned the so-called timed arrest. That is, officers may not unreasonably delay the apprehension of an accused merely to invade his home in the hope of extending their search to the premises he had occupied. If, however, a residential arrest is justified on the basis of other factors, the delay is reasonable. Thus, officers, with an arrest warrant for Smith, observe him walking home. Smith is part of a suspected drug ring, and his arrest on the streets would alert his accomplices. If the officers delay apprehension until he is inside his residence, the delay is reasonable and justified. Anything seen in plain view, once the officers are inside, is admissible as evidence. Items within Smith's reach, in the room where he is apprehended, can be lawfully searched.

Tensions in a community, which sometimes result in civil disturbances, can often be avoided by inconspicuous apprehensions. If hostile attitudes are prevalent in a neighborhood, delayed residential arrest of a local resident would be justified.

(4.6) *SEARCHES OF VEHICLES*

Automobile searches are in most cases an exception to the rule requiring issuance of a search warrant. For many years the courts have been more lenient in car searches because the very mobility of the automobile creates something like an emergency situation, making it impractical to get a warrant in most cases. (*Carroll* v. *U.S.*, 267 U.S. 132 [1925]).

In addition, the Supreme Court has pointed out that people have less expectation of privacy in a motor vehicle because of the public nature of travel and because the automobile itself is ruled by various governmental regulations. (*South Dakota* v. *Opperman,* 428 U.S. 364 [1976]; *Cardwell* v. *Lewis*, 417 U.S. 583 [1974]).

Only on rare occasions are warrants now necessary to search an automobile. However, random stops of vehicles cannot justify automobile searches, even if there is probable cause to search a car that has been so stopped. (*Delaware* v. *Prouse,* 440 U.S. 648, 59 L. Ed. 2d 660 [1979]).

If the stop is justified, a vehicular search without a warrant may be legal under the following set of circumstances:

1. The officer has probable cause to search the vehicle.
2. The officer has probable cause to arrest the driver for a custodial offense of an evidentiary nature. That is, the offender must be booked, not released on citation, and the offense is one in which physical evidence may be present.
3. The officer has probable cause to arrest the driver for a custodial offense of a nonevidentiary nature. Here, the scope of the vehicle search is limited by the *Chimel* ruling.

Warrantless vehicle searches are now the usual method. Inventory searches after an arrest are commonly done. Lower court decisions have split over the right of the police to open suitcases or other closed containers in cars.

The Supreme Court, in a 1979 decision, *Arkansas* v. *Sanders*, 442 U.S. 753, ruled against the warrantless opening of a suitcase taken from a car unless there is probable cause *and* exigent circumstances. Some state decisions have differed over the right of police to open a car's trunk. California, for example, banned it in 1976 (*Wimberly* v. *Superior Court,* 128 Cal. Rptr. 641). The best rule is to obtain a search warrant before opening any closed container found in a vehicle and to get warrants to open car trunks in those states that require this procedure.

a. Custodial and Evidentiary Offenses

When an officer makes a custodial arrest for a crime of an evidentiary nature, it is possible that the fruits of or the evidence of the offense, such as weapons or contraband, will be in the car. No special proof of the existence of these items is necessary to justify a complete warrantless search of the vehicle. However, New Jersey, Pennsylvania,

Rhode Island, Hawaii, and the 8th Circuit limit car searches to the area within the driver's immediate control if incident to an arrest. (*State* v. *Welsh,* 419 A. 2d. 113 [N.J. 1980]; *State* v. *Robalewski,* 418 A. 2d 817 [R.I. 1980]; *Commonwealth* v. *Timko,* 417 A. 2d. 620 [Pa. 1980]; *Accord, State* v. *Jenkins,* 619 P. 2d 108 [Hawaii 1980]; *U.S.* v. *Benson* [8th Cir. 1980]).

When a custodial arrest is made for a nonevidentiary offense, the scope of the permissible search is limited by the *Chimel* decision to the area immediately around the arrestee. A custodial arrest is occasionally made for a traffic offense. They are normally of a nonevidentiary nature. If, however, the apprehension is for drunk driving, the arresting officers may search for intoxicants.

Most traffic offenses are handled by the issuance of a citation, and a custodial arrest is not involved. In these cases, a search "incident to arrest" is not justified. If, however, the officer issuing the citation reasonably suspects that the driver may be armed and dangerous, he may frisk the occupant. Though the scope of the frisk of someone occupying a vehicle is broader than that permitted of a pedestrian, it parallels that allowed in searches incident to arrest. A gun kept under the driver's seat is just as accessible to the driver and as dangerous to the officer as one concealed in the driver's clothing—perhaps more so.

(4.7) *HOT PURSUIT AND EXIGENT CIRCUMSTANCES*

Two exceptional situations make a search warrant unnecessary. The first is the so-called hot pursuit exception. An officer who chases a fugitive, or is in fresh pursuit, does not need a search warrant to continue his chase into homes or offices, and anything found in the course of the pursuit and incident to it is an admissible item. In order for the incident to qualify as this type of exception, the officer must have legal grounds to make an arrest, the suspect must be fleeing to avoid imminent capture, and the pursuit must be promptly started and continuously maintained. It is not necessary that the fugitive be constantly in sight of the officer or, for that matter, in sight at all. Certain interruptions are justified, such as calling for assistance, temporarily resting if the pursuit is on foot, or stopping for gas or directions if it is by car.

Since fresh pursuit, in the absence of a statute, is a common-law rule, an officer must stop at the territorial limits of his jurisdiction. If, during the course of the pursuit, the officer finds incriminating evidence, contraband, or weapons, he may seize these items without a warrant.

The second exception is exigent circumstances. If a true emergency exists, or is reasonably believed to exist, officers may enter the premises without a warrant. The most common example is the situation in which there is the threat of a bomb. Another is when officers believe a person may be in need of aid. The urgency of the incident justifies entry without a warrant, and, in most jurisdictions, anything seen inside in plain view may be seized without a warrant. In a few states the officer must return with a warrant for the actual seizure, but the entry and search without a warrant are lawful when they occur. The Supreme Court has made it clear that police officers cannot create their own exigent circumstances. These circumstances must exist independently. The following is an example of this. Officers had an arrest warrant for Vale and knew where he lived. Outside his home they witnessed him conduct an apparent narcotics transaction. They arrested Vale and searched his house. The search could not be justified on exigent circumstances since the police themselves created the circumstances (*Vale* v. *Louisiana*, 399 U.S. 30 [1970]).

(4.8) *CONSENSUAL SEARCHES*

Nothing in the Fourth Amendment requires the issuance of a warrant when the party in possession of that which is to be searched validly consents to the search. There is nothing immoral or unethical about asking a suspect to give his consent. As a matter of fact, the majority of police searches are made on this basis. The "waiver" is simply the voluntary relinquishment of a known right—the right to demand a search warrant. Consensual searches are convenient because of several factors.

1. The search need not be based on probable cause or a lesser amount of proof.
2. The search does not have to be related to a valid arrest.
3. The officer does not have to name or particularly describe the property sought.
4. The search may be commenced long after the leads have become stale.
5. The premises to be searched do not have to be particularly described.
6. Extensive paperwork and judicial approval are unnecessary.
7. The search may be conducted outside the officer's jurisdiction.

a. Voluntariness

The consent must be freely given, without coercion or deceit. Once incriminating evidence or contraband is found, the suspect's only realistic defense is to challenge the legality of the consent itself. It is important, therefore, that officers document facts surrounding the giving of consent. It may not be enough simply to warn a suspect that he has the right to refuse to give his consent. Below are some factors that tend to prove the voluntariness of the consent.

1. The suspect actively assists the officers in conducting the search.
2. The suspect verbally incriminates himself.
3. The suspect expresses a belief that nothing incriminating will be found.
4. The suspect is the first to suggest that a search be made.
5. The suspect is well educated or holds a responsible position.

Factors that tend to prove a consent was not given voluntarily include the following.

1. The suspect is an alien or is semiliterate.
2. The original entry into the premises was illegal.
3. The consent was taken while the subject was at gunpoint and was handcuffed.
4. The officers made "implied threats" such as "You'll be better off if you cooperate."
5. The suspect was forcibly arrested and suffered minor injury, such as lacerations.

Exculpatory statements expressing belief that nothing will be found tend to support a finding of voluntariness. This is so because of the recognition that many suspects use affirmative means to suggest their innocence. Similarly, a suspect might believe that the items sought are well hidden and will not be discovered. The courts have also recognized that denials of ownership or a stated lack of authority to give consent are simply efforts to use an alternative defense.

The Supreme Court has held that an officer may not falsely state that he possesses a search warrant in the hope that he will obtain consent. Such action constitutes coercion and would invalidate the consent as "freely given." Officers may state that if consent is not given they will apply for a search warrant. They may also express the belief, if it is reasonable, that a warrant will be issued at their request. They can, moreover, advise the suspect that, unless he voluntarily consents to an immediate search, his premises will be placed under surveillance while they attempt to secure a search warrant.

If a detective posed as a building inspector and sought to search a place for "building code violations," the search would be illegal. Deceit differs from "infiltration," which rests on another theory. If an officer works undercover or poses as a criminal, such action does not legally constitute deceit. Although deception is necessary, it is the "misplaced trust" put in the officer that leads to the finding of evidence or contraband. The officer is actually *invited* onto the premises. In the incident of the building inspector, he is *permitted* to enter the place to be searched. As an example, officers, posing as customers, enter a pawnshop and ask to see "better buys." The owner takes them into the back room and displays stolen wares. The officers were invitees the owner mistakenly believed were genuine customers. The items observed in plain view are thus admissible.

The simplest method of ensuring that a suspect knows he has the right to refuse his consent is to tell him so. It is not essential that this be done. The Supreme Court has stated (*Schneckloth* v. *Bustamonte*, 93 S. Ct. 2041, 2059 [1973]) that the "prosecution is not required to demonstrate such knowledge as a prerequisite to obtaining a voluntary consent." A distinction should be made when the suspect is under arrest and in custody. At that stage, a suspect is entitled to a recital of the *Miranda* warnings because of the "inherently coercive atmosphere" associated with custodial questioning. It is recommended that officers obtain written consents to search from suspects who have been arrested. Such waivers indicate that the suspect knows he has the right to refuse his consent.

The burden of showing that a consent was involuntary rests on the defense. Nothing in the *Miranda* decision applies to consensual search cases. Some courts have, nevertheless, enlarged on a suspect's rights under the Fourth and Fifth Amendments as they are embodied in their respective state constitutions.

b. Scope and Capacity

Officers frequently assume that once consent is given it applies to all of their subsequent actions. This is untrue, and the courts will limit the areas of permissible search to the scope of the given consent. Authority to look in a glove compartment does not extend to a locked trunk. Consent to frisk a suspect does not include the right to rummage through his wallet. A suspect may limit the places that can be searched, define the time limits, direct the numbers or classes of searching officers, and revoke his consent at any time.

Consent may be given by juveniles as well as adults. Courts often hold, however, that a person lacks the capacity to give his consent when he is drunk, high on drugs, very youthful, mentally retarded, injured or in pain, illiterate, or hysterical.

Consensual searches are not limited to goods and chattels. A suspect can lawfully consent to the taking of his fingerprints or footprints; urinalysis; hair, blood, and seminal samples; handwriting and voice exemplars; paraffin and other skin tests; breath and pupillary examinations; and nalorphine injections (the nalline addiction test).

c. Third-Party Consent

At common law, a husband, as head of the household, could consent to a search of the family residence. Over half of the states have ruled that the wife can also consent to a search of the family residence. Five states (Arizona, Florida, Mississippi, North Carolina, and Oklahoma) have ruled, however, that wives lack the authority to allow police officers to enter the family's premises to search for evidence (*see Annotation*, 31 A.L.R. 2d 1078, Sec. 10). It is generally felt that one spouse has as much right as the other to control the household, in the absence of the partner. The Supreme Court has recently held that a wife may consent to the search of the family home under the Fourth Amendment, but states are free to fashion a more restrictive rule based on their state constitutions.

Some courts have examined the subject's marital situation to see if it was harmonious or antagonistic. Most courts have upheld the legitimacy of the consent if both parties live on the premises, since they have equal control or right of control over the property. It may be another situation when the spouse has moved out of the suspected home. If the vacating party has retained a key and has lawful access to the home, the consent is probably valid. On the other hand, if the vacating party returned the key to the other spouse on separation, a forcible entry based on the consent of the vacating spouse is of dubious validity.

So-called common-law marriages and temporary liaisons often result in relationships of convenience. The test of the validity of a consent is control and access. It is unnecessary to prove that one person authorized another to give his or her consent to a search. The following serves as an example. William Matlock lived with a woman in a large home. Officers who were investigating a bank robbery asked the woman for her consent to search Matlock's room, which she shared with him.

Matlock was in custody, and his consent was not sought. The woman pointed out Matlock's room, and the officers confiscated a large quantity of money. The Supreme Court upheld the woman's consent and the subsequent seizure. Although the woman's statements were hearsay, the court found them inherently believable, made against her interests because she could have involved herself, and were thus admissible in a suppression hearing (*U.S.* v. *Matlock*, 415 U.S. 443 [1971]).

It is possible that one spouse may not have access and control over some property of the other, regardless of the length of time they have been married and cohabiting. Examples include a safe, a safe-deposit box, or a file cabinet that is locked and exclusively used by one spouse.

Regardless of the age of a child, his room may be searched with the consent of a parent who owns or leases the premises. Even if the child pays his parents something for support, the room he uses does not, in most cases, take on the context of separately rented property. When, however, a child lives with his spouse in separate quarters over which the parents have voluntarily relinquished control, the situation is different. The situation is similar when a parent moves in with an emancipated child. In that case, the parent can only give consent to the search of his room and jointly occupied rooms. On the other hand, if the child owns or leases the home, he can usually grant consent to officers to search the entire premises, including rooms occupied by a parent, brother, or sister. Normally a brother or sister could not consent to the search of a sibling's private room, only to shared and commonly occupied rooms.

Roommates can give consent for the search of their own rooms and those occupied in common, such as the kitchen, bathroom, basement, garage, and hallways. This situation frequently arises in college towns and in communes.

Hosts may normally consent to the search of rooms occupied by visitors. If, however, the houseguest has a reasonable expectation of privacy, the consent will not be binding. Things left on the dresser of an unlocked bedroom are not within the zone of privacy. Things put in drawers or left in suitcases normally would be. Jointly used drawers, closets, and storage space do not create an expectation of privacy.

The concept of the expectation of privacy is a limited one. The expectation is not that a roommate, host, or cotenant will not consent to a police search. The expectation must be that this person will not have access to these places. Thus, the question is an expectation from an intrusion by the other party, not an expectation that his consent will not be given the police.

Landlords do not have the right to consent to a search of occupied property they have leased to another person, even if the tenant is in arrears. Once the tenant has vacated or given up occupancy, the landlord may consent to a search. Although a landlord might have a right to enter a tenant's premises to make repairs, to inspect for damage or hazards, and to show the premises to future tenants, this right is a limited one, and it cannot be extended to police officers for another purpose.

Hotel rooms that are occupied by guests, even past checkout time, are treated no differently than premises leased for longer durations. If a maid, bellhop, valet, or any other employee sees contraband or weapons in a room and notifies the police, the police should refrain from entering the room until a search warrant is obtained. If the officers responding to a call reasonably believe that evidence or contraband will be destroyed or removed, they may, of course, act immediately because of the exigent circumstances surrounding the event. Courts do not lightly uphold exigent searches and will often demand strict compliance with the warrant requirement.

Employers normally have the right to inspect lockers and work areas that are assigned to employees for the mutual convenience of workers and employers. Employees usually cannot expect immunity from employer-instituted searches of company property, including desks, file cabinets, and company-owned vehicles.

Employees do not have an unrestricted right to consent to the search of an employer's property. A manager, of course, has broader discretion in authorizing a search than a clerk. Partners, who at law are joint owners, may consent to the search of the company's premises, files, books, and other property. Silent partners in a limited partnership ordinarily do not have unlimited access and authority and cannot authorize such a search.

Schools, which are somewhere between employers and parents, have the power to authorize a search by police of lockers and other areas that are used by or assigned to a student. Dormitory rooms occupied by college-age students do not fall within this exception, and the school is relegated to the status of a landlord in these situations.

(4.9) *BORDER SEARCHES*

Several federal statutes authorize searches at our nation's borders. It is unnecessary to demonstrate the existence of probable cause to justify such searches. This does not mean, however, that the border patrol and customs and immigration officers have complete freedom to conduct warrantless searches. They still must comply with the test of reasonableness as set down in the Fourth Amendment.

The mere fact that a person crosses a border is justification for a customs search. Officers may not subject an individual to indignities and intrusions on human privacy unless there is a reasonable suspicion that he is smuggling contraband or items subject to duty.

Recent court decisions have restricted the right of federal agents to conduct random searches at some distance from the actual border. For example, the occupants of a vehicle seen near but not crossing the Mexican border may appear to be Mexican nationals. This is not sufficient reason for federal agents to stop them to determine whether they are actually aliens. Probable cause is not necessary, however, at a fixed checkpoint some distance from the border.

(4.10) *"SHOCKING" SEARCHES*

Some types of searches may "shock" the conscience of the reviewing court and are therefore illegal. The landmark case is *Rochin* v. *California*, 342 U.S. 165 (1952), where the Supreme Court invalidated the use of a stomach pump to retrieve narcotics the suspect had swallowed. The use of an emetic, given by medical personnel, has, however, been upheld. This is particularly true when the suspect swallows a balloon filled with narcotics, the contents of which could have fatal effects.

The Supreme Court also allowed, in *Schmerber* v. *California*, 384 U.S. 757 (1966), the extraction of blood from a suspect, under medically supervised conditions. Another case in California, *People* v. *Kraft*, 84 Cal. Rptr. 280 (App. 1970), held that the application of a scissors lock on the suspect's leg and holding his arm immobile constituted excessive force and was, therefore, an impermissible search.

Several courts have maintained that a successful attempt to prevent a suspect from swallowing apparent contraband is not an illegal search. This includes choking the suspect or inserting fingers into his mouth. (*State* v. *Young*, 550 P. 2d 689 [Wash. App. 1976]).

Searches of a suspect's rectum or vagina have been upheld when they are done in a "dignified manner" and when police have reasonable grounds to believe contraband has been concealed in these body cavities. Routine inspections of these areas are not permissible.

"Strip searches" of suspects arrested for minor offenses are generally held to be unreasonable. (*People* v. *Seymour*, 398 N.E. 2d 1191 [Ill. App. 1979]; *Tinetti* v. *Wittke*, 620 F. 2d 160 [7th Cir. 1980] Affg. 479 F. Supp. 486 E. D. Wisc. 1979). But strip searches and visual inspection of body cavities after a contact prisoner visit have been approved by the Supreme Court. (*Bell* v. *Wolfish,* 441 U.S. 520, 25 Cr.L. 3053 [1979]).

(4.11) *STANDING*

"Standing" refers to the legality of a person's status to file a motion or seek other relief. Before 1960, if a defendant denied possession or ownership of seized items of evidence he had no "standing" to move the court to suppress it. The rule was then changed by the Supreme Court decision of *Jones* v. *U.S.*, 362 U.S. 257, which gave any defendant an automatic "standing" and allowed defendants to move to suppress evidence without having to admit that they owned it or possessed it.

In one of the moves that further weakened the exclusionary rule, the Supreme Court has overruled the *Jones* case and in a series of decisions now holds that a suspect must have standing before he can move to suppress evidence in that he must (a) have a privacy interest in the article seized and (b) he must also have a personal right of privacy in the *place* searched. (*Rakas* v. *Illinois; Rawlings* v. *Kentucky,* 27 Cr. L. 3245 [1980]; *U.S.* v. *Salvucci,* 27 Cr. L. 3245 [1980]).

The defendant's testimony at the suppression hearing, where he must admit an interest in the items seized, cannot be used as evidence against him at the subsequent trial. (*Simmons* v. *U.S.*, 390 U.S. 377.) But it is still an open question whether his suppression evidence can be used to impeach his testimony if he chooses to take the stand at his trial.

(4.12) *MISCELLANEOUS SEARCHES*

When a search warrant is used, can individuals found on the premises be personally searched? *Ybarra* v. *Illinois,* 63 L. Ed 2d 838 (1979), involved an Illinois search warrant for narcotics in a tavern and on the bartender. In executing the search warrant, the police also did a pat-down for weapons on customers and found narcotics on one of them.

The Illinois statute allowed a search of any person on the premises. The Supreme Court, however, suppressed the narcotics evidence in spite of the Illinois statute, pointing out that the bar cutomers had a "legitimate expectation of privacy" of their persons while in the tavern and that there was not even a "reasonable suspicion" in this case to justify a *"Terry"* type pat-down. (*See* also *People* v. *Summers,* 243 N.W. 2d 689 [Mich. 1976]).

The widespread use of administrative searches done for building inspections, industrial inspections, and the like has been restricted by decisions regarding OSHA inspections. For the latter, the courts now either require a consent from the owner or else a showing of probable cause from the government and the issuing of a warrant authorizing the search.

(4.13) *SUMMARY*

The Fourth Amendment, made applicable to the states by the Fourteenth Amendment, applies to people, not to things or places. It has been continuously interpreted in light of modern phenomena, such as motor vehicles. Aside from its literal meanings, it prohibits unreasonable searches and allows those that are reasonable. There is no absolute warrant requirement, for example, and the test of reasonableness applies. The amendment is applied in criminal cases by the enforcement of the exclusionary rule. It is an absolute rule. There are not gradations in sanctions based on the gravity of the unlawful character of a policeman's acts. The rule does not consider either the good faith of an officer or its total absence. It only theoretically deters police "misconduct."

Not every act that uncovers evidence, contraband, or other seizable items is a "search." Open lands are quite different from homes. Moreover, an officer does not have to close his eyes to things he observes in plain view, in a place he has a lawful right to be. He may use technical aids, such as field glasses, in his surveillances and accomplish lawfully what he could not do directly through trespass.

Decisions related to the Fourth Amendment no longer follow strict concepts of property. If a person has a reasonable expectation of privacy, any warrantless intrusion upon this right will give rise to the exclusion of evidence. Again, the test is the reasonableness of an individual's expectation of privacy, and no absolute lines are drawn. Officers can no longer justify their actions on the basis that they had a legal right to be where they could observe illegal activity.

Concepts of property are still important when they involve abandonment or consent. The Supreme Court has relaxed many of the technical aspects surrounding consent searches and has imposed the overall standard of reasonableness.

Vehicles are still treated differently than homes. Because they are movable and because their contents are more readily subject to removal, concealment, and destruction, a warrant is usually unnecessary. Though the Fourth Amendment still protects people without regard to the place searched, the rule of reasonableness recognizes the exigent circumstances that surround a vehicular search. Two types of searches are covered by distinct rules. Border searches do not require evidence of suspicious conduct unless the suspect is asked to disrobe or other significant intrusions are attempted. Inventory inspections are not really searches at all, at least in the criminal sense; they are justified by the duty of officers to safeguard property in their keeping.

chapter 5

No. P.N.D.A. - 1597.

Name Geo Cassidy alias Butch Cassidy alias

Alias Ingerfield. right name Robt. Parker

Age 32 Height 5 ft 9" Weight 165

Complexion Light Hair Flaxen

Eyes Blue Beard ______ Teeth ______

Nationality American

Marks and Scars 2 cut scars back head

Small red scar under left eye.

eyes deep set. Small brown

mole calf of leg.

Arrested for Grd. Lar. Fremont Co. Wyo.

Remarks July-15-94. Pardoned Jan 19-96

by Gov. Richards

Home is in Circle Valley, Utah

Sandy beard & Mustache if any.

8166

P70-44

(Courtesy of Wyoming State Archives, Museums and Historical Department.)

BUTCH CASSIDY AND THE RECORD OF HIS ARREST ON JULY 15, 1894

Arrest and Search Warrants

As mentioned in chapter 4, physical evidence is not admissible unless it has been lawfully collected. In many cases, the defendant goes free because of a faulty seizure of evidence. To avoid the consequences of the exclusionary rule, officers must be expert in the laws of arrest, search, and seizure.

The subject of arrest and search warrants has never received more attention than it is now. In recent years, the U.S. Supreme Court has emphasized the importance of interposing the determinations of a "neutral and detached magistrate" between the police officer and the citizen. Early in 1976, the California Supreme Court said that unless there are exigent circumstances, police officers must obtain a warrant before arresting a person in his home. Failure to do so would result in the suppression of evidence seized incident to the arrest. (*People* v. *Ramey*, 127 Cal. Rptr. 629 Cal. [1976]).

In 1980, the Supreme Court (*Payton* v. *New York*, and *Riddick* v. *N.Y.*, 63 L. Ed. 2d 639) ruled in this same area that a warrantless nonconsensual entry into a *suspect's* home to make a *routine* felony arrest violates the Fourth Amendment.

This decision did not consider whether exigent circumstances would validate such an arrest, nor did it pass on warrantless felony arrests in the home of a third party. However, other decisions have collectively held that probable cause, warrantless felony arrests in *any* private home can only be done if there is an emergency situation. (*U.S.*

v. *Williams*, 26 Cr. L. 2421 [3rd Cir. 1976]). Warrantless arrests in *public* places are always valid if on probable cause. (*U.S.* v. *Watson*, 423 U.S. 411 [1976]).

The standards for a warrantless arrest or search are, moreover, the same as for the issuance of a warrant in either case. At the time an officer applies for a warrant, all the supporting facts and circumstances must be set forth in the affidavit itself, which means the facts must be in writing or otherwise recorded. The prosecution then is bound by the contents of the affidavit. This is the so-called "four corners" rule, (*U.S.* v. *Damitz*, 495 F. 2d 50 [9th Cir., 1974]).

The showing of probable cause must be contained within the four corners of the piece of paper given to the magistrate. Supplementary material cannot be supplied later to validate the warrant's issuance. In many jurisdictions, even oral statements given under oath cannot be a consideration by the issuing magistrate. (*U.S.* v. *Anderson*, 453 F. 2d 174 [9th Cir., 1971].)

If there is a *warrantless* arrest, however, probable cause does not need to be shown until the time of a preliminary court hearing or a trial. This gives the police time to gather additional facts pointing to guilt, but the prosecution still cannot use post-arrest information to justify the original arrest.

(5.1) *PROBABLE CAUSE*

Both search and arrest warrants must be based *on the probability* that a crime has been committed. In addition, for an arrest warrant, the suspect must be identified. Where the name is unknown, Joe Doe warrants, coupled with a description, are permissible. A search warrant need not identify the suspect, but it must show probable cause that the physical evidence of the offense will be found at a particular place and time. Nearly all states provide also that a search warrant may be issued for a described person.

For a search warrant, the affiant should express his belief, based on stated facts, that the things sought will be found in the location to be searched. (*People* v. *Prall,* 145 N.E. 610 [Ill. 1924].)

However, it is not necessary to assume that particular goods will exist if the crime is the kind involving a turnover of items, and the ones found are of the same general class. Surveillances may indicate, for example, that a suspect has taken bets on horses over a period of several weeks. Officers do not have to assume that the older betting records still exist. They need only allege that the crime requires the keeping of records.

Though staleness is always a significant factor that may imperil the validity of search warrants, arrest warrants are good indefinitely, subject only to the statute of limitations.

(5.2) *GROUNDS FOR ISSUANCE*

Search warrants are not among the warrants, writs, and other processes recognized by common law; they are wholly statutory. The Fourth Amendment requires that all warrants must be supported by probable cause, under oath, and they must particularly describe the person or things sought and the person or place to be searched. Most states require the request to be written, but transcribed testimony is constitutionally acceptable if it is allowed by statute. It is imperative that the affiant, sometimes called a complainant, state that he has been placed on his oath or affirmation.

Search warrants can only be secured for enumerated offenses, whereas arrest warrants can be issued for any crime unless a statute demands issuance of a summons or citation. Only the things listed in the statute can be named in the warrant. Recent legislation tends to simplify the list to include the following:

1. contraband, the possession of which is unlawful;
2. instrumentalities used to commit any crime;
3. fruits of crime;
4. items that are evidence of the commission of a crime or the identity of the perpetrator.

Prior to 1967 some states did not allow the issuing of search warrants that sought "mere evidence," which might be a blood-stained undershirt, mud scrapings from shoes, a diary or plans, powder burns on a cuff, or innumerable other things that could only be listed in a statute by category. These things could only be seized incidental to a valid arrest. A serious problem arose because of the restrictions imposed on the scope of searches incident to arrest in the *Chimel* case. The Supreme Court made clear in *Warden* v. *Hayden*, 387 U.S. 294 (1967), that "mere evidence" could be seized by warrant, assuming there was a statute authorizing such searches. Unfortunately, not all states acted promptly after the Hayden case and relied on pre-*Chimel* standards.

(5.3) *PARTICULAR DESCRIPTION*

The requirement that an item be particularly described is flexible. It means the best-known description of the thing sought, not necessarily a unique description. Officers should mention the specific things sought, plus the generic name, so as to authorize seizure of similar items found but not named in the warrant. For example, contraband can be loosely described as narcotics, illegal weapons, or counterfeit currency, but it is preferable to state heroin, cocaine, and other narcotics; a sawed-off shotgun, automatic rifle, and other illegal firearms; or counterfeit twenty-dollar notes and other U.S. tender.

Some courts have permitted a vague description in the warrant if a more precise description appeared in the affidavit and vice versa. Ordinarily, however, care should be used to repeat the descriptions exactly.

Many of the cases with suppressed warrants involve misdescribed premises to be searched. A street address is sufficient where a single-family residence is involved, but it is preferable to state that the premises are a one- or two-storied single-family residence and to describe the home. One might state, for example, "a red brick structure with a front and rear entrance, green front door, and pitched roof covered by gray shingles." Rural property must be so clearly described that there can be no doubt about which place was meant.

Some rooming houses do not number floors, much less rooms, and so they must be described in a way similar to the following: "past the front door and up two landings, south thirty feet and up one landing, south down the hallway to the third door on the left (east side of hall)." At least one court decision (*Morales* v. *State,* 170 N.W. 2d 684 [Wis. 1969]) has approved of the inclusion of a photograph of the premises, attached to the affidavit, and referred to in the warrant. A minor defect in the description will not invalidate the search unless it means that two or more places fit the description. Even in that case, if the affiant or other officer who conducted the surveillances also serves the warrant, the search will be upheld in most jurisdictions.

It is important that the affidavit and warrant list the parts of the building to be searched, unless there is probable cause to believe the things sought could be anywhere in it. This becomes critical when two or more unrelated persons or families share a residence. Only ingenuity can identify which person or family lives in the back, the basement, or the attic. If the officers learn they have named the wrong portion of the building once they have entered it, they should seal the exits and obtain a new warrant quickly.

As mentioned previously, search and arrest warrants may be obtained for persons as well as places. A name is ordinarily sufficient for an arrest warrant, and the name and address for a search warrant. If a physical description is known, however, it is preferable to include it in the warrant and the supporting affidavit. A physical description, photograph, or other method of identifying the individual must be part of a John Doe warrant. For example, a search warrant could be issued for the following: "a negro male, dark complected, balding, middle aged, who accompanies [name] on Monday mornings when money is picked up and sits on the right side, front seat, of the red over white 1976 Mustang Lic. ASD-701."

The affiant should be described in such a manner as a police officer, victim, or eyewitness. In cases where only circumstantial evidence is present, it is essential that the affiant's background be set forth in detail. It is one thing for a priest or postman to see two people conversing; it is quite another for an experienced narcotics officer to observe this same conversation. Police officers may rely on their specialized training and experience when they are interpreting their surveillances and disclosures by informants. Chief Justice Warren Burger, speaking for two other justices in *U.S.* v. *Harris,* 403 U.S. 584 (1971), stated: "We cannot conclude that a policeman's knowledge of a suspect's reputation—something that policemen frequently know and a factor that impressed such a 'legal technician' as Mr. Justice Frankfurter—is not a 'practical consideration of everyday life' upon which an officer (or magistrate) may properly rely in assessing the reliability of an informant's tip." Factors bearing on an officer's expertise include such items as the number of arrests, raids, surveillances, or particular types of police activities he has taken part in.

An officer does not have to compile an impressive arrest record personally; it is sufficient that he participated in arrests or raids in order to gain the necessary expertise to give an opinion in a search or arrest warrant affidavit. Certain activities give important clues to the individual with expertise. The following examples illustrate what such a person might ascertain.

1. A gambling detective observes a suspected bookmaker carrying sheets of an off-white colored paper into an apartment. This could be nitrocellulose fibered rag, known as "flash paper," which instantly burns without residue; it is frequently used by wire room operators.

2. A gambling detective observes a suspected bookmaker carrying a plastic bucket, wooden salad fork, and bottle of liquid drain opener into an apartment. Gelatin paper, which is used extensively by wire room operators, rapidly dissolves in water. Decomposition is assisted by liquid drain openers. A large wooden fork quickens destruction in a plastic bucket.

3. A narcotics detective observes a suspected pusher giving tinfoil packets to a suspected addict and receiving money. Heroin and cocaine are often sold in aluminum foil or cellophane packets.

4. A narcotics detective observes a suspected pusher buy a large bottle of sleeping capsules at a drugstore. These capsules can be easily taken apart, filled with cut heroin, and recapped.

Burglars are known by their tools; gamblers and addicts are known by their associates; prostitutes and some homosexuals are known by the parts of town they frequent. Even if an officer-affiant is not personally acquainted with such facts, he can include them in his affidavit. The collective wisdom of the entire police department can be referred to in supporting pleadings. To reiterate, the important point to remember is that an officer's background should be particularized in the affidavit.

(5.4) *USE OF INFORMANTS*

Informants often supply the basis for warrants of both types. Confidentiality is frequently needed to protect the informant. The police may obtain a valid warrant on confidential information but must show under oath that the informant is reliable, based on past incidents.

The accused will often contest the validity of either type of warrant used against him, question the reliability of the informant, and demand the revelation of his identity. These factors raise problems for the court. Informants may be "stoolies," "good" citizens, or police officers. All three may need the protection of confidentiality.

Police agencies should keep careful records on confidential informants, referring to each by a code number. Each time an informant furnishes information, a report should be written and an attempt made to verify the facts. A running record should be kept on all criminal informants because their tips cannot furnish the basis for probable cause unless prior reliability is demonstrated.

Proving an informant's reliability can be accomplished in a number of ways. The usual method is to allege that the informant has provided information in the past and that he has proved himself trustworthy. A single arrest that results from prior information can provide the necessary reliability, if one of two conditions is met: First, a conviction resulted from the arrest. Second, evidence was seized at the time of the arrest even though a conviction was not obtained for some reason or the prosecution is still pending.

Multiple arrests, regardless of whether evidence was seized and although the prosecution of the cases is still pending, also demonstrate reliability. Surveillances provide another way of verifying an informant's disclosures. If independent observations by police officers corroborate the information, reliability is established, as it is when a second informant independently corroborates the facts of the first informant.

A preeminent case on disclosures by an informant is *Spinelli* v. *U.S.*, 393 U.S. 410 (1969). The Supreme Court affirmed prior decisions that held that a police officer may obtain a warrant, based on the word of a confidential underworld informant, if, first, the affidavit states how the informant obtained his information, and, second, the word of the informant is sufficiently corroborated from past instances of reliability, surveillances, or other supporting sources. The problem is particularly acute when an informant who does not qualify for good citizen status is being used for the first time.

Courts abhor "hearsay on hearsay." Even if an informant has provided good leads a hundred times, the investigating officers must determine whether the latest disclosure is based on personal knowledge. Without such assurances, the information will not in itself support a conclusion that probable cause exists. The problem facing law enforcement officers is that an informant cannot always permit this information to be written into an affidavit without jeopardizing his anonymity. If, for example, an informant was the only person who saw a suspect in possession of stolen goods, the affidavit might as well give the informant's name to indicate how he knows the suspect to be in possession of the goods. There is no problem if several individuals saw the suspect in possession of the goods, unless, of course, the exact time was stated.

An affidavit can be intentionally vague concerning the way an informant obtained his information if the facts disclosed are in sufficient detail that a court can presume the knowledge is firsthand. The following is an example of such a statement. "A confidential informant told me that Jones has a quantity of heroin in his apartment at 234 Main, suite B. He said that the heroin is kept in red balloons and is concealed in a green vase. The vase is on a walnut bookshelf on the east side of the living room of said apartment. The informant has personal knowledge of the truth of this information."

Informants usually provide information in a particular area such as gambling, narcotics, or hijacking, but if they are reliable in one area they are usually reliable in another. It is not necessary that the informant's reliability be based on past experience in the activity under investigation.

The so-called good citizen informant receives greater respect from the courts. Thus, it is not necessary for the police to establish tested reliability, and the person's disclosures do not need independent corroboration. The Supreme Court concluded in *U.S.* v. *Harris*, supra, that a person who lacks experience as an informer and is not part of the criminal community can furnish probable cause to law enforcement officers. As with the *Spinelli* case, he would have to disclose how he learned of the suspected activity. The affidavit, in such cases, must affirmatively establish that the citizen is not a part of the scheme, does not have a criminal record, fears for his safety, and witnessed evidence of the offense. Statements from witnesses that they participated in an illicit act are also entitled to credibility since, in the words of the Supreme Court, "people do not lightly admit a crime . . . ." In the *Harris* case, which involved bootlegging, the citizen informant stated that he had recently purchased moonshine from the suspect.

The courts preserve the confidentiality of informants. To do otherwise would jeopardize their lives, their safety, and their privacy. In 1967 the Supreme Court clearly held that confidential, nonparticipating informants may establish probable cause for the police to make an arrest or to conduct a search. Their identities should not be disclosed as a matter of public policy. Though their disclosures may furnish underlying probable cause to support the search or arrest upon which the prosecution is predicated, they may not be used against an accused at his trial. In limited cases, however, courts will order production of an informant or revelation of his identity. Should this situation arise, the prosecution can either comply or drop the charges. The informant's confidentiality will not be breached unless disclosure is necessary to a fair trial or the informant actually participated in the offense being prosecuted. (For further elaboration of this subject, *see* chapter 8.)

Confidential information received from other police officers is intrinsically reliable. It is unnecessary to establish a history of tested disclosures or to corroborate the information through surveillances. The knowledge of one officer, at law, is the knowledge of the whole police department, and officers are presumed, at law, to be truthful and to have a duty to exchange information. They are more likely to use care in repeating things overheard, and their hearsay is more likely to be valid. Information furnished among officers does not lose any credibility because of repetition; such exchanges are merely conduits of "official" knowledge. Though police officers normally want to testify against a suspect, there are valid reasons for preserving confidentiality. Undercover agents might be identified, working relationships with other informants might be impaired, and other unpleasant consequences might result.

The law distinguishes between named and confidential informants. This is because a named informant may be subpoenaed to a deposition, and he can be called to testify at the trial by either side and can be cross-examined. Most victims of and witnesses to a crime are named informants. They may, however, be treated as confidential informants. If they are credible public citizens, no showing of prior reliability is necessary, particularly when the victim or witness will be produced at the trial or when the information will only be used to develop probable cause for a search warrant.

In larger communities an anonymous informer may occasionally give information to police officers through the mails or over the telephone. Such informants cannot be accorded the good citizen presumption, and prior reliability must be shown. Reliability can be established where, in repeated instances, the anonymous informant is recognized by his handwriting, his voice, or through the use of a code name (*People* v. *Cain,* 15 Cal. App. 3d 687 [1971]).

(5.5) *SURVEILLANCES*

Surveillances are used by police for a variety of purposes. They often supply the information needed to carry out an efficient and safe raid. Sometimes they are conducted to keep tabs on known criminals or terrorists. They may explain motives of suspects or ensure that no other persons are involved. They are often necessary to establish probable cause for a search or arrest warrant. Surveillances may also be required to corroborate information from a criminal informant.

Police officers may lawfully follow a criminal suspect in public areas and make still or motion pictures of his activities (*see* chapter 4 for a discussion of "Searches"). Binoculars, telescopes, and infrared scopes may be used to observe criminal suspects in public and semipublic places. Fluorescein powder, which is excited and becomes visible under ultraviolet light, may be employed. Electronic tracking devices (such as bumper beepers) can be attached to a private car; some courts have found, however, that a suspect's reasonable expectation of privacy may be invaded by their use, and so they should be employed only with the advice of counsel. Surveillances conducted by helicopters and covert rest room observations may, by their nature, be a violation of a suspect's reasonable expectation of privacy.

Police may enter open fields to observe property. A fence designed to keep animals in or erected for apparently aesthetic reasons will not change an open place into a closed one. Areas in multiple-unit dwellings, such as common garages, hallways, and jointly used trash containers may be lawfully observed without a warrant.

A person living on the ground floor in a populous area who leaves his shades up and drapes open does not have a reasonable expectation of privacy. Officers may not peer into windows if doing so involves trespassing. It is also illegal for them to look from a rooftop, use a fire department snorkel truck, or utilize a telescope from a distant building.

Agents using a "high-powered" telescope from across the street looked into a private apartment to watch drug activities. Based on this, the police obtained a search warrant. The resulting drug evidence was later suppressed by the court, which held that the police telescopic view into a private home violated the Fourth Amendment. (*U.S.* v. *Taborda,* 491 F. Supp. 2d 50 [U.S.D.C.E. N.Y., 1980]).

An officer should not completely rely on these generalized guidelines; he should, rather, seek the advice of a prosecutor in all important investigations.

Nothing prevents an officer from assuming the identity of an addict or other criminal, a salesman or customer, or ordinary citizen and from visiting a criminal suspect. A person who carelessly places his trust in another does so at his own peril. Deceptive pretenses, including the furnishing of the motive, opportunity, and means to commit a crime, are all lawful police activities.

Most surveillances do not involve police participation in an offense or overt observations. They usually consist of a list of names, addresses, and license plate numbers, information that is, on the surface, neutral. Once such observations have been completed, corroborative detail must be added by checking available records. Occupancy of a premise can be established through subscription records to telephone, newspaper, water, trash, electric, or gas services, tax rolls, licenses, and building permits. Vehicle registrations are available from the department of motor vehicles, secretary of state, or department of public safety. The identification of persons as "known" gamblers, narcotics users or peddlers, burglars or fences can be made through checks of criminal history with the FBI and state law enforcement agencies. Arrest records of suspects or their associates can assist in the development of probable cause, even though such information is hearsay and is inadmissible in a subsequent trial. Expert opinion of police officers can be used to interpret otherwise innocent facts.

There is a growing tendency for courts to expand concepts concerning privacy. As noted earlier, if a person has a reasonable expectation of privacy, the surveillance is illegal under the *Katz* decision (*Katz* v. *U.S.*, 389 U.S. 347 [1967]).

New methods in the fields of surveillance and search are continually being developed, and the courts must deal with these. For example, many retail stores now use electronic sensory devices to detect stolen merchandise when the customer passes the cash register without paying. At least one court decision has held this is not an unreasonable search or surveillance (*Lucas* v. *U.S.*, 26 Cr. L. 2442 [D. C. Ct. App. 1980]).

(5.6) *EXECUTION AND USE OF FORCE*

Arrest and search warrants are limited to a class of officers named in the statutes. There is no inherent right of a municipal or state police officer to serve all classes of criminal process, and, in some jurisdictions, only the sheriff and his deputies can serve warrants. A warrantless arrest can be made, using an arrest warrant as the basis for believing probable cause exists for the apprehension. Evidence seized incident to that arrest would be admissible in another case. Serving a search warrant, without legal authority to do so, would nullify the warrant.

Statutes or rules of court set the durational limits on serving search warrants, usually 72 to 240 hours. There is no similar restriction on arrest warrants. Some jurisdictions forbid serving any warrant at night unless it is so specified by the court on the warrant.

A warrant does not have to be promptly served if there are good reasons for delay. A search warrant, for example, is normally served when an individual, usually the suspect, is on the premises. This makes it easier for the prosecution to prove a possessory offense, if contraband or fruits of a crime are located. On the other hand, officers may want to delay serving a search warrant until the suspect leaves, if they believe this would lessen the possibility of resistance. It is not improper to delay serving an arrest or search warrant so that more suspects will be present or so that other evidence will be found.

The Supreme Court, in *Cupp* v. *Murphy*, 412 U.S. 291 (1976), affirmed a murder conviction where the defendant's wife had been killed in her bedroom by strangulation. Her husband voluntarily came to the police station for questioning. During his stay there, the police did have probable cause to detain him. He refused to allow his fingernails to be scraped. The police scraped the fingernails anyway without his consent and found skin, blood cells, and fabric from his wife's nightgown.

The defendant was then released and not arrested until a month later. In sustaining his conviction, the court held that because of the "evanescent nature" of the scraping evidence, plus the fact that no full search took place, the search was valid. The delay in the arrest was passed over without comment by the court.

A police officer is required to identify himself, announce his purpose, and request entry into the premises, unless those acts would be futile or dangerous. If his knock is unheeded or if entrance is refused, he may forcibly enter the premises. If the officer has a search warrant, it makes no difference whether or not the items sought are dangerous, whether or not they are feloniously possessed, or whether or not the offense under investigation is a misdemeanor or a felony. In the case of an arrest warrant, the crime can be of any magnitude, and it is not necessary to obtain a search warrant to enter the residence of the accused.

Under the laws of some states, an elaborate procedure has been established for the procurement of "no-knock" warrants. Once the requirements are complied with, a warrant so endorsed can be served by an unannounced forcible entry into the premises.

(5.7) *SCOPE OF SEARCH*

The scope of a search incident to an arrest is the same in warrant situations as in warrantless arrests. (*See* chapter 4 for discussion of the *Chimel* rule.) Search warrants specify the rooms, floors, and areas that may be searched. Officers must restrict themselves to the items sought, even though they suspect other evidence might be found. This does not mean that they must close their eyes to the obvious. If they are lawfully in a place looking for one class of goods or contraband and they see in plain view another class of seizable goods or contraband, the search is lawful. It is advisable in cases where "mere evidence" of an offense is occasionally seen to secure the premises and to obtain a second search warrant. Contraband, weapons, and fruits of a crime can be immediately seized. This type of seizure is not by authority of the warrant, however; it is due to necessity.

A wise officer will always list small items to be sought with a search warrant. For example, currency is the fruit of many crimes. In possessory offenses, evidence of occupancy, such as rent receipts and mail addressed to the occupant, can be sought. Inclusion of these items will authorize officers to search desks, files, and storage boxes in minute detail. Once, however, officers have located the principal items sought and have established occupancy, the search must cease.

An officer would not ordinarily be authorized to remove paneling, rip up carpeting, or tear open chair cushions, but when he is dealing with experienced drug dealers, extreme measures may be called for. In one case, federal agents removed outer shingles, parts of the roof, and dug trenches in the yard of a house worth $65,000. They found nothing and were later sued. The Justice Department paid $160,000 to the owner for physical and mental damages.

It is important that all items seized be properly inventoried on the search warrant, which is returned to the clerk of the court that issued it. A copy of the warrant, together with a receipt for all items taken, must be given to the owner or party in possession of the premises.

(5.8) *ELECTRONIC SURVEILLANCE WARRANTS*

Title III of the Omnibus Crime and Safe Streets Act of 1968 regulates the issuance of warrants authorizing wiretapping and bugging. Most serious offenses are mentioned in the statute, including kidnapping, murder, sabotage, extortion, bribery of public officials, and certain other federal offenses. State attorneys general and district attorneys may personally apply for intercept orders, or authority to wiretap or to bug, in state court.

Not all eavesdropping situations require an intercept order. A person can unilaterally permit police officers to overhear conversations on his telephone, either on an extension or by an alligator clip receiver. A citizen or an officer can wear a concealed radio transmitter or tape recorder without an intercept order. Normal conversations can be taped in this fashion.

Use of a pen register (a device that records the numbers called on a telephone) has been approved by the Supreme Court, who held that it was not a "search." (*Smith* v. *Maryland*, 61 L. Ed. 2d 220 [1979].)

Video tape surveillances have generally been court approved, all the way from the Abscam investigations to their use in such situations as videotaping a police officer in a bar talking with known criminals (*Sponick* v. *Detroit Police Department*, 49 Mich. App. 162 [1973]). A dentist was suspected of sexually molesting his women patients after injecting them with drugs for tooth extraction. Police obtained a warrant to secretly install a TV camera in his office and then videotaped his actions with a female undercover policewoman (*People* v. *Teichner*, 90 Misc. 2d 395, affd, App. Div. 1st Dept. [1980]). The Federal Rules of Evidence 1001 (2) now includes the use of videotapes.

Whenever police officers or federal agents have bugged or tapped a defendant in a criminal case without legal sanction, neither the conversations nor derivative evidence obtained by listening to the conversations can be admitted into evidence. A defendant is entitled to discover the tapes or transcripts and to have a hearing to determine whether any evidence presented against him was tainted by the illegal surveillances. *Kolod* v. *U.S.*, 390 U.S. 136 [1968], mandates an adversary hearing, and a dismissal will be granted if the prosecution fails to produce the transcripts.

Motions to suppress evidence obtained by electronic surveillance are handled in the same manner as motions to suppress physical evidence. An overheard party has standing to challenge the evidence if he can show a violation of *his* rights under the Fourth Amendment. A defendant could not usually challenge with any success the illegal interception of another's home or telephone.

(5.9) *SUMMARY*

Although warrantless arrests and searches are judged by the same standards as those conducted pursuant to warrants, the courts have always expressed a preference for the latter. The procedure requires a police officer to seek out a neutral and detached judicial officer, usually a lawyer, and establish a prima facie case against a suspect.

Warrants are issued upon a statement made under oath, usually a written affidavit. Most courts have adopted the four corners rule, which requires that all elements that comprise the underlying probable cause be within the four corners of the written affidavit. Once a warrant is issued, it is too late for an officer to add additional facts he had mistakenly overlooked. The warrant process forces police officers to arrange their facts and arguments carefully.

The Fourth Amendment requires "particular descriptions" of the person to be seized or searched, the place to be searched, and the things that are sought. The supporting investigations must be complete, and skill in verbal expression is demanded.

Informants and surveillances are often needed to come to the conclusion that probable cause exists. Often the two are intertwined, since neither an informant's disclosures nor a raw surveillance may alone be sufficient.

Care must be used in the execution of warrants, and statutory procedures cannot be avoided. Even a search warrant is a limited authority to intrude upon a suspect's rights. The scope of a search warrant is restricted to the items named and the nature of the offense under investigation.

chapter 6

(Courtesy of the Des Moines Register and Tribune Company.)

THE BARROW GANG CAPTURED AT DEXTER, IOWA, JULY 24, 1933

Interrogations, Confessions, and Nontestimonial Evidence

A. INTERROGATIONS AND CONFESSIONS

(6.1) *THE EXCLUSIONARY RULE IN GENERAL*

In 1964 the U.S. Supreme Court revolutionized the law of confessions and interrogations with the famous case of *Escobedo* v. *Illinois*, 378 U.S. 478 (1964). Danny Escobedo was a murder suspect who was being held in custody by the Chicago police. He had an attorney, but the officers concerned with the case refused the attorney access to his client. Escobedo made damaging admissions, which were later used at his trial. He was thus convicted of the crime. In reversing his conviction, the Warren Court ruled that once an investigation had "focused" on a particular suspect, he was entitled to specific warnings before he could be interrogated.

Two years later, in *Miranda* v. *Arizona*, 384 U.S. 436 (1966), the court ordered an addition to the warning. The "focus" test was all but abolished. Instead, the court adopted the concept of "custodial interrogation." This means that a defendant's pretrial statements are not admissible in evidence to prove his guilt if those statements were obtained by state officers during an interrogation and while the defendant was in custody, *unless* he was warned of his rights under the Fifth Amendment and properly waived them.

The penalty for failure to comply with the requirements of the *Escobedo* and *Miranda* decisions is the exclusion of the statements from the trial, which could prove the guilt of the accused. In the past, trustworthy statements were always admissible, regardless of the ignorance of the accused, his ability to pay for a lawyer, or the hopelessness of his custody.

(6.2) *VOLUNTARINESS OF STATEMENTS*

As was indicated above, prior to the *Escobedo* case, trustworthy statements voluntarily given were always admissible. Needless to say, if a confession was beaten out of a suspect, or if he was coerced into confessing under the duress of a threatened beating, lynching, or other violence, the confession was tainted.

Sometimes there is a fine line between "clever tactics" and coercion. Police officers are not required to be "friendly" with a suspect. They may ask questions in an indignant or hostile manner. They may express belief that the suspect is lying. They can interrogate a suspect using teams of officers, some friendly, some antagonistic. They can play on the suspect's conscience. Officers may act confident that the suspect is guilty and suggest reasons why they believe him to be lying. They may sometimes even express sympathy for the suspect and contempt for the victim. When two suspects are in custody, one can be played against the other.

Statements made by persons who have been falsely arrested are subject to exclusion by the courts. Even a voluntary confession given to the police after the proper *Miranda* warnings will be suppressed if it is a result of an illegal temporary detention (*Dunaway* v. *N. Y.*, 442 U.S. 200, [1979]). The fact that a false arrest is followed by valid *Miranda* warnings and that the interview was free from physical duress is not enough to remove the taint of illegality. In *Brown* v. *Illinois*, 95 S. Ct. 2254 (1975), the Supreme Court ruled that the mere recitation of *Miranda* warnings does not sufficiently interrupt the process to render a confession legal. As in a prior Supreme Court case, the officers had made an arrest without probable cause and had forcibly entered the defendants' homes. Such actions, said the justices, affect the voluntariness of confessions, which cannot, therefore, be the products of a "free will."

The court went on to say that the burden of proving that an illegal arrest did not taint a subsequent confession falls on the prosecution.

(6.3) *THE MIRANDA WARNINGS*

The *Miranda* warnings are four in number, usually read from a pocket card by the police. They advise the suspect that he has a right to remain silent, that anything he says can be used against him in court, that he can consult a lawyer and have one present, and that he will be given a free attorney if he cannot afford one.

After reading the warnings, the officer normally asks formal questions to be sure that the suspect understands his rights. If the accused then goes ahead and talks, the statement is valid. If he refuses or asks for an attorney, any further questioning will result in court suppression of that material.

Officers should always *read* the warnings from a printed card they carry at all times. A jury is more likely to believe that the warnings were complete if they were read, as opposed to their being recited from memory. The *Miranda* card is also admissible into evidence at the trial. The card should be read to the suspect and not simply handed to him to read for himself.

Some courts have split hairs over the second warning. A few departments warn suspects that statements "may" be used against them. Others say they "can" be used. A few state they "will" be used. The theory is that "may" implies that leniency is possible, or even likely, if the suspect confesses.

Miranda applies to both exculpatory and inculpatory statements. Thus, should a suspect admit to being present when a criminal act was committed but not having taken part in the act, officers cannot later testify that the suspect acknowledged his presence at the scene of the crime, if the warnings were absent or defective.

If the warnings are defective, the procedure should be repeated, and anything said after the correct warnings are given will be admissible. When officers begin the interrogation process, they should make sure that proper warnings were given recently and that waivers were obtained. If there is any doubt, the admonitions should be repeated. The officers who first gave the warnings will have to appear in court if the waiver is challenged. It is preferable, therefore, for them to conduct the questioning since it minimizes the number of witnesses needed to prove a confession.

(6.4) *WHAT IS CUSTODY?*

Not every admission or confession must be preceded by a warning of rights. As mentioned above, the *Escobedo* case used the "focus test," that is, whether the investigation focused on the suspect. *Miranda* reinterpreted a suspect's rights under the Fifth Amendment and applied the rule to "custodial interrogations." The court defined this phrase as meaning those circumstances when an accused "is deprived of his freedom in a significant way."

Usually the arresting officers read a suspect the warnings at the time of his actual arrest. It should be noted that an accused does not have a constitutionally protected right to receive these warnings. Rather, his induced statements will be inadmissible in the absence of the warnings. Most departments require that arrested felons be promptly advised of their rights at the time of the arrest. This does not mean, however, that a person who forcibly resists arrest should be warned during the time of his resistance.

Arrests are often made because a police officer observes the offense taking place in his presence. In many such cases, statements received from the suspect are of little value, and it is unnecessary to question him at the time of the arrest. For example, if a demonstrator smashes a window in front of an officer, the individual should be arrested and booked without interrogation. After the arrest and booking, he should be read the warnings before he is questioned. Nothing in the Fifth Amendment requires an officer to demean himself in the presence of a group of demonstrators.

Should the officers who are transporting the suspect engage in conversation with him, they ought to warn him of his rights unless they are sure this has already been done and by whom. Prisoners frequently become talkative at this stage of the process. They may, for example, express regret that they struck an officer. If they later plead self-defense, accusing the officers of aggressive acts, such statements are invaluable.

Once a suspect has been placed in a cell block or is taken to the detective bureau for questioning, he should again be warned of his rights, and a clearly expressed waiver should be taken before questioning begins. It makes no difference that the questioning is not accusatory in nature. It is irrelevant that the suspect is in jail for one offense but is being questioned for another crime. If, however, the officers who are conducting the questioning are from an agency other than the one that first arrested him and are investigating an unrelated case, subsequent statements may be admissible even though the inmate has previously invoked his right to remain silent (*Jennings* v. *U.S.*, 391 F. 2d 512 [5th Cir. 1968]).

Miranda causes the most problems when the suspect has not been placed under formal arrest. A police station may create an inherently "coercive atmosphere." Warnings should always precede questioning at the station house, even if the person is not a strong suspect, or if he or she voluntarily came to the station without invitation. This does not mean, of course, that everyone who visits a police station should receive *Miranda* warnings. Persons who are reporting the theft or loss of property, who are completing accident reports, or who are seeking assistance obviously should not. But if the visitor is a potential suspect in an unsolved crime and officers plan to question him about that crime, the warnings should be given. Sometimes the existence of a crime will be unknown when an individual goes to a station house. For example, Smith goes to a police station to report a stolen car. During the time his report is being taken, a desk officer learns that the car, driven by a man matching Smith's description, was involved in a holdup. Smith should be given the *Miranda* warnings at this time, and questioning should cease until a valid waiver is obtained. Anything said up to this point would, however, be admissible later.

Miranda warnings should always be given when a suspect is asked to go to a station house to be fingerprinted, to take a polygraph examination, to appear in a lineup, or to give a physical specimen (such as hair or blood).

Persons are frequently asked to get inside a police car for the purpose of giving preliminary information about an incident. Whether the interrogation is custodial or not does not always depend on whether the person was arrested. A coercive atmosphere can also exist in a squad car. If, however, cold weather, rain, darkness, or convenience dictate the location of the questioning, the interrogation is less likely to be considered "custodial."

Most sidewalk confrontations are not covered by *Miranda* until the suspect has been formally arrested. If an officer intends to arrest a suspect regardless of what he says, or if he is questioning him at gunpoint or while the suspect is spread-eagled against a wall or made to lie facedown, coercive factors will, of course, be present and will probably invalidate statements made without warnings.

When a crime occurs, the officers on the scene often direct

everyone present to remain on the premises or at the location and not leave without permission. The Supreme Court made clear in the *Miranda* decision that they did not intend to "hamper" the "traditional function of police officers in investigating crime." Thus, general "on-the-scene questioning" as to facts surrounding a crime is not covered by the *Miranda* ruling. This is true even though the exits are temporarily sealed. Circumstances will affect this rule. A possible suicide at a crowded party will be handled differently from the case where the victim is shot six times in the back and only one person is present at the scene.

Though it was originally thought that residential questioning was never covered by the *Miranda* decision, a case in 1969 (*Orozco* v. *Texas*, 394 U.S. 324 [1969]) made clear that this was not always true. Four officers entered the suspect's bedroom at 4:00 a.m. and interrogated him there. They asked him about a shooting that had taken place earlier and sought to inspect his gun. The lateness of the hour, an uninvited intrusion, and the number of officers present, each standing alone, will not require the admonition of the *Miranda* rights. In combination, however, these factors can create a coercive atmosphere that would require the warnings.

In many cases, the fact that the arrest occurred sometime later than the questioning will avoid the necessity of *Miranda* warnings. Though no rigid rule exists, the courts look more favorably on admitting statements if the arrest occurs on a subsequent day rather than shortly after the crime is committed. If, however, interrogating officers already have probable cause to make the arrest and delay the actual apprehension for reasons of convenience, the statements will be inadmissible.

Places of employment are sometimes the sites of police questioning. An employee under the scrutiny of superiors, subordinates, and fellow workers is in a compelling—if not a coercive—atmosphere. The situation is less coercive if the crime being investigated took place on the premises, and everyone understands why police officers are present. This is particularly true if the investigation results from the officers' appearance on the scene immediately after the commission of the crime.

Routine business inspections do not come under the protection of the *Miranda* decision. These include such occurrences as visits to pawnshops by the theft and burglary details, ID checks in establishments licensed to dispense intoxicating beverages, and the like.

Persons who are present where a search is being conducted pursuant to a search warrant should be advised of their *Miranda* rights if they are prevented from leaving, if they are asked to participate in the search, or if they are questioned by officers who are making the search. Once contraband or other evidence is found, there is a more compelling reason to warn persons at the scene of the search.

(6.5) *WHAT IS INTERROGATION?*

Not every question asked by a police officer constitutes interrogation. There should be some connection between the question and the offense or suspected offense. General questions asked before an officer discovers that a crime has been committed are less likely to be considered interrogation than similar questions asked after a crime has been discovered. This is often the case when suspicious persons are encountered on the streets and in alleys.

Interrogation has been defined as "any questioning likely or expected to yield incriminating statements." General on-the-scene questioning, as mentioned above, is not likely to be held "interrogation." Thus, officers responding to a silent burglar alarm notice a man sitting in a van near the premises. The hour is late, and the street is dark. They ask the man to explain his presence. Such generalized questioning is only preliminary and does not constitute "interrogation." The man's initial answer would be admissible, even if the officers blocked his van and detained him temporarily.

At some point, general questioning may become accusatorial questioning. This comes about in one of two ways. First, the questions become less general and focus on incriminating conduct. Second, the conversation systematically eliminates noncriminal explanations, leaving only a conclusion of criminal conduct. For example, officers respond to a call concerning a shooting. They find a young man, seriously wounded and comatose, and an older man. General questioning reveals the wound was not self-inflicted, that no other persons were present, that the shooting was not accidental, and that self-defense was not involved. As the various noncriminal alternatives are eliminated, suspicion deepens that the older man shot the younger man without apparent justification. At this stage, all questioning should cease until the *Miranda* warnings are given. The conversation is no longer general and therefore constitutes interrogation.

Statements that are volunteered are admissible, even though the person making the statement is in custody. This is because volunteered statements are not the product of interrogation. A "volunteered" statement is different from a "voluntary" statement. The first means the utterance came forth without prompting. The second refers to a statement that is free of duress and coercion but is usually brought out by questioning. Volunteered statements are frequently spontaneous and may take officers by surprise. The following are examples of volunteered statements.

1. A man walks into a police station and says, "I just murdered my wife."
2. Police officers knock on a suspect's door, seeking permission to search the premises for narcotics. The suspect says, "That won't be necessary. The dope is under the front seat of my car."
3. A man being driven to the morgue to identify a woman thought to be his wife suddenly says to the officer accompanying him, "Stop. I can't bear to see her. I killed her, and I'm sorry."

"Threshold confessions" are also admissible since they are not the product of an interrogation. They are so called because they are often made as officers cross the threshold of the premises and ask, "What happened?" Once an incriminating statement is volunteered or made in response to a threshold question, further questioning must cease, and the *Miranda* warnings must be given. Anything said up to this point is admissible without the *Miranda* warnings. Most courts have held that an officer does not have to interrupt a person who is in the process of volunteering a story or responding to a threshold question. The longer the story continues, however, and the more pauses contained in it, the more likely it is that an officer must interject with the *Miranda* warnings.

One of the exceptions to *Miranda* is the situation in which an officer is working undercover at the time a crime is being perpetrated. The person talking or answering questions will not be under arrest, but he will be arrested immediately after the conversation is completed. The officer is not required to interrupt the progress of the crime to warn the person of his *Miranda* rights. There must, however, actually be an offense in progress or about to take place for this exception to apply. Thus, it is not permissible to pose as a criminal to interrogate an inmate housed in a jail or prison.

Miranda warnings need not be given to persons responding to questions in an accident report or a similar incident. This is true even if the citizen is suspected of having committed a felony. The purpose of the interview must, of course, be legitimate, such as the completion of a report form. If, during the interview, the citizen makes damaging admissions that are unconnected with the report, the *Miranda* warnings must be given at that point.

(6.6) *WHAT IS A STATE OFFICER?*

The *Miranda* decision only applies to "state action." This means that interrogation by nongovernmental personnel falls outside its mandates. With the exception of Maryland, private security officers in all states are exempt from the *Miranda* decision even if they possess a commission as a special officer or deputy sheriff. Shopkeepers, under many state shoplifting laws, are granted powers of arrest or detention, but these laws do not transform private action into state action. Citizens' arrests are wholly outside the protection of *Miranda*.

Statements made by an arrested felon in response to questions asked by civilians are similarly admissible. Some courts have ruled suspects' statements as inadmissible when an officer requested the civilian to ask certain questions or even when the officer was present at the time the questions were asked. To state the matter simply, the courts will not tolerate subterfuge.

Also outside the scope of *Miranda* are statements made to nonpolice officials, such as physicians and nurses in city hospitals, school administrators, firemen, and similar personnel. It would be a travesty of justice to exclude such admissions because nonpolice officials and employees would not know the *Miranda* warnings or when to give them. Exclusion of these statements would not punish police misconduct, but would only allow inculpatory remarks to be made outside the "coercive" atmosphere of police interrogation.

(6.7) *APPLICABLE OFFENSES*

A survey by the International Association of Chiefs of Police in 1972 indicated wide variance among law enforcement agencies in the interpretation of *Miranda*. Though the decision applies to all felonies, many states have ruled that misdemeanors are excluded from its protections. There is merit to this interpretation if the offense is a petty one, punishable by fine only, or a jail term of short duration (less than six months). Nearly everyone agrees that traffic offenses are outside the scope of *Miranda*, although some courts have extended its protections to serious traffic offenses, such as driving while one is intoxicated.

Officers in states that have not resolved this issue should give the *Miranda* warnings to all persons with an offense punishable by incarceration. This policy will eliminate unnecessary appeals and avoid problems with civil liberties groups.

(6.8) *CAPACITY OF SUSPECTS*

Statements taken from the insane, from persons who are drunk, who are under the influence of drugs, or who do not speak elementary English may not be admissible. A suspect must make a knowing and intelligent waiver. At what age and level of intelligence a person becomes legally capable of understanding his rights and knowingly waiving them is not subject to definition. The mere fact that a suspect is a juvenile will not invalidate the waiver. In one case a waiver by a thirteen-year-old boy was upheld, as was, in another case, a confession by a fifteen-year-old who was "mildly retarded." In other cases, courts have failed to find a knowing and intelligent waiver when the suspect had an IQ of sixty, an IQ of seventy-two at age fifteen, and when age and retardation or other factors impaired the suspect's judgment. The testimony of a psychiatrist that the suspect understood the warnings will go a long way in validating the confession.

Insanity may be a complete or partial defense in a crime, but it does not automatically invalidate a confession. One case upheld a waiver by a paranoid schizophrenic. Another admitted statements by a suspect who had the mental state of a six-year-old.

Most courts have refused to exclude statements made under the influence of alcohol or mild tranquilizers. Addiction to heroin is more likely to invalidate a confession, depending on the amount used, the degree of withdrawal, and other factors.

Whether a suspect was suffering from impaired capacity at the time he made incriminating statements is based on the "totality of the circumstances test." There is no "per se" rule unless it is enacted in the penal or evidentiary code. For example, a law in Colorado forbids the police to question juveniles in the absence of their parents.

Police officers who have custody of a suspect who is willing to talk but whose capacity is dubious, should use the following procedure. First, the statement should be taken, accompanied by other questions that tend to indicate the suspect's mental capacity. If the statement is later excluded from evidence, no harm has been done since the alternative is not to interrogate at all. If the impairment is temporary, officers should attempt to take a second statement at a later time. If this can be done, the second statement should not be induced by reference to the prior statement. This is because the first statement might be excluded. The court might conclude that the second statement was obtained by referring to the first statement, and thus the second statement could be excluded.

Even if the statement is of dubious validity, it might encourage a suspect to plead guilty in the hope of being given a lesser punishment, which is certainly better than a straight acquittal.

(6.9) *IMPEACHMENT AND OTHER DERIVATIVE USES OF INADMISSIBLE CONFESSIONS*

The Supreme Court decided in *Wong Sun* v. *U.S.*, 371 U.S. 471 (1963), that police could not use the results of inadmissible statements to garner additional evidence. In that case federal agents forced their way into the residence of a man named Toy, arrested him without probable cause, and obtained a statement that implicated Wong Sun and Johnny Yee. The statements led to the arrest of Yee and Wong Sun. Wong Sun later confessed his guilt to the agents. The court concluded that the case against Yee was the result of illegal police conduct, "Fruit of the Poisoned Tree." Wong Sun was convicted because his subsequent confession was so "attenuated" from the original illegality that all "taint" was "dissipated."

Thus, evidence that is seized or statements that are subsequently obtained as a result of an inadmissible confession are themselves subject to exclusion, as the "poisoned fruit" of the initial illegality. In order for evidence to be admissible, the prosecution must show one of two things: that the police would have obtained the evidence anyway and without the use of the tainted statements, or that the connection between the original misconduct and the subsequent evidence was too remote to require its exclusion.

Another example of the use of evidence derived from statements made in violation of *Miranda* came to light in *Michigan* v. *Tucker*, 94 S. Ct. 2357 (1974). In its decision, the Supreme Court upheld the following evidentiary scenario: Tucker, the accused, was given defective *Miranda* warnings. His alibi involved Henderson. When Henderson was questioned, he did not support Tucker's alibi; rather, Henderson's testimony further incriminated Tucker. The court ruled that although

Tucker's statements were inadmissible, the police could properly use this information to gain additional evidence against the accused.

In its majority opinion, the Supreme Court said that the law does not require that policemen "make no errors whatsoever. The pressures of law enforcement and the vagaries of human nature would make such an expectation unrealistic." Most lawyers interpret the result in *Tucker* as a loosening of the harsh results of the exclusionary rule rather than as a relaxing of the Poisoned Tree doctrine.

Statements taken in violation of *Miranda* may be introduced at the criminal trial for the purpose of impeaching the credibility of the defendant as a witness if he takes the stand. Suppose, for example, a suspect admits selling heroin but later denies it at the time of his trial. If the statement is tainted because of a *Miranda* violation, it nevertheless may be read to the jury. The purpose of the prior statement is to impair the believability of the accused, not to prove his guilt. It is admitted to contravene his testimony because, said the Supreme Court (*Harris* v. *New York*, 401 U.S. 222 [1971]), "The shield provided by *Miranda* cannot be perverted into a license to use perjury by way of a defense, free from the risk of confrontation with prior inconsistent utterances."

(6.10) *EFFECT OF IMMUNITY OR CONVICTION*

The basis for all restrictions on confessions and admissions is the Fifth Amendment, which prevents a person in a criminal case from being a witness against himself. Once an individual is given immunity from prosecution, he can be compelled, under penalty of contempt, to answer questions put to him. The immunity usually takes effect at the time the person is called before a grand jury. The process is later repeated in the criminal trial.

The Supreme Court has ruled that a person is not entitled to "transactional" immunity; he is limited to "use" immunity. This means that the individual may still be prosecuted for the offense if the police gain their evidence from sources independent of the self-incriminating statements. This has happened occasionally. Thus, under use immunity, the statement itself and the fruits of the statement cannot be used against the accused in a criminal trial. An example follows.

Bruno is granted use immunity before a grand jury and admits that he participated in a counterfeiting scheme. He reveals the location of the printing press (in New Jersey) and the plates (in New York). An accomplice later surrenders himself and brings in the plates from New

York. The surrender is not connected with Bruno's statement. Federal agents could not introduce Bruno's statement against him in a criminal trial, but they could introduce it in prosecuting the accomplice. And the accomplice can testify against Bruno. The printing press, if seized on the basis of information in Bruno's statement, cannot be used in Bruno's trial but could be used in the prosecution of the accomplice. The plates could be used in Bruno's trial since they were turned over to the agents independent of the immunized statement. Had the accomplice been located by using information in Bruno's statement, nothing could be used against Bruno. Had the agents been able to find the accomplice and the plates anyway, Bruno's use immunity would not have prevented the admission into evidence of the plates and the testimony of the accomplice.

Although prosecutors rarely use this technique, a convicted defendant can be called to the witness stand and be required to give testimony that incriminates himself and others. This tactic has been employed occasionally when one party to the offense has received a light sentence and the others are yet to be prosecuted. The reason it is seldom used is because, in most cases involving multiple defendants, one of them offers to plead guilty and testify against the others in the hope of receiving a reduced sentence.

B. EYEWITNESS IDENTIFICATION

(6.11) *LINEUPS AND THE SIXTH AMENDMENT*

In 1967 the Supreme Court ruled in three cases (*Wade, Gilbert,* and *Stovall,* 388 U.S. 218, 263, 293) that an indicted defendant is entitled to the presence of counsel at lineup. In 1972 the Court in *Kirby* v. *Illinois,* 406 U.S. 682, stated the present rule about lineups, saying that after "criminal procedings have been initiated, that is after indictment, prosecutor's information, arrest by warrant or arraignment, once he is 'formally charged' this right to lineup counsel attaches," and the defendant is entitled to have his lawyer present.

There is no reason why a defendant cannot waive his right to counsel. Waivers are routinely given in police departments in large cities, often on the advice and with the consent of the public defender.

A very thorough written report should be made immediately following the lineup. Questions asked of each witness and their responses should be transcribed or recorded. Officers must use great care not to suggest the identification of any particular participant. Each witness should be interviewed separately and told not to discuss possible identifications with each other.

Rare is the lineup that includes five whites and one black suspect. Serious problems have resulted, however, when the police attempt to find five or six people with peculiar characteristics. It would be difficult indeed to find six Oriental males in their thirties, who are six feet tall, have brown hair, walk with a limp, speak with a lisp, and have a French accent. Obviously, some matches cannot be done, and professional reasonableness must be the ultimate test. If, for example, the suspect is very fat, everyone should wear a coat. If the suspect has a large mole on his nose or a tattoo on his cheek, special effects, makeup, or bandages can be used. Several courts have held that officers do not have to go to such lengths when truly unique features are involved. Cases upholding the admissibility of lineup identification, notwithstanding certain physical disparities, are: *State* v. *Tidwell,* 500 S.W. 2d 329 [only one with chin whiskers]; *People* v. *Allen*, 327 N.E. 2d 387 [only one with a natural hairstyle]; *People* v. *Broadnax*, 325 N.E. 2d 23 [only one bald-headed, all participants wearing hats]; *State* v. *Tomizoli,* 519 S.W. 2d 713 [only one had "weather-beaten" appearance]; *Conner* v. *Deramus*, 374 F. Supp. 504 [ages of other participants were eighteen, nineteen, twenty-four, and twenty-eight; the defendant was forty-seven]; and *Payne* v. *State,* 210 S.E. 2d 775 [defendant was seven feet, two inches tall, and stuttered].

To avoid problems of suggestive lineups, officers should arrange to have five or six persons participate. If one individual has to wear jail clothing, all should do so. It is never permissible for a suspect to wear garments resembling the clothing worn by the perpetrator, unless all participants do so. Similarly, five detectives in conservative suits will impair the effectiveness of a lineup if the suspect is wearing casual attire. Finally, the suspect or suspects should be randomly placed in the lineup.

To minimize the number of officers who will have to appear in court, it is advisable that a single officer conduct the lineup, complete the reports, interview the witnesses, take the photographs, and perform the clerical tasks. Polaroid photographs will minimize the problems concerned with the chain of evidence, and the officer in charge should initial the print and staple it to the reports.

To avoid unexpected problems connected with the viewing procedures, it is recommended that witnesses be given a printed sheet explaining the system. A typical information sheet would advise the witnesses not to speak unless asked a question by an officer and not to display recognition of anyone until those individuals in the lineup are interviewed by an officer. It would, in addition, explain that they are under no obligation to identify anyone and that, if they do, certainty of identity is not required.

The attorney representing the accused should be permitted to view the entire proceedings, including the interview of the witnesses. This will help ensure that the lineup and the subsequent interview process are free of suggestive influences. Attorneys for suspects ought to be told that they should communicate any suggestions or objections to the officer in charge of the lineup, but that they will not be permitted to obstruct the procedures. They should not be allowed to interview the witnesses before, during, or after the procedures. If they want to take the deposition of a witness, they should follow the state's rules of criminal procedure designed for that purpose.

(6.12) *RIGHT TO COMPEL ATTENDANCE*

A suspect does not have a constitutional right to refuse to appear in a lineup, providing there is sufficient cause to believe he is a suspect. A lesser standard of proof is sufficient and will support the legality of the proceedings.

It is fairly common to reduce the number of suspects in a case to not less than three of five individuals. In these cases, officers should apply to a court of competent jursidiction for an order compelling the attendance of these persons if they do not appear voluntarily. An affidavit in support of the order must be filed. The affidavit is similar to that required for the issuance of an arrest warrant, though the proof may be substantially diminished.

A lineup order may be issued for several suspects when only one of them could be guilty or issued for a single suspect based on less proof than is required for an arrest warrant because the intrusion on the rights of a participant in such a lineup is less than the intrusion on the rights of an arrested suspect. The lineup procedure takes about an hour; it can be arranged to take place at a convenient time. A suspect is not booked, individually photographed, jailed, or required to post bond. The stigma of guilt associated with an arrest is not present.

As an example of the above, a drugstore was robbed by a gunman who was dressed in the uniform used by deliverymen of the Baker Department Store. Three drivers for that company fit the description and were in the area of the drugstore at the time of the holdup. A court order should be obtained requiring each of the three drivers to appear in a lineup in order that employees of the drugstore might determine whether one of them was the robber.

Although a suspect cannot lawfully refuse to appear in a lineup, there is no practical way to force him physically to do so. What if he must be dragged onstage, screaming and cursing? This will clearly focus attention on him and away from the other participants. On the other hand, a resisting suspect misbehaves at his peril, and he should not be allowed to complain later that he was identified solely because of his performance. Thus, each participant is free to appear as nonchalant and obedient as he chooses. If he intentionally misbehaves, he waives any rights he might have to object to an identification tainted by his own behavior.

(6.13) *CONFRONTATIONS WITH SINGLE SUSPECTS*

Although identifications of single suspects tend to be suggestive, there are three situations where they are completely lawful. The first is when the suspect is located near the scene of the crime at about the time the crime was committed. Most police departments define this time as sixty minutes and set the location as the distance that can reasonably be traveled in that period. The greater the distance from the scene and the greater the time elapsed since the crime, the stronger the case is for a due-process lineup. There is also less likelihood of a faulty identification when the suspect is presented shortly after the commission of the offense. That is, the process is more reliable. Sometimes several suspects may be stopped because they fit a general description. It would be unfair to hold a half dozen persons until a lineup could be put together.

If, on the other hand, a single suspect is stopped and there is other evidence that he committed the crime, it is a better practice to book him and arrange for a formal lineup. Such other evidence would include a large amount of money or a gun found on his person or in his car, or a confession. A lineup of a single suspect should be avoided when the witness is injured or is extremely upset. It would be a bad practice, for example, to take a suspect back to a grocery store for identification by a woman whose husband was fatally shot by the robber. If this is the only choice without risking a false arrest, it must, of course, be done. When suspects are returned to the scene of the crime, they should not be hauled in at gunpoint or wearing handcuffs. Both of these practices are too suggestive of guilt. If there is more than one witness, each should be asked to step outside to make an identification. This avoids the risk of one witness shouting out his or her identification in the presence of others and thus influencing them.

The second situation justifying a confrontation with a single suspect occurs when a witness is in danger of dying. In these cases the suspect should be taken to the hospital or wherever the witness is for immediate identification.

The third situation is the accepted police practice of having a witness get into a patrol car while the officers ride around the neighborhood looking for the suspect.

It is sometimes thought that a single-suspect confrontation is permissible when the witness knows the identity of the suspect. Examples of this would include a former employee, a resident of the building in which both live, or a relative. It is permissible for the witness to point out such a suspect for the purpose of apprehending him. If the suspect is already in custody, however, the prosecutor should be consulted before allowing a confrontation with the single suspect.

(6.14) *USE OF PHOTOGRAPHS*

Police have resorted to the rogues' gallery since the invention of the photograph. There are many reasons why books of photographs are used instead of lineups. First, the police may not know the identity of the suspect, and it is thought that he may be a prior offender. Second, the suspect may have fled, or his whereabouts are unknown. Finally, the police may have the person under surveillance and not want him to know he is suspected of the crime.

Photographs only portray how a person looked at a particular time. Aging, facial hair, a different hairstyle, baldness, and a number of other factors tend to make the process less reliable than a lineup. Nevertheless, such viewings of photographs frequently take place in larger police departments. If no particular person is a suspect before the viewing takes place, it is proper to permit the witnesses, on an individual basis, to look through a book consisting of known burglars, robbers, rapists, or other categories of criminals.

If, however, a particular person or persons are under suspicion, the following procedure should be utilized.

1. All photographs of the suspects should be removed from the books or files in which they are kept.

2. The suspects' photographs should be mixed with pictures of persons with similar features. It is not absolutely necessary that these individuals have been arrested for the crime under investigation, but, if at all possible, they should be.
3. "Mug shots" should not be mixed with other photographs unless there is no alternative.
4. The date of arrest and other ID data that might appear in a mug shot should be covered up. This will minimize the chance that the witness will pick out a recent arrestee when the witness knows that a suspect has been picked up.
5. If a particular person is suspected of the offense, and he is in jail or facing charges, the prosecutor should be consulted. He may want to notify the suspect's attorney of the scheduled viewing.
6. After an identification is made, the officer in charge should record the ID numbers of each photograph shown the witness if the photographs are displayed separately. If the witness picks the suspect from a book, the pages viewed should be noted. This procedure will enable the officer to reconstruct the viewing process in court if it becomes necessary.

Many police agencies use a photocomposition process to build a likeness of the perpetrator. Several identification kits are on the market and employ drawings of many types of eyes, ears, noses, and mouths that can be placed together. Their usefulness and legality have been upheld in several court decisions. The officer using such devices should be trained or educated in the proper techniques, and he must be prepared to be cross-examined on this process.

C. OTHER NONTESTIMONIAL EVIDENCE

(6.15) *BLOOD AND BREATH SAMPLES*

When the procedure is done by or under the direction of a licensed physician, blood samples may be taken from the body of a suspect even if he objects. Because it is an extraordinary remedy, probable cause is a necessary condition when the individual makes an objection. Samples are usually taken to determine the influence of alcoholic beverages or narcotics. In order to avoid civil liability and not violate the prerequisites of the Fourth Amendment, a court order should be sought and obtained before a suspect is forcibly strapped down and blood is drawn from him. If the objections are merely verbal and not physical, a court order is not necessary. The motor vehicle code may provide for forcible samplings under certain conditions. A person can, of course, always consent to the taking of a blood sample. Moreover, it is wise to administer such a test if the suspect insists on it.

A person may be required to breathe into a device that measures his intoxication or other conditions. Again, the motor vehicle code may provide that such a test be given, and a court order can be obtained if he forcibly resists.

In justifying such actions, courts have said the following:

1. There is no privilege against self-incrimination since the evidence is obtained by the labors of the prosecution.
2. There is no right to counsel. Since the suspect does not have a right under the Fifth Amendment to refuse a blood or breath test, he cannot have the right to counsel under *Miranda,* which was decided on the basis of the Fifth Amendment.
3. The action is not an unlawful search and seizure. There is reason to believe the evidence will be destroyed by natural bodily processes unless the tests are administered promptly, and the methods used in extracting the evidence are not unreasonable. No body cavities are searched, and the process does not shock the conscience of the courts.

Not all courts agree on the issue of the degree of force that may be used. In a California case decided in 1970, the officers kept a scissors lock on the suspect and held his arm immobile while he was lying on the floor (*People* v. *Kraft*, 3 Cal. App. 3d 890, 894 Cal. Rptr. 280 [1970]). Though the suspect was "defensive," the officers were aggressive beyond all need. Thus, in California, if excessive force is applied, the evidence will be suppressed.

(6.16) *OTHER PHYSIOLOGICAL MEASUREMENTS AND EVIDENCE*

Samples of hair, fingernail scrapings, urine samples, and the like can be taken over the objections of a suspect. Seminal stains or bloodstains from a suspect's clothing may be taken by force if necessary.

For several years legal philosophers have debated whether a bullet could be forcibly removed. Suppose that a policeman is found shot to death with his gun in hand and a single bullet missing. Suppose, further, that a former offender is found a few minutes later in the next block, suffering from a bullet wound. Suppose, finally, that the gun that fired the fatal shot was found next to the officer, wiped clean of prints and, again, with a single bullet missing. On the basis of such evidence, could a search warrant or court order be obtained to extract the bullet from the suspect? If the bullet is removed to preserve his life or well-being, it would, of course, be admissible. By the same token, if removal of the bullet would imperil his life, the court cannot order that it be done. If a decision is made by the prosecutor not to seek a court order, if the suspect refuses to consent to an operation, and if medical evidence all concurs that the bullet could be removed safely, would it be lawful for the prosecution to introduce these facts into evidence against the accused?

As mentioned in chapter 5, police may not forcibly pump the stomach or forcibly examine the rectal cavity of a suspect. Cases have upheld the administration of an emetic by a physician and the use of such evidence derived from the procedure. If a stomach pump or rectal probe is administered by a physician as a necessary procedure to save the life or preserve the well-being of a suspect, anything recovered during these processes would be admissible.

In general, urine samples may be required of a suspect (for alcohol or narcotics tests). They cannot, however, be forced by inducing the suspect to drink liquids. Because of the problems of dilution, a suspect may be required to urinate in the presence of an officer, with his back toward him (*Quesada* v. *Orr*, 14 Cal. App. 3d 866, 92 Cal. Rptr. 640 [1971]).

(6.17) *SUMMARY*

Prior to 1964 the only test governing the admissibility of a confession or admission was the voluntariness of the statement. The *Escobedo* and *Miranda* decisions put the lawyer in the middle of the interrogation process. They mandated a litany of warnings that must be recited when the suspect is in "custody."

In recent years the lawbooks have been filled with cases that have searched for the "proper" warnings and have speculated at what point in time the warnings were necessary. Recitation of the warnings is not enough; a "knowing and intelligent" waiver must precede an admissible statement. At what age and in what mental condition a suspect must be have never been precisely defined. Jurisdictions have differed on whether misdemeanors and traffic offenses are includable under the *Miranda* decision.

The Warren Court seemed to infer that full compliance with *Miranda* in every respect was a necessary prerequisite to the admissibility of a statement. The Burger Court has been more flexible and has carved out several exceptions to *Miranda*. For example, statements in violation of *Miranda* may be admitted to impeach a suspect's credibility if he testifies at his trial. The Poisoned Tree doctrine will no longer be automatically applied to tainted confessions.

The Warren Court also put lawyers into the lineup procedures in police stations. The Burger Court qualified that holding and limited this requirement to situations following the initiation of adversary criminal proceedings.

Lineups, blood tests, and other physiological measurements are nontestimonial in nature. A person does not have a constitutional right to refuse to participate in these procedures if there are reasonable grounds to compel his participation.

chapter 7

Two lie dead outside of a dance hall the morning after a dance in Bear Town, Wyoming. (Ca. 1865)

Shoes used by Wyoming criminals to leave misleading footprints during escapes. (ca. 1880)

Mr James Stirling. Ex Sheriff

You are hereby invited to be present at the execution of

GEORGE A. BLACK,

which will take place at the Court House, in Laramie, Wyoming Territory, on the 26th day of February, 1890, at the hour of 11 o'clock, A. M.

Not transferable.

CHARLES YUND,

Sheriff Albany County.

Invitation to a hanging. (1890)

(Courtesy of Wyoming State Archives, Museums and Historical Department.)

EVIDENCE OF CRIME IN THE OLD WEST

Discovery

(7.1) *DISCOVERY IN GENERAL*

"*Discovery*" is the inspection of opposing evidence prior to trial. "At common law, discovery before trial was generally unavailable in both civil and criminal cases" (*State* v. *Cook*, 43 N.J. 560 [1965]). Even in relatively recent judicial history, the criminal trial was usually run with neither side revealing anything to the other in advance. Secrecy of the prosecution was upheld on the theory that pretrial revelation of police witnesses or prosecution evidence could lead to intimidation or possible physical danger or death of witnesses. There was also a subconscious reason for secrecy. Everyone considered the criminal trial a legal contest with prescribed rules in which each side tried to beat the other—not as a vehicle for seeking the truth.

Even in civil cases, pretrial discovery of evidence was only narrowly allowed. This attitude in civil suits has now been completely reversed. Experience has shown that if each side understands the strengths and weaknesses of the other, cases are often settled without necessity of a trial.

This experience in civil cases has greatly affected the court's attitude toward pretrial discovery in criminal matters. In fact, the old idea against pretrial criminal discovery is now rapidly being discarded. The U.S. Supreme Court decision of *Jencks* v. *U.S.,* 353 U.S. 657 (1957), started this trend. Beginning with *Jencks*, a series of court decisions and statutes has opened the way for pretrial discovery of evidence in criminal cases. The present attitude on pretrial criminal discovery is best summarized in a statement from *Williams* v. *Florida*, 399 U.S. 78 (1970): "The adversary system of trial is hardly an end to itself, it is not yet a poker game in which players enjoy an absolute right always to conceal their cards until played."

Coupled with this changing attitude toward pretrial criminal discovery has been an increased emphasis in the courts on protecting the criminal defendant's rights. Now by court decision, rules, and statutes, criminal defendants are being allowed much wider pretrial access to the prosecution's evidence (*see* statutes in Arizona, Idaho, New York, Vermont, and Wyoming; Federal Rules of Criminal Procedure, 6 [e], 16 and 17; *State* v. *Ford*, 108 Ariz. 404, cert. den. 409 U.S. 1128 [1973]).

The more liberal discovery rights in criminal trials should not be confused with depositions (*see* section 7.7 on "Depositions of Third Parties"). "Discovery" and "depositions" are not the same. "Deposition," the testimony of a witness reduced to writing, is not as broad a term as "discovery." Depositions have been allowed in the past in a narrow area. Now, both discovery, the disclosure of facts known to the opposing party, and deposition, the taking of testimony, are more widely allowed in advance of the trial itself.

Many older court decisions deny criminal pretrial discovery. These cases should be relied on only with caution in view of the changing attitude allowing broad pretrial criminal discovery. Because of this changing attitude, the only safe conclusion is that a defendant's right to pretrial discovery of the prosecution's evidence will get broader and broader. The prosecution's right to pretrial discovery of defense evidence will lag behind considerably; but it, too, will gradually be enlarged by court decisions and rulings.

(7.2) *POWER TO COMPEL DISCLOSURE*

Because pretrial criminal discovery was not accepted in common law, the older cases held that the courts were without power to order it (*Rex* v. *Holland*, 4 Durn. & E. 691, 100 Eng. Rep. 124 [K.B. 1792]). Even as late as 1958, the U.S. Supreme Court held that denial of pretrial criminal evidence to the defendant did not violate due process (*Cicenia* v. *LaGay,* 357 U.S. 504 [1958]). A general rule now adopted by state courts is that the court can compel pretrial discovery of prosecution evidence (*State* v. *Superior Court of Cohise County,* 90 Ariz. 133 [1961]).

The court can also, within constitutional limits, allow prosecution discovery of defense criminal evidence. Discovery in federal cases is detailed in the Federal Rules of Criminal Procedure.

(7.3) *PROPRIETY OF COMPELLED DISCLOSURE*

The accused, even in the modern view, is not entitled to discovery as a matter of right or as a constitutional guarantee (*Palermo* v. *U.S.,* 360 U.S. 343 [1959]). In some jurisdictions, however, it is now spelled out by statute (*People* v. *Muñoz*, 11 A.D. 2d 79, affd. 9 N.Y. 2d 638 [1961]; *Goldman* v. *U.S.,* 316 U.S. 129 [1940]; *U.S.* v. *Fioravanti,* 412 F. 2d 407, cert. den. 396 U.S. 837 [1969]).

In general, discovery by the criminal defendant will be allowed if it is a matter of fairness and if it is a factor in the search for truth. Thus the trial court determines whether to allow the defendant to employ discovery, and the judge is not in error if he refuses to do so unless he has clearly abused his discretion.

The defense counsel must show that the evidence sought is actually needed and is not being requested in the hope that he can learn something useful (*People* v. *Miller*, 42 Misc. 2d 794 [N.Y. 1964]). The courts have, in fact, denied a blanket request by the defense that the state supply copies of all statements in its possession (*People* v. *Terry,* 57 Cal. 2d 538, cert. den. 375 U.S. 960 [1963]). A subpoena to the prosecutor requiring him to bring all statements from his files was also disallowed (*State* v. *Colvin*, 81 Ariz. 388 [1957]). A defense request for all police reports resulted in the same decision (*People* v. *Newville,* 220 Cal. App. 2d 267 [1963]).

A number of older cases hold that only evidence that is admissible can be obtained by discovery (*Fryer* v. *U.S.*, 207 F. 2d 134, cert. den. 346 U.S. 885 [1953]; *Griffin* v. *U.S.*, 183 F. 2d 990 [1950]; *People* v. *Schmitt*, 1 Cal. App. 87 [1957]; *People ex rel Lemon* v. *Supreme Court*, 245 N.Y. 24 [1927]; *People* v. *Riley*, 46 Misc. 2d 221 [N.Y. 1965]). Where not superseded by court rule or statute, these older decisions must now be considered as the minority rule only.

Courts still carefully consider any valid arguments by the prosecution that pretrial discovery of prosecution witnesses or evidence might be dangerous to a witness, might improperly reveal the name of an informant, or might otherwise be unfair. In these situations prosecution matters will be protected; the general court attitude concerning them is set forth in *People* v. *Lopez*, 60 Cal. 2d 223, cert. den. 375 U.S. 994 (1963). "There must be a balance of the right of a defendant to discover potentially material witnesses with the probability that such discovery might lead to the elimination of an adverse witness or the influencing of his testimony. In balancing these competing factors the trial court must be allowed great discretion."

(7.4) *MATTERS IN THE PROSECUTOR'S FILES*

a. Statements by the Accused

Older case law withheld any pretrial discovery of the defendant's own confession. Under present-day practice, he can gain access to it in almost every court. Part of this change came about as a result of *Jackson* v. *Denno*, 378 U.S. 368 (1964). This decision by the Supreme Court required the judge to hold a separate hearing to determine the voluntariness of the confession. Decisions in various states (such as *People* v. *Huntley*, 15 N.Y. 2d 72 [1965]) have followed this decision, and now pretrial hearings on the voluntariness of confessions are common. Because of such hearings before the trial, defense counsel usually has access to the confession itself. Federal Rule 16 now requires that the U.S. attorney give the defendant access to his statements. A number of states have enacted similar statutes (for example, N.Y. Criminal Procedure Law, 240.20). Aside from these statutory requirements, courts now generally recognize that, as a matter of fairness, the defendant should be allowed to have a copy of his own confession before he goes to trial. Even corporations charged with criminal offenses have been allowed access to pretrial testimony of their employees before the grand jury (*U.S.* v. *Hughes*, 413 F. 2d 1244 [5th Cir. 1969]; *People* v. *Leto Bros.*, 70 Misc. 2d 347 [N.Y. 1972]).

Unless there is a rule or statute to cover the situation, the courts are split on the question of discovery of statements by a codefendant or an accomplice.

b. Statements of Witnesses

Once a witness testifies at a trial, opposing counsel has the right to a copy of any prior statement the witness has made. He can then use this information on cross-examination for impeachment purposes (18 U.S. Code 3500; *Jencks* v. *U.S.*, supra). This rule is accepted everywhere by all courts.

The more important question is whether the defendant can obtain the statements of a prosecution witness before trial. Some courts relax pretrial inspection and give the defense access to statements of all witnesses that the state has obtained.

Accessibility of information before a trial takes place can indeed endanger prosecution witnesses. Some courts will, therefore, not allow pretrial defense examination of statements by prosecution witnesses (*State* v. *St. Peter*, 63 Wash. 2d 495 [1963]), and it is forbidden by statute in federal courts (18 U.S. Code 3500).

c. Statements of Victims

Neither rule nor statute generally differentiates between the availability of a victim's statement and that of any other prosecution witness. Where the court has discretion, it is reluctant to require the pretrial availability of a victim's statement. Should there be a preliminary hearing at which the victim testifies, the defense can, of course, obtain a transcript of the testimony before the trial begins. If there is not such a hearing, the court will usually protect the victim by refusing the defense access to his statement. This is particularly true for victims of sex crimes (*State* v. *Circuit Court*, 16 Wisc. 2d 197 [1962]).

d. Statements of Police

If a police officer was a *witness*, his statement in the departmental files is as that of any other witness. A statement by a police officer concerning his investigation and a summary of evidence are different matters. They are not generally given to the defense in advance of trial. The court may, however, make them available at the trial itself to be used in cross-examination of an officer. Indeed, the Federal Rules of Criminal Procedure, 16 (e), expressly mentions these matters. Thus, except for such things as the defendant's statements, criminal record, and reports of physical and mental examinations, "This rule does not authorize the discovery or inspection of reports, memoranda, or other internal government documents made by the attorney for the government or other government agents in connection with the investigation or prosecution of the case . . . ."

Police statements summarizing evidence are exactly what they say they are—summaries. They are not actual statements of witnesses. They can be used in evidence only as possible tools for cross-examination impeachment of the officer making the report. Police statements often discuss problems of prosecuting the defendant. Such material will not, of course, be allowed defense discovery (*U.S.* v. *Pfingst*, 477 F. 2d 177, cert. den. 412 U.S. 941 [1973]).

e. Transcripts and Recordings

Investigators are making increased use of tape recordings for taking statements. The fact that the statement is done electronically rather than in writing has no legal effect on its availability to the defense. If the defendant is entitled to a copy, he may be furnished his transcript or be allowed to hear the recording and make his own copy from it. This rule goes as far back as 1950 (*Cash* v. *Superior Court*, 346 P. 2d 407 [Cal. Sup. Ct. 1959]). An undercover agent posing as a coburglar took secret recordings of the planning for the burglary. Court decisions made his recordings available to the defense. New York allows the availability of this type of evidence by statute, except in cases where there was a legal wiretap (N.Y. Criminal Procedure Law, 240.20). It is safe to say that tape recordings are normally now made available to the defense (*U.S.* v. *Marshak*, 364 F. Supp. 1005 [1973]).

f. Medical Reports

A report by a coroner or medical examiner is admissible evidence in most courts. In jurisdictions where this is true, the court can make such a report available to the defense before trial. In some jurisdictions, however, the coroner's report may not be made available for technical reasons (*Pinana* v. *State,* 352 P. 2d 824 [Nev. Sup. Ct., 1960]). Reports of physical or mental examinations ordered by the prosecution can normally be obtained by the defendant as a necessary tool in preparing his defense (Federal Rules of Criminal Procedure, 6 [e], 16, and 17.1; N.Y. Criminal Procedure Law, 240.20).

g. Laboratory Findings and Reports by Experts

Courts will usually order that the defendant be given copies of police laboratory reports. This is true even when the report itself cannot be used in evidence and the technician must testify in person.

There are innumerable kinds of these reports. The prosecution can normally use photographs as evidence, and pretrial access to such materials will be given the defendant. Reports by experts and technicians on handwriting, ballistics, fingerprints, and blood will also be ordered shown to the accused. Even organs and bodily specimens may be made available to the defense for examination and testing (*People* v. *Sauer,* 163 Cal. App. 2d 740, cert. den. 359 U.S. 973 [1959]; *People* v. *Dinan,* 15 A.D. 2d 786, affd. 11 N.Y. 2d 350, cert. den. 371 U.S. 877 [1962]; *People* v. *Seaman*, 64 Misc. 2d 684 [N.Y. 1970]; *People* v. *Garner*, 57 Cal. 2d 135, cert. den. 370 U.S. 929 [1962]; *State* v. *Thompson*, 338 P. 2d 319 [Wash. Sup. Ct., 1959]).

Today only an unusual set of circumstances would persuade a court to refuse a defendant access to a laboratory report held by the prosecution.

h. Grand Jury Transcripts

Grand jury proceedings are confidential hearings at which only the state's evidence is normally given. The purpose of the hearing is to determine if the prosecution has sufficient evidence to accuse the defendant of a felony. This process is designed to prevent an individual from being unjustly accused by the state.

There are a number of reasons why grand jury hearings are secret. One is for the protection of witnesses. Another is to provide a way of charging the accused and issuing an arrest warrant for him without his knowledge, should he not be in custody. Most jurisdictions consider unauthorized revelation of grand jury testimony contempt of court or even a criminal offense (N.Y.P.L. 215.70; 18 U.S. Code 3333; Fed. Rules of Crim. Procedure, 6 [e]).

Once a witness has testified at the actual trial, a copy of his testimony before the grand jury will be given to the defense counsel. He may use it as possible impeachment material in cross-examination.

Though pretrial access to grand jury transcripts will not usually be allowed by the court, in some cases a witness who has given evidence before a grand jury may be allowed to see his own testimony before trial (*People* v. *Rosario,* 9 N.Y. 2d 286 [1961]; *Jencks* v. *U.S.*, supra; *re Minkoff*, 349 F. Supp. 154).

i. Names of Witnesses

According to the old rule, neither side in a criminal trial was required to reveal the names of its potential witnesses. Modern procedure requires the prosecution to supply the names of its witnesses unless it can show a valid reason for concealing them. The court must balance the arguments and decide whether to keep the names confidential (*People* v. *Lopez*, 60 Cal. 2d 223, cert den. 375 U.S. 994 [1963]; *U.S.* v. *Jordan*, 466 F. 2d 99, cert. den. 409 U.S. 1129 [1963]).

j. Criminal Records

If the prosecution is allowed to keep secret the records it has of criminal convictions of the defendant or of any potential witness, the defendant is at a disadvantage. Knowing that a criminal record can have an adverse effect on a jury, the accused may have a problem in determining whether he can safely use a potential witness or even take the stand in his own behalf. Because of this, the defense should have pretrial information on such criminal records. Courts ordinarily grant a defense request for such information. As a matter of fact, several states (such as Arizona, Vermont, and New York) now have statutes requiring the prosecution to furnish such information without a request by the defense (*Losavio* v. *Mayber*, 486 P. 2d 1032 [Colo. Sup. Ct., 1972]; *State* v. *Coney*, 272 So. 2d 550 [1973]).

k. Work Product

The "work product" of an attorney consists of such matters as summaries of evidence, trial strategy, and research. It is part of the pretrial investigation and is not subject to pretrial discovery by either side. Sometimes it is debatable whether an item is evidence or a work product. If the court determines it is the latter, it will be protected (N.Y. Criminal Procedure, 240.10 [3], Federal Rules of Criminal Procedure, 6 [e], 16).

(7.5) *POLICE FILES AND RECORDS*

In the past, defendants were denied access to police reports and records compiled by police officers whether they were official or investigative. Courts now are increasingly allowing discovery in this area. Police incident reports are generally not withheld. The follow-up reports written by detectives often contain conclusions or leads, so this material may not be made accessible to the defense.

Police personnel files are often sought when police officers are going to be witnesses. Personnel files are internal confidential matters. The accused, though, is looking for derogatory material in the personnel file that he can use to impeach the police witness. In states having "Sunshine" laws, these files may be available as public records. In other jurisdictions, the defense must allege existence of the derogatory material and show a fair basis for giving him access to it in order to persuade the court to order its production.

(7.6) *MATTERS IN DEFENSE FILES IN GENERAL*

The idea of letting the state discover matters from the defense has been slow to develop. Some of the older cases, which are probably now obsolete, refused discovery on grounds it would violate the defendant's right against self-incrimination as set forth in the Fifth Amendment

(*State* v. *Tune*, 13 N.J. 203 [1953]). In addition to this reason, there was the argument that the prosecution has sufficient pretrial weapons, such as police investigations, grand jury proceedings, and preliminary hearings.

The growing area of pretrial criminal discovery is now allowing both sides more latitude, and it is becoming necessary for the defense to give up information. Statutes in some states require defendants to appear in lineups, give physical samples such as blood, submit to physical examinations, and provide samples of handwriting. Federal rules can require both sides to give the names of their witnesses.

a. Alibis

Most states have statutes requiring prior notice by the accused of a proposed defense based on an alibi. The defense can be required to give the names of proposed alibi witnesses as long as the state, in return, must furnish the names of any witnesses it proposes to use to rebut the claimed alibi (*Warduis* v. *Oregon*, 412 U.S. 470 [1973]).

b. Defense Witnesses

There is, as noted, a growing tendency of each side to furnish the names of its witnesses. Unless there is some compelling reason against it, such as possible danger for a prosecution witness, the courts will generally require that the names be revealed to the other side (*People* v. *Lopez*, 60 Cal. 2d 223, cert. den. 375 U.S. 994 [1963]). The courts have moved so far in the direction of allowing the prosecution discovery that in one case the state was furnished copies of a statement by a defense witness for cross-examination, even though the defense counsel had written out the statement and his witness had not signed it (*State* v. *Montague*, 262 A. 2d 398 [N.J., 1970]).

c. Fingerprints, Handwriting, and Photographs

Fingerprinting and photographing the defendant can be constitutionally required in all felony cases. If these things are not done initially, the courts will order them on application from the state. The accused can also be ordered to give examples of his handwriting, blood samples, and the like. In one case the state was working on a possible criminal charge involving $25,000 in faked automobile insurance claims. The prosecution moved to require a suspect to appear in his office and give handwriting samples. The court ordered that this be done. It pointed out that, while no criminal action was pending, the state's moving papers showed probable cause to identify the suspect as the defendant. He could, therefore, be required to furnish the handwriting samples (*U.S.* v. *Harris*, 453 F 2d 1317, cert. den. 412 U.S. 927 [1973]; *U.S.* v. *Thomann*, 609 F 2d 560 [1979], fingerprinting ordered; *In re Melvin,* 550 F 2d 674 [1977], appearance ordered at lineup).

As early as 1962, the courts in California allowed wide discovery to the prosecution (*Jones* v. *Superior Court of Nevada County*, 58 Cal. 2d 56 [1962]). A rape charge was involved. The defendant claimed that he was impotent and asked for time to get medical evidence and reports on an old injury that had caused his condition. A discovery order was granted the prosecution. It made the defendant surrender the names of the doctors he planned to call and any doctors' reports or X rays he intended to use in evidence. The court excluded only medical reports that had been made for the defense counsel. In its decision, the court gave the pioneering statement on prosecution criminal discovery, which is now generally regarded as the proper rule.

(7.7) *DEPOSITIONS OF THIRD PARTIES*

Some states are still reluctant to allow pretrial taking of depositions of third-party witnesses. This seems to be a vestige of the old practice where neither side revealed its evidence to the other in criminal cases. Some jurisdictions do provide for this by law (Florida Rules of Criminal Procedure, 3.220 [d]; N.Y.C.P.L., 660.10–680.80). Pretrial depositions do aid greatly in the prompt disposition of pending cases, and their use is now becoming more widely accepted.

(7.8) *EFFECT OF NONCOMPLIANCE*

If either side refuses a court-ordered pretrial discovery, contempt of court is always an available remedy. Though contempt of court can result in fine or imprisonment, this alone might not deter some individuals. The court, therefore, has additional remedies. It can adjourn proceedings until the court order has been followed. If the state has failed to grant discovery, the charges may be dismissed. This has been done, for example, in espionage cases, where the government has felt it could not reveal its informant. What is most common is for the trial judge to refuse to receive the evidence where a discovery order has not been complied with. The court may, in addition, use any other legal remedy it deems appropriate (*U.S.* v. *Kelly*, 420 F. 2d 26 [2d Civ. 1969]).

(7.9) *SUMMARY*

The original common-law rule forbade any pretrial discovery in criminal cases. It is now generally agreed that courts do have the power to allow such discovery, and so the modern trend in all courts is to be increasingly liberal in this area.

The accused does not have an absolute right to discovery, and it is still within the court's discretion. Informants for the prosecution, victims of criminal acts, and witnesses who are subject to possible criminal pressures are still protected from defense discovery.

Most evidence in the prosecution's files will be made available to the defense if it can show good cause. Thus, the accused will be given pretrial access to confessions, statements by witnesses, criminal records, laboratory and experts' reports, and similar material.

The defense usually asks for much of the material in police files. Police reports, interviews, and records of internal affairs may be requested. Though courts allow some of this type of material to be used at the trial for cross-examination of an individual police witness, they are generally reluctant to allow pretrial access to it.

The prosecution is gradually being allowed some discovery from defense files. Alibi claims with the names of supportive witnesses, handwriting samples, medical reports, and physical specimens are examples of material that the court will generally order the defense to reveal to the prosecution before trial.

Refusal to grant discovery can result in contempt, dismissal of charges, and other sanctions.

chapter **8**

(Courtesy of Media Services Subunit, Federal Bureau of Investigation.)

BONNIE & CLYDE BARROW

Privileged Communications

(8.1) *COMMON LAW AND STATUTORY*

A variety of privileged communications cannot be revealed in court. They range from military secrets to communications between husband and wife. The rule of evidence that communications between certain parties should be confidential and immune from testimonial compulsion is based on public policy. Some, such as confidential communications between attorney and client, are historical and part of the common law. Others, such as the confidentiality between doctor and patient, are of modern origin and are usually found in statutes.

"Communication" in these situations is not confined to what one person has told another but may include such things as written material or observations that could be seen and heard by the person involved in the confidential relationship.

From time to time interested groups seek to enlarge the field of privileged communications by having new laws passed that grant them testimonial immunity. Newspaper reporters, for example, are promoting legislation in some jurisdictions that grants them limited immunity for refusing to reveal their news sources.

For any communication to be excluded from court, the general rule is that it must have some aura of confidentiality about it, and there has to be the required relationship between the parties. If, however, only part of the testimony is privileged, this does not bar the witness from testifying; it only excludes the part that is privileged.

The rule of confidentiality applies to all proceedings, pretrial hearings, grand jury sessions, and the actual trial. There are various exceptions and legal refinements in all areas of privileged communications. Though no constitutional problems are involved, local statutes and court decisions must be consulted in every case to be sure of the particular rule.

(8.2) *MARITAL PRIVILEGE*

An old English rule disqualified one spouse from testifying *for* the other. This has been completely changed through the years so that now in some cases a spouse cannot testify *against* the other. Only a few remnants of this outmoded English rule remain in a small number of states. The general rule of evidence that forbids one spouse from testifying against the other in criminal proceedings known as "confidential communication" grew up by court decision and became part of our common law. Though the reasons for the rule are obscure, the usual rationale is that "it prevents disruption of the home." In this day of women's liberation, equality of the sexes, and divorce by consent, there is no longer any real basis for retaining the husband-wife immunity rule.

It is interesting that a brother was always allowed to testify against a brother and a father against a child without the court feeling that this was socially disruptive, and yet this could be as disruptive of family harmony as a situation involving a husband and wife.

A New York trial court (*People* v. *Fitzgerald*, 422 N.Y.S. 2d 309 [1979]) decided that there should be a parent-child privilege and refused to compel a father to disclose the confidential communication from his twenty-three-year-old son regarding a hit and run accident that the son had been involved in.

The husband-wife testimonial privilege does, however, cause problems for law enforcement personnel, and it promotes more injustice than almost any other rule of evidence. Law books are full of frustrating examples where the rule suppressed the truth and freed guilty defendants.

In a case in Ithaca, New York (*People* v. *Daghita,* 299 N.Y. 194 [1949]), a policeman was charged with stealing from the Montgomery Ward retail store. The store's janitor testified that Officer Daghita often drove him to work in the early morning hours and would go in the store and take merchandise. Many times he carried it away in cardboard boxes. At his larceny trial, the state called Daghita's wife and, over objection by the defense, had her testify against her husband. She said that he often brought home articles in his own car or in the police car at four or five in the morning. She further told how he carried in rugs, clothing, jackets, pillows, and bath towels, often in cardboard boxes. He hid them in the cellar and brought them upstairs later in the day. The husband was convicted and appealed. In New York a statute barred a husband or wife from testifying as to a "confidential communication between them." The appellate court held that even if no word is spoken, the husband's acts done in the presence of the wife were covered and that her testimony in this case was barred. Thus, the conviction was reversed.

Most states do have laws providing for the marital privilege in criminal cases. Following are factors that these statutes generally have in common.

a. Valid Marriage

The parties must actually be married. A mistress or paramour will not qualify, nor will the partner to a bigamous or incestuous marriage or one where there was no marriage license (*People* v. *Glab*, 13 C.A. 2d 528 [1936]). A common-law marriage, where recognized, does, however, qualify for the exclusionary rule.

The general rule is that no privilege attaches to communications before the marriage takes place or after it has been terminated. There are, nevertheless, exceptions. In many jurisdictions, a marriage ceremony after the crime will make the earlier communications privileged. Some states even preserve the confidentiality of marital communications after a divorce. The law of the locality must be consulted in case of a premarital or postdivorce situation.

b. Necessity of Confidentiality

Court decisions are split as to just what husband-wife communications are protected. Most state statutes have attempted to narrow the privilege to cover "confidential communications" only. The prosecutor's problem is that various courts have given a wide interpretation as to the meaning of both "confidential" and "communication." A police investigator may think he has an airtight case because the wife saw some of her husband's criminal activity and no confidential words came from him. When the case comes to trial, the officer may be shocked to find that her testimony is not allowed because it is considered to be privileged.

Many court rulings have regarded conduct observed by a spouse as a "communication." Further, since the acts were done in the presence of the spouse, they are "confidential" because the other spouse committed them in the confidence that he was in the privacy of the marriage situation.

Thus, in barring the testimony of Officer Daghita's wife when she testified about her husband's bringing home stolen goods, the court stated (*People* v. *Daghita*): "Confidential communication . . . means more than oral communications or conversations between husband and wife. It includes . . . disclosive acts done in the presence [of] the other which would not have been performed except for the confidence so existing."

A criminal indictment was dismissed by a court because a wife testified that she found a pistol in her husband's pocket (*People* v. *Sullivan*, 42 Misc. 2d 1014 [N.Y. 1964]). In another, the wife called police to her home and gave them a loaded pistol her husband had hidden in their liquor cabinet. She was not allowed to so testify (*People* v. *Helmus,* 50 Misc. 2d 47 [N.Y. 1966]). One wife was forbidden to testify that she had found a bag of checks that her husband had hidden in the house. The court held that he must have hidden them there because of his reliance on his marital status (*People* v. *Monahan*, 21 A.D. 2d 76 [N.Y. 1964]). In a murder case, an important clue was a piece of cloth found near the victim's body. The defendant's wife testified that her husband left home in the morning of the murder wearing an overcoat of similar cloth and that he had come home that night wearing a different coat. The state's highest court considered this privileged communication, and the testimony was stricken (*People* v. *Woltering*, 275 N.Y. 51 [1937]).

Courts have argued over whether a wife's diary is privileged and even over whether she should be allowed to identify her spouse's handwriting. There is further division concerning the legality of a spouse's testimony in regard to the other spouse's intoxication or mental condition. Merely calling the spouse to the witness stand and making her claim the privilege may be ruled as prejudicial, unless it is done in good faith (*People* v. *Wade,* 53 C. 2d 322 [1959]).

Courts agree that the marital privilege disappears when a third person capable of understanding what is going on is present. In such a situation, confidentiality is lost (*People* v. *Ressler*, 17 N.Y. 2d 174 [N.Y. 1966]). Courts quibble, however, when, for example, the husband was talking to a third party and the wife overheard it. A court in Texas even barred a wife from testifying that she had heard her husband threaten to kill a third person (*Gant* v. *State*, 55 Tex. Cr. 284 [1909]).

c. Exceptions

There are some court-approved exceptions where the marital privilege does not apply. If, for example, a husband commits a crime against his wife, she may testify freely against him. In most jurisdictions this exception has been extended to cover any offense against a family member, such as incest, child abuse, or assault. The exception is based on the theory that such a family offense is in reality an offense against the other spouse (*Commonwealth* v. *Maroney*, 414 Pa. 161 [1964]). According to the same theory, one spouse has been allowed to testify against the other regarding sexual misconduct with any third party.

d. Waiver

The marital privilege can be waived. The problem is how? The federal rule is that the testifying spouse alone has the right to claim privilege, but many of the states allow the accused spouse to claim privilege against the adverse spouse's testimony (*Trammel* v. *U.S.,* 26 Cr. L. 309 [1980]).

(8.3) *MEDICAL PRIVILEGE*

Privileged communication between doctor and patient was unknown in common law. The idea began with a nineteenth-century statute in New York. Most states have passed similar laws, so that, in general, communications between doctor and patient are privileged. Federal courts do not recognize any medical privilege (*U.S.* v. *Meagher*, 531 F 2d 752 [5th Cir. 1976]). The term *doctor* includes psychiatrists and other medical specialists. As is to be expected, the privilege has produced many unjust results. An example of this is shown in *People* v. *Decina*, 2 N.Y. 2d 133 (1956).

At 3.30 p.m. on a bright, sunny day, Decina was driving alone in his car on a city street. Suddenly he swerved to the wrong side of the road and then to the right and mounted the sidewalk at fifty to sixty miles per hour. On doing so, he plowed through a group of young schoolgirls, killing four of them. The car finally crashed through a brick wall. When he was pulled out of the car, he appeared "dazed" and said "I blacked out from the bridge." The police took him to the hospital under guard. An intern examined him and took his history, all of which was overheard by a police officer stationed at the door of the hospital room. The accused told the doctor, who later testified, that he had suffered from convulsions since childhood when he had sustained a brain injury. Further, for nine years he had been subject to seizures in which his right hand "jumped." Just prior to the accident his right hand acted in that way. Decina was convicted of criminal negligence. The appellate court ruled, however, that even though the intern was not hired by the defendant, the doctor-patient relationship existed, and the information the doctor received was privileged. The conviction was reversed.

Thus, four people were killed by a driver with a long history of epilepsy, and this information was kept out of court. Such a result vividly illustrates the need to reexamine this rule for criminal cases. There is now less reason than in times past to bar evidence of a person's physical condition during a criminal proceeding. Little harm, if any, can come to the individual and much public good can result from revealing the truth where a crime has been charged.

In criminal cases, the statutory rule against revealing information that passes between a doctor and his patient is, nevertheless, widespread. Only a few states do not let the medical privilege apply to criminal cases (California Evidence Code, Sec. 998; *Oregon* v. *Belts,* 225 Or. 127 [1963]).

Where the doctor-patient privilege is upheld in criminal trials, there are certain general requirements.

a. Relationship with Patient

There must first be a genuine doctor-patient relationship. The doctor must either be a duly licensed physician or the patient must have, in good faith, believed him to be such. In respect to the privilege, a consulting physician stands in the same position as the regular doctor. The doctor's nurse or the paramedical assistant is generally included.

b. Privileged Subject Matter

Medical privilege is based on the idea that the patient is confiding in the doctor in order that he might be treated. Where the patient is seen for observation only, not to be cured, the information is normally not privileged. A court-ordered physical or medical examination falls into this category. Blood alcohol tests, for example, are not given for treatment. The results are, therefore, admissible (*People* v. *Cook,* 205 N.Y. Supp. 2d 489 [1960]). The same is true of autopsies, since the doctor obviously is not going to treat the corpse.

The doctor-patient privilege covers much more than any confidential matter the patient discusses with him. It includes all information the doctor obtains from the patient that enables him to act (*Renihan* v. *Dennin,* 103 N.Y. 573 [1886]).

c. Exceptions

Some results from applying the doctor-patient privilege have been so extreme that the courts have made exceptions. One of these exceptions is given below.

A physician operated on and removed the bullet from a woman who had been shot. The state had a statute concerning the doctor-patient privilege. It also required doctors to report all gunshot wounds to the police, which the physician did. At the criminal trial the prosecution called the doctor to testify. The defense objected on the basis of privilege, pointing out that the doctor was testifying about treatment. The court overruled the objection and allowed the testimony to stand, stating that the privilege statute was not intended to protect the criminal and that the matter was public information anyway since the physician had to report the wound to the police (*People* v. *Lay,* 254 A.D. 372, affd. 279 N.Y. 737 [1938]).

Another doctor treated an individual who was poisoned. The patient died, and the doctor was allowed to testify rather than protect the murderer (*Pierson* v. *People*, 79 N.Y. 424 [1880]).

d. Waiver

Only the patient can waive the doctor-patient privilege, since he is the one protected. A stranger to the privilege will, therefore, not be allowed to claim it. In a criminal prosecution for driving while intoxicated, the defendant moved to inspect the hospital records of the deceased accident victim. The prosecution claimed that the victim's death resulted from an embolism that developed from a leg fracture. The defendant wanted his medical expert to examine the hospital records in order to determine whether the blood clot was the result of a nonaccidental factor. The district attorney objected on the grounds of doctor-patient relationship. The court allowed the inspection, holding that the People were strangers to any claim of medical privilege and had no standing to object (*People* v. *Christiano*, 53 Misc. 2d 433 [N.Y. 1967]).

The patient can either expressly waive the privilege, or he can fail to object at the trial. He may also lose his privilege by voluntarily disclosing the information to a third party. The courts do not unanimously hold that the privilege is lost if a third party is present during the examination by the doctor. They do agree, however, that the presence of the doctor's nurse or other employee does not waive the privilege.

The patient can lose his privilege if he "opens the door" at his trial by introducing evidence concerning his physical or mental condition where this is an issue. If his defense is insanity, and he introduces medical evidence to demonstrate his condition, the state will even be allowed to bring in a psychiatrist who previously treated him for insanity. The rationale is that the introduction of defense evidence on mental condition opens the entire field for full exploration (*People* v. *Al Kanani*, 33 N.Y. 2d 260 [1973]; *People* v. *Edney*, 39 N.Y. 2d 620 [1976]).

e. Miscellaneous

Medical privilege generally applies to all matters within the hospital, such as hospital records, X rays, and nurses' notes. Interns and hospital residents are within the area of privilege if they treat the patient, even though they are employed by the hospital. Police may, for instance, overlook the fact that a resident in an emergency room who treats a drunken driver and takes a blood sample in the process may be prevented from testifying.

(8.4) *LEGAL PRIVILEGE*

The rule of confidentiality of communications between lawyer and client is of ancient origin and does not depend on statute. It is found in civil law in the codes of continental Europe. In English law its history can be traced to the time of Queen Elizabeth.

The rule originated to maintain the honor of the attorney, not to protect the client. At first the counselor was the only one who could waive it because his honor was involved. As time went on the idea of protecting the lawyer was rejected, and the theory evolved that the privilege belongs to the client. Indeed, the lawyer is now duty bound not to reveal privileged information given by his client and can do so only if the latter consents (*People ex rel Vogelstein* v. *Warden*, 150 Misc. 714, affd. 242 A.D. 611 [N.Y. 1934]).

The privilege applies whenever legal advice is sought from a lawyer and the client makes a confidential communication to him for that purpose. Such information is permanently protected from disclosure, unless the client consents to its revelation.

a. Attorneys within the Rule

"Lawyer" here includes any attorney who is admitted to practice in any state, not necessarily the state where the crime was committed or where the communication was made. The modern trend is to allow the privilege if the client believes that the individual he consults is a licensed attorney (*Wigmore on Evidence,* Vol. 8, Sec. 2302). If the communication was made to the attorney's agent, such as his legal secretary, investigator, or clerk, it is also protected. A law student is not, however, within the protection of the rule, nor is the judge who is consulted as a judge.

b. Relationships within the Rule

The lawyer must be consulted as a lawyer, though it is not necessary that he actually be retained or later hired. "Curbstone advice" is thus not protected.

c. Confidential Communication

Any information the client gives the lawyer for consultation purposes is protected. It need not be labeled "confidential." "Communication" includes words, conversations, or letters from the client.

"Acts" or observations the attorney makes of his clients are somewhat more difficult to classify. An accused thief may pay his lawyer from a large roll of bills. Can the attorney refuse to reveal this? If insanity is an issue, can the lawyer refuse to testify concerning his observation of his client's mental condition? Usually these two questions must be answered in the negative. Facts that anyone could observe are not immune simply because the lawyer saw them (*Oliver* v. *Warren*, 16 C.A. 164 [1911]). If, for the purpose of consultation, the client gives his attorney a voice sample or exhibits a scar, this would be protected.

At times the client may ask a lawyer to do things a layman could do just as well, such as having him witness a bank deposit or listen to a conversation. In this situation there is no privilege.

Lawyers have even claimed that the names of their clients were protected, but courts generally have refused to recognize this. (*U.S.* v. *Gordon-Nikkar*, 518 F. 2d 972 [1975]).

A more difficult area is one in which a lawyer receives information regarding physical evidence of a crime. *People* v. *Belge,* 83 N.Y. Misc. 2d 186 (1975), is an example of this situation. Robert Garrow was charged with the knife slaying of an eighteen-year-old boy. His defense was insanity. During preparation for trial, Garrow told his lawyers that he had killed two other people about a year before, and he described the location of their bodies. Though the lawyers located the bodies, they did not notify the authorities. The police did not find either body until three months later. At that time, Garrow publicly confessed to the two slayings when he testified in his own behalf at his murder trial. Criminal charges were brought against the lawyers but were later dismissed at the trial court level.

It is still the law, however, that a lawyer cannot conceal actual physical evidence of a crime that his client has given him. A lawyer was suspended from practice because he saw a sawed-off shotgun and money that came from an armed robbery and intended to conceal this information until after the trial under a claim of attorney-client privilege. (The general rule is set forth in *People* v. *Lee*, 3 C.A. 3d 514 [1970]; the shotgun case is *In re Ryder,* 263 F. Supp. 360, affd. 38 1F. 2d 713 [1967].)

d. Exceptions

Lawyer-client communication ceases to be protected and loses its confidentiality if there is a third party present who is not in the attorney's employ, who is not a codefendant, or who is not closely associated with the defendant (*People* v. *Kor,* 129 C.A. 2d 436 [1954]). A letter from a third person delivered to the attorney is not confidential, nor is a message from the client to the attorney directing him to deliver it to someone else.

If a lawyer is a party to a crime, or if he is a participant in a conspiracy, there is no privilege. The same is true if the client communicates with the attorney about a proposed crime (*Abbott* v. *Superior Court*, 78 C.A. 2d 19 [1947]).

If the communication itself is criminal, it is, of course, not protected, as illustrated by the case of *People* v. *Farmer,* 194 N.Y. 251 (1909). Mrs. Farmer was indicted for murdering Sarah Brennan. Evidence was presented that she passed herself as Sarah Brennan and signed that name to a deed of Sarah's property. At Mrs. Farmer's murder trial, the attorney who prepared the deed was called by the prosecution. He testified that Mrs. Farmer pretended to be the deceased and signed the name Sarah Brennan before him in his capacity as a notary public. The court approved of the testimony, stating that the communication itself was a criminal act on the part of Mrs. Farmer and that "the seal of personal confidence can never be used to cover a transaction which is in itself a crime."

e. Waiver

Since immunity belongs to the client, he must be the one to waive it. In a case in Minnesota (*State* v. *Madden*, 161 Minn. 132 [1924]), a prosecution witness was being cross-examined by defense counsel regarding inconsistent statements the witness had made to an attorney. Because the witness made no objection to the questions, the prosecutor did, saying that whatever the witness had told the lawyer was privileged. The court overruled the objection, stating the privilege belonged only to the witness and not to the prosecutor.

If a defendant chooses to take the stand, his act of testifying does not waive any attorney-client communication that he may have had. Should part of his testimony concern a communication with his lawyer, he has then "opened the door" on the whole subject and has, in effect, waived his privilege.

The privilege survives the death or the discharge of the attorney. Once a communication is protected, it is protected forever, unless it is waived.

(8.5) *PARAPROFESSIONAL PRIVILEGE*

Some professional fringe areas claim the right of privileged communications. These are occasionally the subject of court decision. Newspaper reporters, as mentioned earlier, are trying to claim the privilege. A privilege of this type ordinarily exists only because a statute grants it.

a. Nurses and Other Medical Personnel

No common-law privilege exists for either of these groups. In some jurisdictions the doctor's nurse is covered under the physician's protective privilege, but the outside registered or practical nurse has no communication privilege unless it is granted by statute. A nurse is allowed to keep a patient's information confidential only when that information is necessary for her to act in her professional capacity (*In re Avery's Estate*, 76 N.Y. Supp. 2d 790 [1948]).

Medical technicians have been excluded from coverage (*Block* v. *People,* 125 Colo. 36 [1951]). Psychologists, psychotherapists, optometrists, and dentists are not included unless they are specified by statute.

b. Hospital Records

Records of hospitals, both regular and mental, are generally included by statute in the area of medical privilege. The rationale is, of course, that these records contain in written form most of the communications between doctor and patient.

c. Miscellaneous

As stated previously, psychologists and psychotherapists are, from time to time, included in statutes concerning privileged communications. This may affect prosecution of juveniles in cases where the school psychologist is barred from testifying.

Accountants have tried without success to be included (*Himmelfarb* v. *U.S.*, 175 F. 2d 924, cert. den. 338 U.S. 860 [1949]).

With the increase of prosecutions concerning drugs and drug-related matters, the question of confidentiality of pharmacists' prescription records occasionally surfaces. Unless he is included by statute, the druggist cannot claim exemption from revealing his records (*Matter of Probate of Will of Annie Miner,* 206 Misc. 234 [N.Y. 1954]; *Green* v. *Superior Court,* 220 C.A. 2d 121 [1963]).

Telephone and telegraph employees, who are generally forbidden by statue from revealing customers' messages, have occasionally been required to disclose such information as trial witnesses (*Morris* v. *State*, 25 Ala. App. 156 [1932]).

Private detectives have at times been compelled by the court to reveal information regarding their clients even when a statute requires them to respect their clients' confidentiality (*People* v. *Roach*, 215 N.Y. 592 [1915]).

(8.6) *DIVINITY PRIVILEGE*

Privileged communication between priest and penitent was unknown in common law, but it is now granted by law in most states. The privilege seems, in fact, to be interpreted in the courts more strictly than any of the others.

a. Relationship of the Parties

The usual statute provides confidential protection if the clergyman involved is a minister of any religion and if the rules of his order forbid him to disclose a confession made to him in his professional capacity.

b. Material Protected

Not every communication with a recognized clergyman is barred. An individual must be consulting him professionally, as he would a physician, and the information must have been given with the understanding that it was to be confidential (*People* v. *Johnson*, 270 C.A. 2d 204 [1969]; see also 22 A.L.R. 2d 1152 [1950]). No promise of confidentiality need be given by the minister, however, as that is understood.

Not every message from penitent to priest is covered. Statements regarding a confederate, codefendant, or other third party are not confessions of the speaker and therefore have no protection. In the same class would be a message that the priest was to give to someone else. By the same interpretation, the privilege does not protect observations the clergyman made.

c. Who Is a Clergyman?

Statutes name "clergymen or priests" and a "clergyman, minister or other person or practitioner authorized to perform similar functions." Problems arise with people who are not officially ministers but are closely related to religious matters. In a homicide trial in New Jersey (*In re Murtha*, 115 N.J. Superior Court 380 [1971]), a nun refused to testify about a conversation she had carried on with a youth. She was convicted of contempt, and the appellate court agreed with the conviction. It was ruled that she did not perform the functions of a priest and that nothing in Catholic doctrine gave her the right to claim the privilege. Presbyterian elders have been included in the area of religious privilege because in that denomination they are "ministers." Elders of other Christian churches, however, are not included (*Reutkemeier* v. *Nolte*, 179 Iowa 342 [1917]; *Knight* v. *Lee*, 80 Ind. 201 [1881]).

d. Waiver

The divinity privilege is generally conceded to be two sided. The person who confesses has the privilege to protect his confession, and the clergyman has a separate privilege because the rules of his church forbid him to speak. Even if the person who confesses waives his right, the law will not force the clergyman to reveal the confession if it violates the rules of his order. Thus, even if the penitent is dead, absent, or does not claim his privilege, the clergyman may still refuse to testify.

(8.7) *PRIVILEGE OF THE POLICE INFORMANT*

There are three kinds of police informants: the good citizen informant, the nonparticipating underworld informant, and the participating informant. Although the identity of the good citizen informant is kept confidential, his reliability must be affirmatively demonstrated in an affidavit establishing probable cause (*see* chapter 5 for a more extensive discussion of this type of informant).

In *McCray* v. *U.S.,* 386 U.S. 300 (1967), the Supreme Court held that the confidentiality of unnamed, nonparticipating informants should be preserved. To guard against perjury by the police, however, the judge at the suppression hearing retains the right to examine the informant in chambers and outside the presence of the accused and his attorney.

Police informants, as discussed in chapter 5, may need to be kept confidential. What they have told the police cannot be used at the trial itself, as it would be hearsay and would be denying the defendant's right to confront the witnesses against him. Their information may be used to support an arrest or a search warrant.

If the informant actually took part in the crime, his testimony bears on the ultimate outcome of the trial, and the accused may be entitled to learn his identity (*Roviaro* v. *U.S.*, 353 U.S. 53 [1957]). This exception poses a real dilemma for police. The prosecutor must be prepared to produce the informant at a later time or reduce the charge to one not involving the participant. Lastly, if confidentiality of the participant informant is of paramount importance, the charge will have to be dismissed.

(8.8) *OFFICIAL PRIVILEGE*

Matters of state, which by their very nature are confidential, are subject to a claim of privilege. When a general is asked questions about a missile, or when a Secret Service agent is asked about precautions taken to protect the president, both may claim executive privilege. If, however, the agent is asked what steps the Secret Service is taking to locate another fugitive or a missing witness, the answer is protected by investigatory privilege. Often the same information will be sought, not in a courtroom but through interrogatories, by depositions, or by subpoenas duces tecum. The same principles of privilege will often prevent discovery (*see* chapter 9).

Several of the Watergate defendants attempted to call former

President Richard Nixon as a defense witness. He resisted their subpoenas to testify on the grounds of executive privilege. The Supreme Court stressed, with repect to the presidential tapes, that a court must accord a high degree of deference to such evidence. A judge must balance this solemn responsibility, however, against the needs of criminal defendants (*U.S.* v. *Nixon*, 418 U.S. 683 [1974]; *U.S.* v. *Mitchell*, 397 F. Supp. 186 [D.D.C. 1975]).

There are varying degrees of official privilege. Military secrets are one thing. Executive privilege is less clearly defined. The court might well decline to call a president or a cabinet officer, yet demand answers from lesser officials. The privilege is not absolute and depends on court discretion.

(8.9) *PRIVILEGE OF THE NEWS MEDIA*

News media privilege is one of the more recently litigated claims. Reporters try to keep from any court revelation of their confidential news sources. There is no common-law right to this, and reporters have been jailed in contempt proceedings for refusing to answer subpoenas seeking their news sources.

Some states have adopted limited-privilege statutes for newspaper, television, and radio reporters. (Calif. Ev. Code, Sec. 1070).

(8.10) *SUMMARY*

Communications between certain people are legally privileged and cannot be used in court without consent.

Communications between husband and wife are protected by many state statutes. Oral and written communications, as well as one spouse's observations of the other, may be covered. Offenses by one spouse against the other spouse or against a family member are not protected.

Doctor-patient communications, when concerned with treatment, are privileged by statute in various states. Hospital and medical records usually are included.

Confidential communications between a client and his attorney are protected from forced revelation in court. The privilege applies whenever the client seeks his lawyer's legal advice, but ordinary observations by the lawyer or actual evidence connected with a crime are not protected.

A communication by an individual to a clergyman is generally protected by statute if the rules of the minister's church forbid its disclosure.

Some miscellaneous privileges are granted by statute to reporters, nurses, and other paraprofessionals. Any of these privileges can be waived, however, and the testimony can be allowed by consent.

Police informants are entitled to maintain their anonymity, and officers can resist demands to identify them on the ground of privilege. If the informant has contributed information bearing on the identity of the accused or on his guilt or innocence, it may be in the interests of justice to refuse the claim of privilege. Where, however, the informant has merely furnished information constituting probable cause to conduct a search, and the guilt of the accused can be shown by direct testimony, the privilege is respected by the courts.

The government has a privilege not to disclose confidential matters of state, particularly military secrets. This privilege also applies to continuing investigations of a criminal nature.

Statutes written for the express purpose of protecting news sources may grant a journalist limited privilege.

chapter 9

Questions, Answers, Impeachment, and Cross-Examination of Witnesses

A. EXAMINATION OF WITNESSES

(9.1) *IN GENERAL*

Witnesses testify first by being questioned by the attorney who called them and then by being cross-examined by opposing counsel. This is often followed by a further brief redirect examination by the first attorney and then a recross-examination by the second.

Testimony is thus produced by questions asked by attorneys and answers produced by witnesses. Sometimes, in the interest of justice or for the sake of clarity, the court may intervene and question the witness. This is quite proper as long as the judge does not indicate his own opinion, does not take the examination out of counsel's hands, and does not himself ask improper questions over the objections of counsel. A juror may wish to question a witness, but the courts are divided on its propriety. The danger is that an improper question may be asked. Trial courts that permit the practice are most cautious in its use.

All testimony is ordinarily given under oath. Rules on the method of administering the oath are not uniform, but where a witness has scruples against taking the oath because of its religious connotations, he will normally be allowed to "affirm" to tell the truth without using a Bible. Some courts allow children or incompetents to testify without taking an oath because they do not understand its meaning.

A subpoenaed witness receives a small fee allowed by law. Expert witnesses, such as engineers, doctors, and the like are normally paid for their services by the party calling them. It is against public policy for any other witness to be reimbursed in any way.

(9.2) *ATTENDANCE*

Some witnesses appear voluntarily. This would be the usual case with police officers. Others are summoned by subpoena, which is, in effect, a court order issued by the judge, court clerk, or attorney, directing the witness to appear in court at a specified time and place. Material witnesses in criminal matters can, in some circumstances, be confined by court order pending trial, thus assuring their appearance when needed.

One can attempt to obtain relief against an improper subpoena by a motion to quash, and this motion will sometimes be granted. Anyone who has material evidence can, however, be compelled to testify, regardless of the inconvenience to the person subpoenaed.

a. Subpoena Duces Tecum

A subpoena duces tecum requires that a person produce physical evidence, such as documents or books. Physical evidence like doctor-patient records or attorney-client communications cannot, however, be obtained in this way. The protection of privileged material is thus maintained.

A problem often arises when incriminating documents are subpoenaed. A defendant cannot be forced to produce incriminating evidence in his possession since this would clearly violate his protection against self-incrimination.

But what about a *witness* who is subpoenaed to bring in incriminating material? A case in point is the following. A grand jury was investigating a criminal charge, and a witness, Ballmann, was subpoenaed to bring in his cashbook, wherein his name apparently was listed with some money transactions. He refused to honor the subpoena, claiming that he could be incriminated in a "bucket shop" gambling charge. The lower court held him in contempt. The U.S. Supreme Court reversed the decision, stating that Ballmann was constitutionally protected and could not be made to produce incriminating evidence by means of a subpoena duces tecum even though it was necessary for the grand jury's investigation (*Ballmann* v. *Fagin*, 200 U.S. 186 [1905]).

The situation differs if the incriminating material is in the hands of a third party who is not involved in any possible criminal activity. In the case of *Couch* v. *U.S.*, 409 U.S. 322 (1973), the Internal Revenue Service subpoenaed the taxpayer's income tax records that he had given to an accountant. When the accountant was subpoenaed, he gave the records to the taxpayer's attorney. A possible crime in relation to income tax was involved. Thus, the claim of possible self-incrimination was made. A federal court found that the accountant was not the taxpayer's employee, refused to honor the last-minute transfer of the records to the attorney, and ruled that the claim of self-incrimination was personal to the accused and held that the accountant could not, therefore, raise it.

Once a subpoena duces tecum is issued, the witness can resort to one of two tactics. He can ask for a protection order, or he can move in court to have the subpoena quashed. The court must then decide if there is any valid reason why the evidence should not be produced. This was the point in question concerning the Nixon tapes, and the courts decided against the president. He made no move to claim the constitutional protection against self-incrimination, and thus his resignation followed.

(9.3) *COMPETENCY OF WITNESSES*

Not every person is legally competent to testify. Age, mental capacity, or other factors can be reasons for disqualification.

a. Children

The trial judge usually makes the decision as to whether children can testify. Some states have statutes stipulating the age a child must be to testify under oath, with younger ones being allowed to testify unsworn if they do not understand the meaning of the oath.

No general rule defines a particular age at which a child is legally capable of testifying. A four-year-old child has, for example, been allowed to testify in a murder case (*Jackson* v. *State*, 239 Ala. 38 [1940]).

b. Mental Incapacity

Often the only witness may be ignorant, illiterate, mentally retarded, or insane. Such a witness is not barred absolutely from testifying.

If he understands an oath and can present a reasonable account, the court will normally allow him to testify. Unless there is a statutory bar against it, even a lunatic may be allowed to testify if he can give an account of events.

A trial in 1845 illustrates the lengths to which courts can go to allow the handicapped to testify. The defendant was convicted of a rape committed upon the person of Mary Marshall. She was then an inmate of the county poorhouse, "about thirty years of age and of imbecile understanding. One witness considered her an idiot." The act occurred in a woods near the highway. Triskett, the poorhouse keeper, found her shortly after the crime. He testified that, although Mary could not talk, "she communicates her ideas by signs" and that he had no difficulty communicating with her. Triskett stated that "her face was bloody and her clothes soiled." When he asked her what had happened, she told him by signs "that she had been violated." The court, in reviewing the trial, found that it was improper for Triskett to have testified for her and said that there was no reason why Mary herself should not have testified "to give evidence through the medium of this witness as an interpreter by signs" (*People* v. *McGee*, 1 Denio 19 [N.Y. 1845]).

The trend today is to let incapacitated witnesses testify for whatever their testimony may be worth. Even a witness who is under the influence of drugs or alcohol is not incompetent to testify. Whether he testifies is determined by the court. The jury's function is to weigh such testimony.

c. Convicts

In early English common law, a person convicted of a serious crime was thereafter completely barred from being a witness. The theory was that such a person was so depraved as to be unworthy of belief. The modern rule is different. Under it, criminal conviction does not make a witness incompetent to testify. It is up to the jury to judge his truthfulness and accuracy, taking this factor into consideration along with all others. A few areas, however, retain the rule barring testimony by convicts, and some jurisdictions forbid testimony by individuals convicted of specific crimes, such as perjury.

d. Relationships

The relationship of the witness to the individual involved in a crime does not bar his testimony. An exception to this rule is the marital privilege, by which one spouse can prevent the other from testifying in court against him. A blood relative, close associate, or friend may be a witness. The owner of the stolen goods that are involved in the case may testify in a larceny prosecution. A witness who will receive a reward should a defendant be convicted is even allowed to testify. None of these relationships to the crime or the suspect disqualify the witness. It is his believability, not the legality of what he says, that is important.

(9.4) *ADVERSARY SYSTEM VERSUS INQUISITORIAL SYSTEM*

In this country the adversary criminal trial system is used. This system calls for evidence to be produced by two opposing sides, with all witnesses subject to cross-questioning by opposing counsel. The inquisitorial system, which is used in other parts of the world, is quite different. There, the prosecution proves its case by asking questions of the accused, as well as by producing any other witnesses it can find. The defendant is thus forced to defend himself in court by answering the state's questions. The adversary system completely rejects this idea. Here, we have gone so far in the other direction that we protect the accused from having to testify at all.

(9.5) *FORM OF QUESTIONS AND DUTY TO OBJECT*

All testimony is given in the form of questions and answers. The witness is not allowed to testify in a block by giving a general narrative of events. He presents his story piecemeal in answer to questions. In terms of brevity and clarity this is a handicap, but it is necessary so that no evidence will come out unless it is valid.

Questions should seek testimony based on the facts known by the witness. The answers sought should be factual, not based on the witness's "understanding" of what happened. Questions should be clear. A compound question containing more than one part is improper. A question may not be so general as to include illegal evidence, and it must not be misleading, ambiguous, or indefinite. Any question that does not fit this description is legally objectionable.

In the adversary system, opposing counsel has the opportunity to make legal objection to the question being asked or to the answer being sought. This method thus prevents the introduction of improper evidence. If, however, opposing counsel does not object, any evidence may be used, even though it may be completely irrelevant or invalid.

(9.6) *IMPROPER QUESTIONS*

Leading questions are generally improper. This type of question suggests the answer, often leaving the witness simply to reply "yes" or "no." Lawyers are not supposed to put answers in the mouths of their own witnesses. Though leading questions will be allowed in preliminary testimony, opposing counsel may properly object to them when the material part of the testimony is reached.

Cross-examination introduces an entirely different situation. Counsel is here seeking to test an adversary witness for truth and accuracy. Leading questions are quite proper, and the witness may be led in any direction and to any degree.

Another improper question is one which states facts that are not in evidence. The reason for this is readily apparent. If unproven assumptions are used in questions, both the witness and the jury may be misled.

Purely argumentative questions are also improper. Lawyers are supposed to question witnesses, not argue with them, although this frequently happens. More leeway is allowed in this area in cross-examination than in direct examination, but it is technically incorrect in both types of examination.

With a few exceptions, questions asking for conclusions are objectionable. The witness is not supposed to give his opinion or his conclusion about the case. If this were not so, a trial could be decided by a parade of witnesses on both sides stating what they thought about the defendant's guilt or innocence.

Often it is not readily apparent that a question is really calling for a conclusion. For example, an assault victim may be asked: "Did the defendant threaten you?" The question can be properly objected to as calling for a conclusion. To avoid the objection, the examiner should draw the witness's attention to the relevant time and place and then ask a series of questions. "What did the defendant do?" "Then what did he do next?" "What did he finally do?" In this way he gets a detailed description of all the actions.

There are, however, several areas involving matters of common observation in which lay witnesses are allowed to make estimates or to state an opinion. (These are discussed in detail in chapter 10.)

The jury, not the witness, draws a conclusion as to what actually happened. When opinion evidence is allowed in any case, either from laymen or experts, the jury is not bound by it. They may reject it or accept it as they wish.

Experts are allowed to state their opinions. The purpose of calling an expert witness is to get his professional or scientific judgment on a matter outside the realm of common experience. Physicians, engineers, and laboratory technicians are common examples of expert witnesses.

(9.7) *IMPROPER FOUNDATION*

In a courtroom one may hear an objection to a question on the basis of "improper foundation," and the objection is often sustained, much to the surprise of the uninformed. What usually happens is that a question is asked prematurely or facts are included that have not yet been proven. In order to make the question proper, counsel must have the exhibit introduced in evidence or bring out the needed basic facts before he asks it again. In fact, the physical exhibit itself cannot be introduced without "laying a proper foundation," that is, without proving its relevance, authenticity, and sameness of condition.

(9.8) *PAROL EVIDENCE RULE*

"Parol" is a short way of saying "word of mouth." The parol evidence rule is one saying that, with few exceptions, a written document is what it says it is. For example, ambiguities in documents, such as technical or trade terms, may be explained by verbal evidence. The law will not normally allow oral proof to take precedence over written proof, however, for the spoken word vanishes with the wind, while the written word remains.

Because this rule has little application in criminal trials, it need not be discussed in detail here. It is mentioned only because of its general application in all court proceedings.

(9.9) *SELF-SERVING DECLARATIONS*

The counsel for the defense is not allowed to introduce in evidence his client's statements demonstrating his innocence. The defendant could write letters in which he declares his innocence to his congressman, the governor, the president, and the newspapers and publicly proclaim his innocence on television. But none of these things has evidentiary value.

Only if a person admits something *against* his interest can any validity be attached to it. People usually do not make derogatory statements about themselves unless they are true. For this reason, a voluntary confession of a crime is considered the strongest type of evidence against an accused. On the other hand, personal protestations of innocence are regarded simply as manifestations of self-preservation and so are not admissible as evidence in one's own defense.

Some textbook writers and judges have criticized this blanket ban against the use of self-serving statements as being too broad. It is possible, therefore, to find court rulings in which a defendant has been allowed to show that he made statements indicating lack of motive or interest, demonstrating goodwill toward the victim, or proving that there was a plan not to perform an act (*Wigmore on Evidence*, Sec. 1732; *U.S.* v. *Dellinger*, C.A. [1972], 12 Cr L 2196).

B. ANSWERS OF WITNESSES

(9.10) *IN GENERAL*

A witness's answers should be exactly that—answers. If he digresses, he runs the risk of introducing illegal evidence that could result in a mistrial. The witness may, for example, argue, give an unsolicited opinion, or volunteer added information. Opposing counsel can object even after such an answer is given and ask that it be stricken from the record. The court will then order the answer to be expunged and instruct the jury to ignore it. Answers of this kind are as improper as questions of the same type and are always subject to be stricken from the record.

(9.11) *REVIVAL OF MEMORY*

Witnesses forget, just as the rest of us do. This is especially true in criminal matters where the normal procedure delays considerably the time of the trial from the original date of the crime. The most effective way of solving this problem is for attorneys to ask leading questions. For example, a witness who cannot recall a date might be asked: "Wasn't it in the winter?" "Do you remember telling me that it was shortly before the end of the school vacation?" Though these questions are leading, they are an acceptable way of refreshing a witness's memory. Another way of jogging a person's memory is to refer to prior statements, testimony, or written memorandums.

(9.12) *PAST RECOLLECTIONS RECORDED*

There are times when leading questions, statements, or memorandums do not revive a lost memory. In that case there may still be a valid evidentiary method to produce the needed evidence. If the witness has a written record of the facts that he made shortly after the event, that record may be introduced in evidence as a "past recollection recorded." The witness is shown his own written memorandum, and if, after reading it, he still has no independent recollection of the event, the memorandum may be used as evidence. Though this may sound implausible, it does sometimes happen.

(9.13) *WITNESS'S USE OF MEMORANDUM OR RECORD*

Doctors, businessmen, police officers, and many others in this photocopy age keep a wide variety of written records and memorandums. We are not concerned at this point with how such records can be used against a witness, but with the way the individual who is testifying can use his written records to strengthen his testimony.

He cannot, of course, offer his prior written record to support what he is now saying. As we have seen, this would be self-serving testimony. Neither can he present a diary entry or police reports that say: "Here is what happened. It's all in my record." It is not possible for opposing counsel to cross-examine a piece of paper.

A witness can legitimately use his memorandums to refresh his memory. Doctors, laboratory technicians, and other expert witnesses could not be expected to recall independently detailed information in individual cases. Such witnesses repeatedly jog their memories by looking at their notes. They are not ordinarily allowed to read directly from these memorandums, but use them only as an aid to memory. When a witness uses a written record to aid his testimony, opposing counsel is entitled to inspect that record.

Police officers or private investigators should be particularly careful about written reports. A faulty one can lose a case. The example of Officer Dwyer is a case in point. This officer monitored telephone taps during an investigation of ticket scalping. He made shorthand notes of the messages, transcribed them into longhand, and then dictated the material to a court clerk who put it all into a criminal complaint.

Officer Dwyer had previously appeared in court and had been subjected to a long, detailed cross-examination concerning his notes. Because of that, he deliberately destroyed all of his original records in the case of ticket scalping. At the trial, Dwyer stated that he had no memory of these calls and admitted destroying his original notes, but said he could testify by using the complaint he had dictated to the clerk. The appellate courts ruled against this, holding that where the destruction of records was deliberate, the witness could not use any other record as an aid to his memory. Thus, the case was lost (*People* v. *Betts,* 272 A.D. 737, affd. 297 N.Y. 1000 [1947]).

And so, any witness in modern criminal trials can expect that opposing counsel will see any personal records he uses in testifying. Further, it is likely that the court will allow inspection of any memorandum or records a witness has made prior to his actual testimony.

C. IMPEACHMENT OF WITNESSES

(9.14) *PURPOSE*

The purpose of impeaching (discrediting) an adverse witness is to weaken the case of the opposing side. It is always proper for the opposing counsel to use this tactic. He may do so by showing that the witness was inaccurate, untruthful, or unworthy of belief. The most common method of demonstrating the weakness of the witness is to cross-examine him. In some situations, counsel may even be allowed to present affirmative proof that tends to throw doubt on the witness's credibility.

(9.15) *COMPLAINANTS AND DEFENDANTS*

It is obvious that both the complainant and the accused are interested in the outcome of the trial. A complainant in a rape case or the victim of a mugging naturally wants to see the defendant convicted, and every defendant is interested in acquittal.

Because both parties are concerned with the outcome, the jury may consider this as one of the factors affecting their credibility as witnesses. It is legal for the attorneys to bring out such self-interest. This may be done by questioning the witness and by presenting legal arguments to the jury. Both methods are intended to impeach the witness. Such witnesses are also subject to the methods of impeachment discussed below.

(9.16) *COMPETENCY*

Evidence of the witness's lack of normal mental capacity may always be shown by way of impeachment. If a child testifies, for example, his age, his progress in school, and his intelligence as demonstrated by test scores can be scrutinized. Proof of mental retardation, senility, or insanity may also be presented in order to discredit a witness.

(9.17) *BIAS AND PREJUDICE*

Evidence tending to show bias or prejudice on the part of a witness is always relevant and can be introduced, even where the witness has denied it. A number of factors may indicate bias. The opposing attorney may show, for example, that the witness was an accomplice, a friend, or an enemy of either the defendant or complainant. He could also be related by blood or marriage. Any financial or business relationship is relevant. Immoral relations between the witness and one of the parties have a bearing on impeachment. The fact that a witness is a private detective hired by one party could easily bring about a charge of bias.

(9.18) *ACCURACY OF DIRECT TESTIMONY*

The most common method of impeachment is to demonstrate any inaccuracies in a witness's direct testimony. A cross-examiner invariably questions the witness on the minute details of his story. He might ask what time the witness heard a shot. If his answer varies from what he stated in direct testimony, the attorney will forcefully point this out, thus discrediting the witness. It is safe to say, however, that no witness remembers the past exactly, and all observers see things in different ways. But, regardless of the problems involved, bringing out inaccuracies and misstatements is a fair way to attempt to discredit a witness. Juries are affected by the tactic, which is, after all, the reason why trial lawyers use it.

(9.19) *CONVICTION OF A CRIME*

It has been the general rule that a witness could be impeached by asking him about any criminal act of his past life. He could be cross-examined concerning the details of such criminal activity as rape, robbery, or burglary as well as the fact of his conviction for that offense. The universal limit on such questioning for purposes of impeachment is that counsel must have a fair basis for doing so. Every witness automatically presents himself as being worthy of belief. This is the justification for the general rule that any immoral or vicious act in his past life should be allowed to be shown as affecting his credibility.

In some states the field of impeachment is narrowed considerably. California law, for example, restricts cross-examination to the details of offenses that were mentioned on direct testimony (*People* v. *Morgan*, 87 C.A. 2d 674 [1948]j). A few states limit impeachment questioning to felony convictions and will not allow inquiries into juvenile adjudications or misdemeanors. All courts bar questions regarding arrests or indictments since they do not involve convictions.

If a defendant takes the stand in his own behalf, he is subject to cross-examination just as any other witness. He can usually be asked about prior criminal convictions within the limitations established by the state in which he is being tried. Should he deny the past conviction, the prosecutor may offer a certificate of that conviction as impeachment evidence.

The attitude of the court toward the use of criminal records as impeachment testimony is currently undergoing change. The new Federal Rules of Evidence (Rule 609, effective July 1, 1975) restrict the use of criminal records to impeach any witness, including a defendant. Barred are the use of convictions over ten years old, juvenile adjudications, misdemeanors, and felony convictions that have been pardoned or granted certificates of rehabilitation. Even felony convictions that are not barred can be excluded as impeachment evidence against the defendant under the federal code. This occurs if the court feels that damage to the accused is greater than the value it might have for the case.

Various court decisions have approved of a procedure whereby defense counsel asks for a ruling in advance of the trial as to which prior criminal convictions can be introduced in evidence. The judge weighs the theoretical prejudice against the defendant and the "probative value" of such evidence and decides which record of convictions, if any, can be used. On the basis of this decision, the defendant with a criminal record can determine in advance of the trial whether or not he wants to take the stand (*Luck* v. *U.S.*, 348 F. 2d 763 [1965]; *People* v. *Beagle*, 6 Cal. 3d 441 [1972]; *People* v. *Sandoval*, 34 N.Y. 2d 371 [1974]).

In all likelihood this trend toward eliminating criminal records for the purpose of impeachment will continue. It is imperative, therefore, that anyone involved in law enforcement keep informed of statutes and current judicial decisions in this field.

(9.20) *DRUG USE*

With the widespread use of drugs, all the way from tranquilizers to heroin, there is an increasing problem with witnesses. Evidence of drug addiction usually impeaches a witness. Some older decisions refuse to allow this evidence to discredit a witness, but the current majority rule is that it may do so. There is, in fact, general agreement that the effect of drugs on a participant at the time of trial can and should be shown, even though it might not be done for the specific purpose of impeachment.

Gary Pray was tried in Vermont for the murder of his brother-in-law. His defense was insanity. At a pretrial hearing, the defendant turned over a table and tried to attack a psychiatrist who was testifying. The state therefore put him on medication, which made him appear quiet, well oriented, and cooperative throughout the trial. Because the jury was never told that Pray was sedated, they found him guilty. The decision was appealed, and the appellate court held that the state had a duty to reveal the defendant's true condition. It stated: "The jury never looked upon an unaltered, undrugged Gary Pray . . . yet . . . his deportment . . . was a part of the basis of their judgment . . . of his defense of insanity . . . . In fact, it may have been necessary to expose the jury to the undrugged, unsedated Gary Pray in so far . . . as safety might permit." Pray's conviction and life sentence were, therefore, overturned (*State* v. *Pray*, 342 A. 2d 227 [Vt. Sup. Ct., 1975]).

(9.21) *IMMORAL ACTS*

A witness may be cross-examined about any immoral acts in his past, as long as the examiner has a fair basis for asking about them. This is based on the assumption that honesty is associated with morality and good character. Thus, inquiry concerning behavior that demonstrates lack of morality and good character is allowed by way of impeachment. Some jurisdictions are more restrictive than this and will not allow cross-examination about past misconduct that did not result in a criminal conviction.

This presents a real problem in the prosecution of a rape case. The victim must, of course, testify regarding the circumstances of the rape. Defense counsel, in the guise of impeaching her credibility, may cross-examine her regarding her complete moral history in both major and minor aspects. Even though the victim's answers give no indication of immorality, counsel suggests past indiscretions simply by asking the questions. He is not actually trying to impeach her credibility but is suggesting that she consented to intercourse. In response to public pressure, some states are enacting laws that limit such cross-examination of complainants in rape cases. Many people have come to feel that this type of question has produced unfair results. These new statutes, therefore, forbid cross-examining the rape victim about past moral history. (*See* N.Y.C.P.L.60.42.)

(9.22) *CHARACTER AND REPUTATION*

There is a major exception to the rule barring self-serving evidence. In criminal cases, the defendant may offer evidence demonstrating good character. This is usually in the form of testimony by third parties concerning the defendant's reputation in the community. If the defense offers evidence of good character, then the prosecution, in rebuttal, can show impeaching evidence by giving similar proof of poor character.

Also, when any witness, including the defendant, has taken the stand, the adversary party may offer evidence of poor reputation for truth and veracity by way of impeachment. This is done by asking the witness who knows of the reputation if he would believe the prior witness when he is under oath. The other side may then introduce rebuttal evidence to the contrary.

(9.23) *PRIOR INCONSISTENT STATEMENTS*

A prior inconsistent statement can always be used to discredit a witness. The examiner must always lay a foundation for using this tactic. First he calls the witness's attention to his prior testimony or statement. Once the witness admits that he made it or outside proof is submitted showing that he did so, the witness may be queried about the discrepancies. Any variations may then be introduced in evidence.

A witness in a criminal trial can expect that his prior testimony before a grand jury or at a preliminary hearing, as well as any of his earlier written statements, will be used against him in this fashion.

(9.24) *USE OF COLLATERAL MATTERS IN IMPEACHMENT*

Questions used in cross-examination by way of impeachment inquiring into past improper acts of a witness are, of course, concerned with side issues that are not involved in the trial before the court. The scope of these impeachment factors must be limited. If it were not, a trial could degenerate into a series of trials within a trial in which opposing counsels would attempt to prove or disprove the alleged indiscretions of the witness. For this reason, a universal rule has been adopted. Except for past criminal convictions, if the witness on cross-examination denies the existence of any alleged disgraceful or vicious act on his part, that ends the matter, and the questioner is bound by the answers.

A case involving stolen property is illustrative of this rule. The defendant testified in his own defense. The prosecutor, on cross-examination, asked the defendant if he had bought and passed counterfeit money at one time. The defendant denied that he had. He was then asked if he had not confessed to doing so at one time. Again he denied the accusation. Though the defendant was shown his signed confession, he continued to deny it was true. At this point the prosecutor read the entire confession to the jury. The defendant was found guilty of the present crime. A higher court set aside the conviction. It was pointed out that though inquiry into the forgery was a collateral matter allowed by way of impeachment, "the cross-examiner . . . is bound by the answers to his questions on collateral matters" and that should have ended the matter. (*People* v. *McCormick,* 278 A.D. 410, affd. 303 N.Y. 403 [1951]).

D. CROSS-EXAMINATION OF WITNESSES

(9.25) *PURPOSE AND CHARACTER*

In contrast to what is portrayed on television, in real courtrooms during cross-examination, witnesses do not break down on the stand and tearfully confess that they committed the crime. One of the general purposes of cross-examination, as has been discussed, is to point out inaccuracies, falsehoods, or collateral matters tending to weaken the believability of the witness. Another general aim of the cross-examiner is to pry out all the favorable information possible from the opposing witness. Police and prosecutors often neglect this area in preparing for trial, forgetting that the defense will attempt to elicit helpful information by cross-examining the People's witnesses.

These two aims, impeachment and the obtaining of favorable information, are the general purposes of most cross-examination.

(9.26) *RIGHT TO CONFRONT AND EXAMINE WITNESSES*

Cross-examination of witnesses is basic to our adversary trial system. The defendant has a constitutional right to confront the witnesses against him and to cross-examine them (*Boykin* v. *Alabama*, 395 U.S. 238 [1969]).

This presents a problem when there are two or more defendants and the prosecution has confessions he can use in evidence. The following hypothetical situation demonstrates this. In a joint trial, the prosecutor uses defendant A's confession, but A does not take the stand. If the confession also implicates defendant B, he loses his chance to cross-question A concerning the incriminating material. The lawyer for B cannot, of course, cross-examine a piece of paper. Under these circumstances, B has a constitutional right to a separate trial from A, where only B's own confession can be used against him. If the prosecution wants to use A's information, it will have to get A to testify in person against B. He will then be subject to cross-examination by B's defense attorney (*Bruton* v. *U.S.*, 391 U.S. 123 [1968]).

(9.27) *SCOPE OF CROSS-EXAMINATION*

Every witness who testifies, including the defendant, is subject to cross-examination. Though there are limits to what may be asked, in general the examiner may question any matter testified to on direct examination. Included within these limits are the usual questions testing credibility. Thus, a cross-examiner is not allowed to question the witness on any unrelated matter. Nor can he badger the witness or otherwise treat him unfairly. It is up to the trial court to limit such questioning, which means that the judge largely determines the area that is to be allowed.

While there is much latitude in cross-examination, it still must be relevant to the issue. Anything concerning the accuracy or credibility of the witness is relevant. Questioning based on his direct testimony must relate to material matters recited by the witness.

(9.28) *PARTICULAR SUBJECTS*

Illegal evidence, such as privileged communications, cannot be inquired about in cross-examination any more than in direct questioning. Nor may counsel cross-examine the witness on matters about which he can have no knowledge. In addition, the Fifth Amendment forbids questions by which the witness could incriminate himself.

Should the defendant testify, he does so at some risk since the prosecutor may cross-examine him regarding any fact that may convict him of the crime of which he was accused. The defendant can, however, still claim his privilege against self-incrimination with respect to any other crime, and the cross-examiner will be prevented from inquiring further into such areas (*see* 35 L.R.A. 518; 21 Am. Jur. 2d Crim. Law, Sec. 358).

Another general area of testimony may be forbidden to the cross-examiner. It arises if he brings out new relevant facts on cross-examination that the witness had not mentioned in his direct testimony. When this occurs, the generally accepted rule is that the examiner has "made the witness his own." In effect, he has adopted this witness as if the examiner had called him. In this event, he can no longer contradict or impeach the witness. Most courts are reluctant to apply this rule rigidly, however, and so some leeway may be allowed in impeachment or contradiction of a witness that one has made his own.

(9.29) *REFUSAL TO ANSWER*

On occasion a witness may refuse to answer. Normally, this would occur during cross-examination, but sometimes a hostile witness may refuse to respond on direct questioning. Refusal to answer an incriminating question is not contempt of court. Failure to reply to a degrading question does not constitute contempt unless the answer is material.

Another exception involves a prosecution witness who can refuse to name an informant unless the court directs him to do so. Any contempt of court that comes about because of a refusal to answer can result in a fine or imprisonment.

(9.30) *SUMMARY*

Our adversary trial system depends on the questioning and cross-questioning of witnesses. Anyone having material information can be subpoenaed to testify and can be made to produce evidence in his possession. The criminal defendant cannot be forced to give testimony.

In direct examination, questions must be relevant, avoid general conclusions, seek facts; they must not be leading or argumentative. In cross-examination much more leeway is allowed in all these areas.

Answers must be responsive and produce valid evidence. Opposing counsel must object to any improper question or answer. If he does not do so, even illegal evidence may be used.

Witnesses are not disqualified solely because of age, incompetency, past criminal history, or even insanity. If the court is satisfied that such a witness is able to give a reasonable account of events, his testimony can be taken. These conditions actually affect credibility, not admissibility, of such testimony. Even unsworn testimony is allowed under certain conditions.

A witness may, if necessary, use a personal memorandum or record to aid his memory, but ordinarily he will not be allowed to read this directly to the jury. Opposing counsel may see the record and use it in cross-examination.

Every witness is subject to possible impeachment by any legitimate means. His competency, accuracy, and truthfulness are all subject to question. The witness's interest in the outcome, his relationship to the parties involved, and his bias or prejudice may be shown as bearing on credibility. Cross-examiners commonly inquire into past criminal history, drug addiction, and immoral acts. A witness may decline to answer incriminating questions, as may a testifying defendant, except in relation to the crime for which he is presently being charged.

Any prior inconsistent statement made by the witness may be used for impeachment. The same is true if he had a poor reputation for honesty. A defendant may use evidence of good character as a defense. If, however, he introduces such evidence, the prosecution may show the opposite.

Every defendant has the constitutional right to confront the witnesses against him and to cross-examine them. Though cross-examiners generally must stay within the limits of the direct examination, they may seek out information favorable to their side and can inquire into any legitimate matter of impeachment.

chapter 10

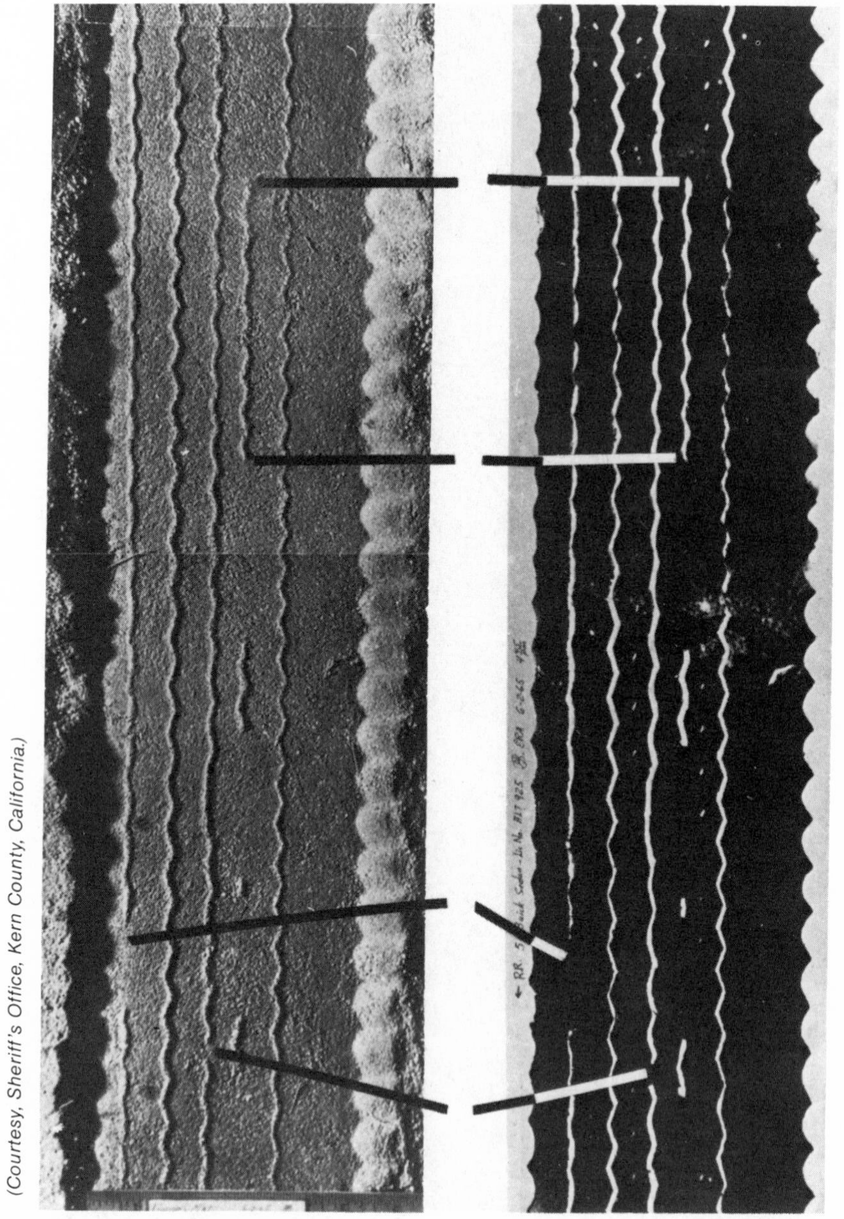

Tire impression left at crime scene in sand.

An inked impression of a suspected tire.

A SUBJECT FOR OPINION EVIDENCE

Opinion Evidence

(10.1) *IN GENERAL*

Witnesses frequently find their testimony blocked because they have stated an opinion rather than an actual observation. All witnesses have opinions as to what happened but are generally not allowed to state them. They must confine themselves to facts.

When opinions are accepted, however, they are not allowed to be so broad as to invade the jury's prerogative of deciding guilt or innocence. Nevertheless, opinions from both laymen and experts are received in many situations where the courts have found this to be practical.

(10.2) *LAY WITNESSES*

A lay witness is any witness who has not been qualified as an "expert witness" or as a "skilled witness."

a. Common Experiences

There are actually large areas where a witness is allowed to state his opinion, mainly in matters of common experience. A layman can say whether it was light or dark and give his estimate of the size, shape, or color of an object. How far away was the defendant? How old was he?

How tall? All of these are proper questions, and the opinion answers are allowed as being common observations. A witness can also estimate speed or measurements without being an engineer.

The testimony offered will often be part fact and part opinion. Many times this will pass undetected, but when an objection is raised, the court must decide on its admissibility. The court usually allows such an answer as being the only way the witness can adequately describe an incident and will admit it as a type of "shorthand rendering of the facts."

In a case involving a charge of assault to commit rape (*State* v. *Collins*, 88 Mont. 514 [1930]), the complainant testified she was at a party when the defendant suggested they go into the bedroom. When she refused, he grabbed her by the wrist, pulled her down the hall into a darkened bedroom, and pushed her onto the bed. When she continued to protest and tried to get up, he threw his left leg across hers and "would pull my dress up." The prosecutor then asked if she knew what the defendant was trying to do, and she answered, "Yes." The defense immediately objected, saying she was being asked to give a conclusion. The objection was overruled, and she was allowed to answer further. She said: "He was trying to have sexual intercourse with me." The evidence was sustained on appeal. It was held that, however justified the opinion rule was, the answer was based on facts previously testified to and "was a compound of fact and conclusion—a 'shorthand rendering of the facts'—and was properly received."

b. Intoxication

Any witness may testify on the question of intoxication. An individual who has observed drunken people—a common sight in everyday life—can testify directly concerning his opinion on the person's drunkenness or sobriety. A better practice, however, is to have the witness in a case of drunken driving describe the erratic behavior of the car and then give details regarding the defendant's personal appearance, such as slurred speech, staggered walk, and odor of alcohol. Then he should be asked directly: "In your opinion, was the defendant drunk or sober?" This is allowable, even though there is no precise measurement of intoxication, and other conditions, such as diabetes or medication, can produce symptoms similar to drunkenness (*Daniels* v. *State*, 155 Tenn. 549 [1927]). In the opinion of *People* v. *Eastwood*, 14 N.Y. 563 (1856), "A child . . . may answer whether a man (whom it has seen) was drunk or sober: it does not require science or opinion to answer the question, but observation merely."

c. Identity

Witnesses commonly are allowed to testify to identify, naming the accused as being the one involved in the crime. Identity is a conclusion about which people often differ; but, regardless of how unreliable it is, such evidence is accepted by the court.

Many years ago in the *Tichborne* case, an English judge, Lord Cockburn, charged the jury in this way:

> Frequently a man is sworn to, who has been seen only for a moment. A man stops you on the road, puts a pistol to your head and robs you of your watch and purse; a man seizes you by the throat and while you are half strangled his confederate rifles your pockets; a burglar invades your house by night and you have only a rapid glance to enable you to know his features. In all these cases, the opportunity for observing is so brief that a mistake is possible and yet the lives and safety of people would not be secure unless you acted on the recollection of features so acquired and so retained and it is done every day.

d. Mental Capacity

Because everyone observes "normal" behavior in others every day, any lay witness is allowed to describe "abnormal" behavior in an individual and to give his opinion as to that person's mental condition. He can state whether he thinks the person is sane or insane or had the mental capacity to understand what he was doing.

The layman's opinion must be based on personal observations and not on an abstract situation. In two cases (*McKenzie* v. *U.S.,* 266 F. 2d 524 [1959]; *Hixon* v. *State* [Fla. App.], 165 So. 2d 436 [1964]), laymen testified on the question of sanity, and the appellate court explained the rules saying that a nonexpert in a criminal case "may be permitted to give an opinion regarding sanity, but it cannot be a general opinion independent of circumstances within his own knowledge." The witness must lay a foundation for his opinion by first testifying as to the "appearances, actions, and conduct . . . of personal knowledge and observation."

It is necessary at this point to introduce a word of caution. While the above is the generally accepted rule of opinion evidence concerning mental condition, some states have statutes limiting this type of evidence in criminal cases. These laws must, therefore, always be consulted.

e. Voices

Testimony on voices is similar to that on identity: A layman may express his view in regard to a person's voice. As long as he has some basis for recognizing the voice, he may give his opinion, even though he never heard the voice before the time of the crime (*Froding* v. *State*, 125 Neb. 322 [1933]; *People* v. *Harris*, 17 Ill. 2d 446 [1959]).

f. Handwriting

Anyone who knows another person's handwriting may give his opinion as to whether the writing in question was made by that person. Because this is also an area of common observation, all courts agree that a layman familiar with a particular handwriting may state his opinion concerning its identity even though he is not a handwriting expert.

Some court decisions hold that a layman can testify on handwriting so long as he has become familiar with the handwriting, even though he has never actually seen the person write (*Phoenix State Bank* v. *Whitcomb*, 121 Conn. 32 [1936]).

g. Demeanor or Appearance

Although some courts take a narrower view, many hold that a witness may describe another's demeanor or appearance by conclusory words such as "agitated," "nervous," "angry," or "disturbed." Clothing can be described as "messed up" or "disheveled." This testimony showing a person's emotions or appearance may be very important as proof of motive or intent. The reason for allowing this type of conclusion is that it is difficult for the average witness to put such descriptions into words, and this is the most helpful way for him to describe such conditions to the jury (*State* v. *Vanella*, 40 Mont. 326 [1910]; *People* v. *Deacon*, 117 Cal. App. 2d 206 [1953]; *Taggart* v. *State,* 143 Ala. 88 [1905]).

h. Miscellaneous

In some areas commonly thought of as requiring expert scientific evidence, laymen have been allowed to give their opinions, and those opinions have been considered facts of common observation. Courts have, for example, let nonexperts present their opinions on blood, powder burns, the similarity of footprints, tire marks, and the like (*Greenfield* v. *People*, 85 N.Y. 75 [1881]; *Commonwealth* v. *Dorsey*, 103 Mass. 412 [1869]).

i. Qualified Answers

A witness often qualifies his answer by saying "To the best of my knowledge," "I believe," or even "I think." Does this make it simply his opinion, rather than a fact, and thus disqualify the answer? Such language will not ordinarily result in eliminating his testimony so long as he was only explaining a faulty memory or admitting his uncertainty.

The court generally allows this type of answer to stand on the ground that it is fully admissible. Its weight, however, is up to the jury (*Losey* v. *Atcheson, Topeka & Santa Fe Railroad*, 84 Kan. 224 [1911]; *State* v. *Wilson*, 9 Wash. 16 [1894]; *Bachelder* v. *Morgan,* 179 Ala. 339 [1913]).

(10.3) *SKILLED WITNESSES*

There is a class of witness between laymen and technical experts, often referred to as a skilled witness, who may be allowed to give his opinion in court within his particular field. A cutlery worker, for example, might testify that the stone and mineral oil found in an accused convict's cell could have been used to grind down a table knife into the murder weapon used in assaulting another convict.

In a trial in Georgia, Clif Byrd was convicted of the shotgun slaying of John Mandeville (*Byrd* v. *State*, 142 Ga. 633 [1914]). A lay witness testified that he examined the gunshot wound inflicted on Mandeville and that, in his opinion, it was done with a "cut shell." The latter, he said, was a shotgun shell with the paper almost completely cut off between the powder and the shot (now often referred to by police as a "wad cutter" shell); thus, when the shot was fired, it stayed together in a lump instead of scattering. He explained that he had fired such shells at objects other than humans and had observed the effects. The court approved the use of his testimony. While not an expert, he was, the court said, a witness experienced in such matters with knowledge on the subject, and he could therefore state his opinion.

(10.4) *THE SCOPE OF EXPERT WITNESSES*

The area where opinion evidence is accepted most widely is that of the expert witness. An individual who has special knowledge, education, skill, or experience is qualified to be such a witness. Doctors, engineers, and chemists are among those routinely used as expert witnesses. Under proper limitations, the expert is allowed to state his opinion, which is intended to aid the jury in making its decision.

a. General Limitations

The expert may, of course, give opinion evidence only within the area of his special knowlege. If, however, the matter involved is one on which jurors of ordinary experience can make a decision, an expert will not be allowed to give his opinion. There is no reason, for example, to call a minister or professor to testify that something is obscene. The jury can decide that as a matter of common experience. Neither can a psychologist give his expert opinion that a witness is lying, because this is also a matter of common knowledge for the jury's determination.

In a prosecution for receiving stolen property (*Girson* v. *U.S.,* 88 F 2d 358, cert. den. 300 U.S. 697 [1937]), the assistant post quartermaster was a government witness. On cross-examination he was handed two pairs of socks, admittedly not stolen, and asked if they did not have the same appearance as the stolen articles. The court properly disallowed the question since this was a matter of common experience that the jury was well qualified to decide.

Many years ago in *Ferguson* v. *Hubbell*, 97 N.Y. 507 (1884), an appellate court stated what is still a correct rule:

> It is not sufficient to warrant the introduction of expert evidence that the witness may know more of the subject than the juries; . . . the jurors may have less skill and experience than the witness and yet have enough to draw their own conclusions . . . where the facts . . . are of such nature that jurors generally are just as competent to form opinions . . . there is no occasion to resort to expert or opinion evidence.

Even where expert opinion is properly used, it is still just that—an opinion. The jurors may accept or reject it. They still are the sole judges of the facts, not the experts.

b. Province of the Jury

An expert cannot give his opinion on the ultimate question to be decided by the jury. Even the most experienced criminologist or investigator is not allowed to testify that the defendant is, in his opinion, innocent or guilty.

While questions of this scope will not be allowed, there is a growing tendency for evidence codes and court decisions to widen this area of expert testimony, even though technically it invades the ultimate issue to be decided by the jury (*People* v. *Ciucci*, 8 Ill. 2d 619 [1956]; *Rabata* v. *Dohner*, 45 Wis. 2d 111 [1969]; Rule 704, Federal Rules of Evidence; Florida Evidence Code).

(10.5) *QUALIFICATIONS OF EXPERTS*

Before an expert can give his opinion, the foundation must be laid for it by showing the expert's qualifications, his education, experience, and training. This is usually done by having the witness recite the facts of his experience and background. Occasionally, counsel will stipulate his qualifications, and his detailed background need not be recited. This commonly occurs when doctors are testifying.

The court must always be satisfied that a witness is qualified before it will allow him to testify. Expert witnesses are normally paid a fee for testifying, and in some cases the amount is very substantial. This is a proper procedure and provides no grounds for disqualifying the expert from testifying.

(10.6) *HYPOTHETICAL QUESTIONS*

A common method of obtaining the opinion of an expert witness is to ask a hypothetical question. This is done by requesting that he assume certain facts about which other witnesses have testified and then ask for his opinion based on the assumed facts. Doctors testifying in homicide cases are routinely questioned in this way. Previous testimony may have shown that the deceased had a split skull and that a bloody ax was found at the scene. Questioning of the doctor might proceed thus:

> Q: Assume, Doctor, that the deceased was found with a wound at the top of the skull approximately four inches long, a half inch wide, and extending into the brain and that this ax, Exhibit 1, was found near the body. Can you state with reasonable medical certainty whether or not Exhibit 1 could have caused such a wound?
> A. I can.
> Q. You may state your opinion.
> A. In my opinion Exhibit 1 could have produced the wound you have described.

In the past, hypothetical questions were universally used to solicit the opinions of experts. Their use causes problems. In the first place, the question itself must be precise, and one can only assume the exact facts already in evidence. If anything beyond this is assumed in the question, both the question and the answer are improper. Secondly, doctors and other expert witnesses have resisted the use of the hypothetical question because they consider it unduly restrictive and a handicap to the presentation of their findings.

Modern decisions and some procedural statutes avoid the hypothetical question on direct examination and simply let the doctor or other expert tell what his examination revealed and what his conclusions are. The hypothetical question is still widely used on cross-examination, however, to test the expert's findings and to try to impeach his conclusions. Opposing counsel may assume only part of the evidence in his question and base his hypothetical questions on his own view of the facts (71 ALR 2d 16–18).

A hypothetical question may be used only with expert witnesses. The nonexpert who is allowed to state an opinion must base it on his own observations and nothing else. Thus, theoretical or hypothetical questioning of a lay witness is improper (*People* v. *Dolbeer*, 149 Cal. 227 [1906]; *People* v. *Vehler,* 114 Ill. App. 2d 171 [1969]).

(10.7) *BASIS FOR OPINION*

The expert may give his opinion from personal observations. When a psychiatrist has made a mental examination, he may base his opinion regarding sanity entirely on this examination. A pathologist who has performed a postmortem examination may give his opinion about the cause of death on the basis of that examination. The lay witness, as has been said, can base his opinion solely on personal observations.

The expert may base his opinion on past medical history and hospital records as well as on personal observations. He can also draw his conclusion entirely from the hypothetical question that assumes the facts and then asks for his opinion.

(10.8) *SCIENTIFIC BOOKS*

Scientific books cannot be used on direct examination to back up the expert's findings. Otherwise each side would present titles of learned tomes to prove the view of each witness, and the jury would be left to read all of the books cited in order to reach a decision. Even if a single book were introduced to prove a point, it would not be allowed because opposing counsel would be denied the right of cross-examination. Only mathematical or mortality tables can be quoted.

The expert can say that his opinion may have been formed in part by his study of scientific books even though he cannot read from them in testifying. The expert must give his own opinion, not that of someone else.

Material from scientific works can be effectively used in cross-examination. Counsel can ask his opponent's expert if he recognizes certain authorities and then point out conclusions in these books that differ from his opinion. The court has discretion in this matter and will not let books be used in cross-examination merely as an excuse to put contrary opinions before the jury (*Pahl* v. *Troy City Railroad*, 81 A.D. 308 [N.Y. 1903]; *O'Connell* v. *Williams,* 17 Misc. 2d 296 [N.Y. 1958]; *People* v. *Riccardi*, 285 N.Y. 21 [1941]). The Federal Rules of Evidence (Rule

803, [18]) has relaxed the general ban against using books as evidence and does allow scientific treatises to be used as evidence under some conditions. (*See* text, sec. 12.3[f].)

(10.9) *SUBJECT MATTER OF EXPERT OPINION*

A number of considerations govern this area. A discussion of each follows.

a. Legal Opinions

Legal opinions ordinarily are not a proper subject for an expert witness. The expert may give his opinion of facts, not of the law. A lawyer cannot be called in to give his opinion as to the meaning of a local law applying to the case. That would be a conclusion of law for the trial judge, not for the witness. There is, however, at least one exception to this rule. If foreign laws are involved in the case, a legal expert might be allowed to give his opinion concerning these laws.

b. Estimates

Opinion regarding value must frequently be given by an expert. Stolen property or buildings destroyed by arson do not have a definite market value; therefore, estimates of value by experts must be used. Because there was no actual sale between a willing buyer and seller to fix the market price, estimated value cannot be exact. Estimated value by an expert in the field is the best possible measure.

c. Time, Speed, Weight, Duration, and Number

Time of death, speed of vehicles, direction, and similar measurements can seldom be determined with mathematical certainty. As stated, lay witnesses can estimate such things on the basis of their observations. The fact that laymen may give such opinion evidence does not mean that experts are not allowed to do the same. The expert may give similar estimates on the basis of both the evidence in the case and his technical background. An accurate estimate of speed may be obtained from such information as the weight and size of the vehicle and skid marks. A contractor or engineer might estimate the number of cubic yards of fill placed on a land area. The direction from which a blow is struck and shots were fired would also be proper subjects for expert opinion (*Hopt* v. *Utah*, 120 U.S. 430 [1886]; *Ford* v. *State*, 96 Ark. 582 [1910]).

d. Mechanical and Agricultural Matters

An endless variety of mechanical and agricultural matters can involve expert testimony. Problems involved with the safety of machinery and with construction, such as the strength of structures, all involve expert testimony. Examples of agricultural items calling for expert evidence include value of a crop loss, whether or not milk has been adulterated, and whether stolen timber came from the complainant's woodlot.

(10.10) *PHYSICIANS AND PSYCHOLOGISTS*

Medical witnesses are the most common of all expert witnesses and cover many general topics.

a. Injuries

Almost all criminal cases involving injuries call for expert testimony from physicians. Is there tissue injury indicating force in a rape case? Was "serious physical injury" inflicted? A doctor's opinion is obviously necessary in this kind of situation. Physicians can give opinion evidence as to type, extent, and cause of wounds and injuries. Some states even allow them to state whether they feel the wound was self-inflicted.

A defendant charged with murdering a woman with whom he had been living argued that her death from gunshot was suicide, not murder. The pathologist who performed the autopsy found that death came from a bullet that entered below the left armpit, traveled across the thorax, penetrated the heart and lungs, and struck the right arm three inches below the shoulder. He was asked if, in his opinion, the wound could have been self-inflicted. Over objection, the court permitted him to reply, and he said it "would be a very unusual pattern for a self-inflicted wound." The court allowed the answer to stand, even though this was the crucial fact in issue. It held that self-inflicted wounds were not such a matter of common experience as to exclude expert testimony (*People* v. *Cole*, 47 Cal. 2d 93 [1965]; *see also* 56 ALR 2d 1435).

b. Physical Condition

There are times when it is necessary to have expert opinion on an individual's physical condition. If, for example, the defense claims a forced confession was beaten from the accused, and the prosecutor says that the man beat his own head against the cell bars, the jail physician who examined the defendant is the most qualified expert witness to help resolve the question. Another example arises when there is a claim of self-defense. In this case the general physical condition of both the accused and the victim of an assault is pertinent. There are countless other situations where medical testimony is required in criminal cases.

c. Mental Condition

Only in rare cases is an individual so obviously deranged that the testimony of a trained psychiatrist, physician, or psychologist is not needed. Though the court usually accepts the expert testimony of a general practitioner on sanity, a few jurisdictions require the opinion of a specialist.

d. X Rays

Laymen are not capable of interpreting X rays. If X rays are to be used in evidence, they must be introduced through expert testimony and interpreted for the jury by either a qualified physician or a radiologist.

(10.11) *CAUSE OF DEATH*

Expert testimony is ordinarily required in statements regarding cause of death. While it is true that laymen often observe death and dead persons, they have no common knowledge as to its various causes.

The pathologist studies tissues and organs to determine the cause, while the medical examiner may discover that the cause was the result of wounds, drowning, burning, and the like. Where special knowledge is necessary to find death's cause, the prerogative of the jury is not violated.

(10.12) *FINGERPRINTS AND DOCUMENTS*

In cases where fingerprints have been found, a fingerprint expert must give testimony concerning them, as only he can explain the points on which he has based his opinions.

Determination of the authenticity of documents—faked stock certificates, wills, letters, and others—requires examination by an expert. Typewriters differ by make, model, and even by individual machine. Here, too, an expert, by careful examination and with the aid of enlarged photographs, can identify and authenticate the typewritten material in question. Laymen can give testimony concerning handwriting, but experts in the field are frequently needed for an examination and a professional opinion.

(10.13) *CHARACTER AND REPUTATION*

So-called "character evidence" is often used by the defendant in criminal trials. This is done by having witnesses testify as to the defendant's good reputation in the community. The theory, which is not terribly sound, is that an individual's misdeeds are generally known by friends and acquaintances. Thus, a good reputation is evidence of one's innocence of the crime charged. Such evidence is generally accepted as sufficient to raise a reasonable doubt among members of the jury.

If the defendant offers character evidence, the prosecutor may introduce evidence of poor character in rebuttal. In addition, character witnesses can be cross-examined as to whether they have heard of specific improper acts on the part of the defendant. In a related area, evidence of a poor reputation for truthfulness and accuracy can be presented as impeachment material against a witness.

No one can testify as an expert on an individual's character and reputation, since the basis for such testimony is public discussion by people in the community. Therefore, those who are qualified to give testimony are laymen, people familiar with the individual's reputation.

(10.14) *MODERN DEVELOPMENTS IN OPINION EVIDENCE*

The field of expert testimony that is accepted by the court expands as scientific knowledge increases. Those who examine questioned documents can now testify freely on typewriter comparisons. Evidence based on breathalizer tests is now allowed to prove intoxication when the test was administered by trained personnel, and the results are in effect conclusory. Expert testimony on voiceprints is now being offered and accepted in some courts. Polygraph investigations are routinely used and relied upon by police forces everywhere. Properly administered by trained and experienced experts, the polygraph has proved itself a reliable guide in the search for truth. And yet, with few exceptions, courts have refused to accept the results of polygraph tests. Only gradually are they being allowed as evidence.

In the area of narcotics, expert opinions on the effects of drugs and the way they are used and administered are increasingly being accepted.

Even nonscientific personnel with experience in the drug field have been allowed to qualify as skilled witnesses and to give opinion testimony (*People* v. *Smith*, 253 Cal. App. 2d 711 [1967]; *People* v. *Moore*, 70 Cal. App. 2d 158 [1945]; *People* v. *Chrisman*, 256 C.A. 2d 425 [1967]).

There is now wider acceptance of expert testimony on modus operandi, where actions that seem normal on the surface are actually methods of committing a crime. Gambling, bookmaking, lottery, and even burglaries are examples. For instance, in a trial in California the defendant was charged with a form of burglary known as "till tapping" (*People* v. *Clay*, 227 Cal. App. 2d 87 [1964]). Testimony indicated that the defendant stood by the store's checkout counter and asked for a number of grocery items that caused the clerk to turn his back. A customer saw the defendant's accomplice withdraw his closed hand from the cash drawer. Testifying as an expert in the area of "till tapping," a police officer stated that this was the usual method of committing such a crime. The court allowed this testimony because the defendant's conduct at the checkout counter appeared normal, and, for this reason, the jury might have found him to have been an innocent bystander.

The theory behind this loosening of the strict ban on opinion evidence was stated in a federal case (*U.S.* v. *Petrone*, 185 F. 2d 334, cert. den. 340 U.S. 931 [1950]). It stated that a blind following of the rule against conclusions "may . . . become a substantial obstacle to developing the truth . . . for our perceptions are always 'conclusions.' The rule should be held lightly and in many cases let the witness state his opinion and leave to cross-examination a searching inquisition to uncover its foundations."

(10.15) *SUMMARY*

Though witnesses are supposed to recite facts, not opinions, there are wide areas in which opinion evidence is accepted.

Lay witnesses may estimate speed of vehicles, distances, time, and other measurements. They are also allowed, solely on the basis of their own observations, to state their opinions on another person's identity, handwriting, voice, sanity, and even his state of intoxication.

An expert witness is in a different class. He is called for the sole purpose of stating his expert opinion about some facet of the case. He cannot, of course, go so far as to decide the case for the jury. They are free to accept or reject his conclusion as they see fit.

Once having established his credentials in court, the expert can give his opinion, not only from his own observations, but also from an assumed state of facts based on the evidence in the case. The expert may sometimes give opinions in the same areas as laymen, such as measurements, handwriting, and the authenticity of documents.

Many areas of opinion evidence, such as fingerprints and scientific, engineering, and mechanical matters, come only from experts.

Physicians are commonly needed for opinion evidence regarding physical condition, types and extent of injuries, and the cause of death.

Character evidence is a common defense in criminal trials. This is nonexpert testimony concerning the reputation one has in his community and is based on discussions of local people. If the defendant produces evidence of good character, the prosecution may offer proof of poor character. A witness may be attacked by evidence of poor reputation for truth. Though character evidence is pure opinion, it is nonetheless legal.

chapter 11

Hearsay Evidence

A. WHAT IS HEARSAY?

(11.1) *GENERAL DEFINITION*

The subject of hearsay is widely misunderstood. This need not be. The generally accepted idea of hearsay is that a witness is forbidden to mention what someone else has told him. This is not so. Many out-of-court statements are allowed in evidence. There is a simple two-step rule that anyone can use to identify hearsay.

"Hearsay" is an out-of-court statement (oral or written) *offered to prove that the statement itself is true.* If the statement is being used for any other purpose, it is not hearsay. It may be objected to on other grounds but not on the basis of hearsay.

This is the most important step in recognizing hearsay and one that even many attorneys miss. The first question to be asked is, "Why is the conversation being offered in evidence?" If the offeror does not care whether the statement is true or false, then it is *not* hearsay.

For example, Davis is being tried for murder, and his defense is insanity. His lawyer offers to prove that shortly before the shooting Davis was seen standing on the corner of Main and Delaware, wearing a cocked hat with his hand in his shirt front, shouting "I'm Napoleon." An objection is raised on the grounds that the statement is hearsay. No one was claiming that he was Napoleon. The statement was offered to prove Davis was insane. Therefore, it was *not* hearsay.

So whenever a question of hearsay arises, remember this Napoleon example. If the conversation is not offered to prove its truth, it is *not* hearsay.

Make your own analysis. Do any of the following situations involve hearsay?

1. A spectator offers to testify that just before the victim was hit with a beer bottle, he shouted at the defendant, "Hit me, you bastard, and I'll kill you."
2. A bank customer, now a witness in an armed robbery trial, offers to testify that he heard the teller say to the defendant, "Don't shoot me. Don't shoot me. I'll give you the money."
3. The charge is blackmail. The prosecution offers a legally recorded telephone conversation in which the defendant said to the victim, "Pay me five bills or I'll tell your wife what went on in room 209 of the Paradise Motel last night."
4. The charge is burglary of the Empire Warehouse. The first officer who arrived at the scene in his patrol car testified that just before this he had received a radio message saying, "Go to the Empire Warehouse at the corner of Main and Elm."

None of these can be classed as hearsay. The offeror does not care whether or not any of the statements is true. The answers to the illustrations are as follows.

1. This was offered to show provocation or self-defense, and it does not matter whether the victim would have killed his assailant or not.
2. The teller's "Don't shoot" statement is evidence that she was giving up the funds under fear of physical harm, which is an element in robbery. Even if the bank robber only had a water pistol and could never have shot her, the statement is proper to show her state of mind.
3. The blackmailer's threat may well have been pure bluff and entirely untrue. True or false, it is only offered to show the threat as part of the crime, and the truth of the threat is immaterial, and so it is not hearsay.
4. The radio call was not offered as proof that there was a burglary, but simply to show why the officer went there. It would not have mattered if the dispatcher had been giving him a false instruction. Since the truth of the message was not involved, it was not hearsay.

Statements that show motive, intent, or bias are not always hearsay but can easily be confused with it. Usually, such statements are offered not to prove the content as being true, but to show a state of mind like the earlier example of Napoleon. For instance, a husband is accused of murdering his wife. The People offer evidence by a neighbor who overheard him calling her a whore just before the fatal shot. The evidence is accepted not to prove that she was immoral, but that he hated her enough to kill her.

In addition, the prosecution might reveal that before the murder, the defendant told a third person he was going to marry a long-time woman friend. Whether or not he was going to marry her is beside the point; a statement is properly received in evidence to prove that he intended to and hence had a motive to murder. Courts normally accept this type of statement for the purpose of showing mental operations.

It is not just oral statements that can be classified as hearsay. A "statement" can be oral, written, or even nonverbal conduct that conveys a message. The basic objection to hearsay is that if it is used, the opponent is denied his right to confront and cross-examine the person who made the statement. It is not possible, of course, to cross-examine an out-of-court statement. This is the reason an expert is not allowed to bolster his testimony by reading from a scientific book. The testimony would be offered to prove the *truth of the matter in the book*, and there is no way counsel can cross-examine a volume. Thus, such testimony is objectionable as hearsay. For the same reason, a case cannot be proven by submitting a sworn affidavit instead of having the live witness. Cross-examination and confrontation would be lost. If the affidavit were offered to prove its truth, it would be objectionable as hearsay.

B. HEARSAY EXCEPTIONS

(11.2) *EXCEPTIONS IN GENERAL*

If the evidence offered involves an out-of-court conversation, document, or message-type action, your analysis must begin with the first step. Stop. Ask yourself "Why is it being offered?" *If offered to prove its truth, it is hearsay.*

This does not end your inquiry. It only begins it. Practicality dictates that many out-of-court statements must be allowed in evidence. Contracts, for example, are often made by word of mouth. Threats and promises are made the same way. So, there are a number of universally recognized exceptions to the hearsay rule.

Having first decided that a statement being offered is hearsay, the next step is to determine whether it falls within any of the exceptions to the hearsay rule.

(11.3) *CONFESSIONS*

People ordinarily do not admit that they have committed a crime. If they do so, it is likely that their statements are true. For this reason, courts accept confessions in evidence. Since the confession is offered to prove the truth of its content, it is hearsay. The confession is an exception to the hearsay rule, one of the most commonly used. All that is required is that the confession be voluntary and meet the necessary constitutional requirements (*see* chapter 6).

a. Admissions

An admission is a kind of miniconfession. Though the accused might never have actually confessed, he might have made a partial admission regarding the crime. Perhaps he told a girl friend that he was at the scene of the crime or showed her a gun that he claimed was used in an armed robbery. If voluntarily made, such an admission can be used as evidence against an accused, as an exception to the hearsay rule.

b. Admission by Silence

On rare occasions there may be an admission or a complete confession simply by silence. There is a widely held misconception about this. Many practitioners think that if a defendant is present during a conversation, then the words can be used as evidence against him. This is not true.

The mere presence of a defendant does not in itself make the conversation admissible. If a statement (not written) is made in the presence of the accused incriminating him *under circumstances calling for his denial,* only then is his silence deemed an admission. For example, if he is arrested, and the lieutenant says, "You stole this gun," the defendant's silence means nothing, for he has a constitutional right to remain silent. Therefore, if the accusation is made in open court or while the man is in custody, his silence is not an admission. If, on the other hand, there is a street fight, and the victim confronts a man saying "You cut me," the man's silence can be taken as an admission of guilt. The statement "You cut me" could be introduced in evidence by any witness who heard it.

There can be no admission by silence unless all the circumstances call naturally for a denial from the accused. Only if the circumstances are so strong that the defendant's silence amounts to an acquiescence may the accusatory conversation of a third party be admitted as an exception to the hearsay rule.

c. Confessions of a Codefendant

As discussed earlier, a defendant's confession can be used only against himself. It cannot be used against a codefendant because it is pure hearsay in regard to the other party. It is admitted only against the person who confesses, as an exception to the hearsay rule, on the common-sense premise that people do not ordinarily admit a crime of their own unless it is true. But there is no reason to be afraid to say that someone else committed a crime. It is only when an individual implicates himself that the statement has the ring of truth.

(11.4) *STATEMENTS OF COCONSPIRATORS*

If two or more people conspire to commit a criminal act, they become partners in crime. Each one then is the agent of the other, and any act done *in furtherance of the conspiracy binds all of them.* The federal rule is generally followed. It holds that the statement of a coconspirator is admissible in evidence against all conspirators under three conditions. First, the conspiracy must be established by independent evidence. Second, the statement must be made in furtherance of the conspiracy. Third, it must be made during the conspiracy. The following cases illustrate this: *Mares* v. *U.S.*, 383 F. 2d 805, cert. den. 394 U.S. 963 (1967); *U.S.* v. *Coppola*, 479 F. 2d 1153 (1973); *Grunewald* v. *U.S.*, 353 U.S. 391 (1957).

In a federal vice case (*Krulewitch* v. *U.S.*, 336 U.S. 440 [1948]) the defendant was accused of conspiring with his wife to transport another woman from New York to Miami for prostitution. After the prostitute had been taken to Miami and the defendant arrested, she came back to New York. This ended the conspiracy. Then the prostitute and the defendant's wife had a conversation in New York. At his trial the prostitute was allowed to relate the conversation she had with the wife in New York as follows: "The wife said 'You didn't talk yet?' and I says 'No' and she says 'Well don't . . . until we get you a lawyer . . . Be very careful what you say . . . It would be better for us two girls to take the blame than Ray [defendant] . . . . He couldn't stand to take it.' " Partially on the basis of this testimony, the man was convicted. His conviction was eventually reversed by the Supreme Court because the conversation took place after the prostitution conspiracy ended. Thus, what the two women said was not binding on the husband and was inadmissable hearsay.

For the same reason a *confession* of one conspirator is not admissible against the others. Because the conspiracy was over by the time the man confessed, his confession, like that of any codefendant, was binding only against himself (*U.S.* v. *Register*, 496 F. 2d 1072 [1974]).

(11.5) *DECLARATION AGAINST INTEREST*

Declarations against interest are out-of-court statements by one who is not a party to the crime and can be used as evidence when a witness is not available.

Ordinarily, a person does not publicly admit things that are harmful to (that is, against) his own interest. If he does, it is a good indication that what he says is true. One example is a declaration against pecuniary interest, such as admitting a debt. More commonly involved in criminal trials is the declaration against penal interest, where an individual other than the defendant admits to a criminal act.

The declaration against penal interest ordinarily constitutes evidence that the defendant tries to use in his own behalf. He offers it to prove that *someone else has admitted committing* the crime he is accused of. In the past the declaration against penal interest was not usually considered an exception to the hearsay rule (*Donnelly* v. *U.S.,* 228 U.S. 243 [1912]). The modern trend of court decisions, however, is to recognize this type of declaration as an exception to the hearsay rule and to admit it under certain circumstances.

The leading decision in this was *Chambers* v. *Mississippi*, 410 U.S. 284 (1973). Chambers was tried for murder. A spectator, McDonald, had fled the murder scene. McDonald returned later and told some friends and Chambers's lawyer that he, McDonald, was the one that had done the actual shooting, not Chambers. At Chambers's trial, McDonald was called as a defense witness, but he denied that he had made the incriminating statements. The defense offered testimony by three of McDonald's friends that they had heard him admit he had done the shooting. The trial court refused to let them testify, ruling that this was hearsay.

The Supreme Court reversed Chambers's murder conviction, saying that McDonald's statements were statements against penal interest and that the people who heard him should have been allowed to testify. The court avoided the usual requirement that the speaker should be unavailable as a witness before his declarations against penal interest could be offered in evidence. They simply said that McDonald was there and could have been cross-examined; therefore, the out-of-court statement should have been used.

In two modern decisions (*Commonwealth* v. *Hackett*, 307 A. 2d 334 [Pa. App. 1973]; *Commonwealth* v. *Colon*, 337 A. 2d 554 [Pa., 1975]), Pennsylvania has accepted the declaration against penal interest as a hearsay exception. Additional states have also done so. The federal courts recognize the exception, and it is part of the Federal Rules of Evidence (Section 804). Some court decisions now approve the use of a declaration against penal interest whether or not the speaker is available to testify.

It is undoubtedly true that with the limitations traditionally applied to the declaration against penal interest, third-party confessions to a crime will increasingly be allowed in evidence as part of the defendant's case.

A word of caution about relying on the use of a declaration against penal interest should be mentioned. It may not be used unless the speaker is actually faced with the possibility that he will be punished. If he cannot be punished for what he says, it is not an acceptable declaration against penal interest. This is graphically demonstrated by *U.S.* v. *Dovico*, 380 F. 2d 325, cert. den. 389 U.S. 944 (1967) (*see also U.S.* v. *Seyfried*, 435 F. 2d 696 [7th Cir. 1970]; *Commonwealth* v. *Colon,* supra).

A man named Dovico and a codefendant were convicted on a drug charge. While the codefendant was in a federal penitentiary, he told a cellmate that he, not Dovico, was the one who had put the cocaine in the trash. The codefendant never testified at Dovico's original trial and died before the case was appealed. Because of the codefendant's death, Dovico sought to use the statement to the cellmate. The reviewing court determined, however, that the statement was not a declaration against penal interest. By assuming all the blame when he made the statement, the codefendant was not subjecting himself to any possible additional punishment. He had already been convicted of the crime, and, because he had never testified in court on the matter, he was not even opening himself to a possible charge of perjury. Since no additional criminal punishment was possible, this was not a genuine declaration against penal interest.

a. Homicide or Suicide?

Declarations of suicide are admitted as an exception to the hearsay rule. They are similar to other declarations against interest on the logical basis that threatening suicide is generally regarded as a disgraceful act that an individual ordinarily would not falsify. It is true that the declaration of suicide is offered to show a state of mind, but normally its purpose is also to prove the truth of the matter contained in the statement. It is unimportant whether the statement is made orally or is in the form of a suicide note. The result is the same. All such statements are hearsay, but are received as exceptions to the rule (*People* v. *Tugwell*, 28 C.A. 348, 359 [1915]; *People* v. *Selby*, 198 C. 426).

(11.6) *DYING DECLARATIONS*

The dying declaration of a homicide victim has long been accepted as an exception to the hearsay rule. In order for the declaration to be considered an exception, however, certain conditions must be met. First, the victim must be "in extremis." Second, he must know that he is dying and that he has no hope of recovery. Third, if he were living he would be competent as a witness. Fourth, his statement must relate to the cause of his death. Courts have based this exception on the theory that if a person knows he is about to die, he is unlikely to lie about who injured him. What he says is thus guaranteed to be true as much as if it had been under oath in court.

People v. *Coniglio*, 79 Misc. 2d 808 (N.Y. 1974), demonstrates a dying declaration. A police officer called to the scene of a shooting found a woman lying on the floor bleeding from bullet wounds. As he bent over her, she said: "Benny shot me. Benny shot my husband and he's dead and I'm going to die too." The officer asked: "Benny who?" She answered: "Benny Coniglio." "Where is Benny?" he asked. She replied: "Around the corner on 11th Avenue." She was taken to surgery and died a few hours later.

The trial court found that her statement met all the conditions for a dying declaration in a homicide case. It ruled, however, that only those portions of the statements bearing on her own death, not on that of her husband, were admissible.

In the absence of authority granted by statute, courts have refused to accept the following types of statements: the dying statement of a burglar that his codefendant was innocent; the dying victim's statement where the crime charged was assault with intent to kill rather than homicide; and the statement of a convicted murderer about to be executed that his codefendant was innocent. None of these statements are true dying declarations in homicide. Neither would they be received as declarations against penal interest, as the dying speaker could in no way be subjecting himself to any further punishment, knowing that his life was about to end.

In the past, the classic restriction on the use of a dying declaration has been to apply it only to homicide cases. Some jurisdictions have now widened the rule to apply to matters other than homicide but limit it to the declarant's description of the circumstances of his own death.

(11.7) *RES GESTAE*

The term "res gestae" (literally meaning "things done") is a general catchall used by courts for admitting various conversations that are connected in some way with a transaction.

One judge complained about the use of the term (J. Hauser dissent, in *Coryell* v. *Reid*, 117 Cal. App. 534 [1931]), saying, "Definitions of the term 'res gestae' are as numerous as the various cures for rheumatism and about as useful."

Courts continue to misuse the term, mistakenly admitting conversations as res gestae exceptions to the hearsay rule when they really are not hearsay at all. The illustration used earlier—of a witness testifying that the bank teller said to the robber, "Don't shoot me. Don't shoot me. I'll give you the money"—would in most courts be admitted as part of the res gestae if there were a hearsay objection. As was previously pointed out, it is not hearsay in the first place and stands in its own right as a relevant proof that the teller was parting with money in fear, which is an essential element in robbery. It was not proof of a shooting.

The best way to handle the problem of res gestae is to realize that judges generally admit conversations, words, or acts that are incidental to and explanatory of the fact in controversy. This is, of course, an ill-defined and inexact way to rule on the admissibility of hearsay evidence. A much better way is to understand that there are three classes of genuine hearsay exceptions under the classification of res gestae: excited utterances, explanatory statements, and verbal acts. It is always preferable to use their correct names even if the judge terms them res gestae.

a. Excited Utterances

A speaker's spontaneous words made while he was under the stress of excitement caused by the event will be admitted *even as proof of the matter contained in the statement*. This type of statement made under stress is reliable because the speaker did not have time to fabricate. Thus, his words are spontaneous, generated by the circumstances themselves.

The key to the admittance of an excited utterance is its spontaneity. In this way it differs from the dying declaration in a homicide case. The validity of the latter is based on the solemnity of the occasion and must meet all the requirements given previously. A murder victim's excited utterance made at the time of the crime is admitted because of its spontaneous nature, even though the victim is unaware of his imminent death.

A good example of this is *State* v. *McClain*, 25 N.W. 2d 764 (1964). The defendant, McClain, returned home at about 3:00 a.m. after a heavy drinking spree. He argued with his wife, hit her, and she fell across the bed. McClain then went into the kitchen and ate two sandwiches. He claimed that he came back to the bedroom, found the mattress on fire, threw it out the window, and went out looking for his wife.

The state's story was quite different. The prosecutor produced a neighbor who testified that he heard the McClain family argument and that the wife came to the neighbor's front porch afterward and asked him to "Call the law." The neighbor refused. The burned wife came out and sat on the steps, rocking back and forth and screaming. She accused her husband, saying: "Don't touch me under here, I'm burned up . . . Mac poured gas on me and burned me up." She died thirteen days later in the hospital. The court ruled that her statement was a spontaneous declaration made under stress, even though it was subsequent to the event, and was properly admitted in evidence as an exception to the hearsay rule. McClain was thus convicted.

The excited utterance is allowed in evidence even if made by a third party because the basis for its truth—spontaneity—is the same whether said by a participant or a spectator (*Swensson* v. *Albany Dispatch Co.,* 309 N.Y. 497 [1956]; *Ollala* v. *State*, 157 Tex. Cr. 458 [1952]; Federal Rules of Evidence, Sec. 803 [2]).

The admission of the excited utterance is gaining wider acceptance in court decisions. It is generally admitted as part of the evidence, whether or not the speaker is available as a witness. Many decisions, like the McClain case, also admit excited statements that are not strictly "contemporaneous" as long as they were made spontaneously under the stress of the event (*State* v. *Ehlers*, 119 Atl. 15 [N.J. 1922]; *People* v. *Costa*, 40 Cal. 2d 160 [1953]).

b. Explanatory Statements

Conversations accompanying the fact in issue will be admitted to explain ambiguous actions even if they are offered to prove the truth of the statement itself. The conversation must actually "explain" the conduct. It must outline and give meaning to the act.

Much evidence of the explanatory type is not hearsay. Like the statement "I'm Napoleon," it is not offered for the truth, but to explain conduct or to show a mental condition.

c. Verbal Acts

"Verbal act" is a term that is frequently used loosely. A contemporaneous type of statement is often admitted into evidence under the label "verbal act" because the statement accompanied the act. This use of the term is too broad. It is more accurate to confine the definition to a statement that is itself a fact and is an integral part of the action under investigation. A verbal act is actually what it says it is—an action by words.

If a pickpocket steals a man's wallet, he has committed a larceny with his hands. If he swindles him out of the same money by a dishonest investment scheme, he has committed larceny by word of mouth. Thus, his conversations on the latter subject would be admissible as a spoken form of larceny, that is, as a verbal criminal act. A criminal conspiracy is a similar example of a verbal act. In this case, every word of the criminal participants is admissible. The words of the conspirators thus amount to an act of crime—a verbal act.

(11.8) *COMPLAINT OF A SEX VICTIM*

A complaint made by a victim of a sex crime will be admitted under certain conditions as an exception to the hearsay rule *as proof that the crime itself took place*. If the statement is made at the time of the attack, it is admissible as an excited utterance, but the type of exception being discussed here is a complaint made after the attack, when the stress of events may have passed.

If there has been a rape or an act of nonconsensual perversion, the victim usually complains about it at the first possible opportunity. Should the woman not complain, one might assume that she was not violated but had consented to the act.

The person who heard the complaint can testify concerning it since the complaint is a natural, instinctive type of utterance and so bears a presumption of truthfulness. It is also allowed to overcome the negative reaction to silence on the part of the victim and to corroborate the victim's testimony if she is impeached as a witness. The victim's statement must not be too remote and must actually be a complaint.

In *Callahan* v. *U.S.*, 240 F. 683 (1917), an adult man was tried for statutory rape, sexual intercourse with a fourteen-year-old girl who was under the age of consent. Shortly after the event, the girl met a friend outside of the house and told her that she had been inside having intercourse with the defendant after he paid her three dollars. The witness testified for the prosecution and related the girl's conversation.

An appellate court reversed the conviction, saying that the girl's statement was not a complaint or expression of outraged feeling or even an excited utterance. It was merely interesting information passed on to an acquaintance, was hearsay, and could not be used by the state as proof that intercourse took place.

Thus, in order for the sex victim's complaint to qualify for this hearsay exception, it must be recent, it must be given voluntarily at the first natural opportunity, and it must be an actual complaint.

(11.9) *BUSINESS RECORDS*

Over the years the courts have developed a set of rules for admitting business records in evidence. Sometimes known as the "Shop Book Rule," it is now usually referred to by a term such as "business records as evidence act."

This hearsay exception has evolved as a matter of practicality. For example, if a merchant suing a customer in regard to his charge account had to produce each clerk who made every sale, the employee who made the delivery, and the bookkeeper who made the account entry, it would clutter the courtroom endlessly and make proof extremely difficult. Thus, the rule has developed over the years allowing records regularly made in the course of business to be admitted in evidence as an exception to the rule against hearsay.

The rule has recently been expanded. It now includes records that are not strictly "business records" if they are made in the regular course of the "business," near the time of the event, and if, in the opinion of the court, the sources of information and the purpose of keeping the record were such as to justify its admission. Under this expanded interpretation, accident reports, police reports, and other regularly kept records not involved in any commercial business are often allowed in evidence in criminal cases. A police report can, however, normally be used only if the writer of the report was a witness to the facts or if the person giving the information to the writer was under any obligation to relate the facts (*Hole* v. *N.Y.*, 32 A.D. 2d 47 [N.Y. 1969]).

In criminal trials the defense ordinarily asks for the production of police witnesses' notes, police records, and the like. As previously noted, the defense uses these in cross-examination. Occasionally, however, the defense may offer such a record in evidence under the business records exception as proof of the actual matter contained in the report.

(11.10) *PRIOR STATEMENTS OF A WITNESS*

Many types of earlier statements made by a witness may be allowed as evidence. If a witness has testified previously in the same case at an earlier trial, at a pretrial hearing, or in an examination before trial, when he could have been cross-examined, the record of his testimony can ordinarily be used in the later trial should the witness be unavailable. His earlier testimony is then used as direct proof of its contents, just as though he were on the stand testifying in person.

In *California* v. *Green*, 399 U.S. 149 (1970), the Supreme Court announced an extension of the rule by allowing the use of earlier testimony in the situation even where the witness was available. In that case a sixteen-year-old boy was arrested on a drug charge, and he named Green as his supplier. He testified to this at Green's preliminary hearing. At the trial, however, the boy took the stand and said he had been taking LSD and could not remember. The prosecution then read from his testimony at the preliminary hearing and had an officer testify that the boy had orally named Green as his supplier. This was the state's only proof that directly linked Green to the drug sale. The Supreme Court approved this evidence, saying that the boy had testified at the trial and could have been cross-examined thoroughly in regard to his prior statements and his present testimony. The court further pointed out that it was not an unconstitutional deprivation of the right of cross-examination to use the prior statements as direct proof of the crime.

The use of a prior statement of a witness often becomes involved in cases of identity, where the witness indentifies the defendant from the stand during the trial and has, of course, identified him earlier at the station house or in a police lineup. The general rule has been that prior identification is equivalent to a prior statement. If the witness had failed to identify the defendant earlier, that fact would be allowed as impeaching evidence to weaken the present testimony. If, on the other hand, it was a consistent identification whereby the witness had identified the same man twice, the prior identification would not be allowed in evidence unless the identity had been attacked and it was necessary in order to rehabilitate the witness.

A rule that is now evolving in court decisions is to admit the evidence of the earlier identification, even if it is consistent, on the theory that it was fresher and more reliable in the first instance than it is during the trial. Judges maintain that this situation is similar to that of *California* v. *Green*. Thus, when the identifying witness is on the stand, he can be thoroughly cross-examined, and, for this reason, the testimony of both identifications should be allowed. States still vary in this interpretation. Some, for example, will not allow testimony regarding prior identification simply to bolster the witness then on the stand. Some states also have statutes governing identity testimony (*People* v. *Rosati,* 39 A.D. 2d 592 [N.Y. 1972]; *People* v. *Caserta,* 19 N.Y. 2d 18 [1966]; N.Y., CPL 60.25).

(11.11) *MISCELLANEOUS EXCEPTIONS*

A number of minor hearsay exceptions—official records, such as certificates of conviction, records of vital statistics, family records, and ancient documents—occur infrequently in criminal cases.

Some states now admit hearsay in general at administrative proceedings or preliminary hearings before indictment. Hearsay is also widely allowed as a basis for arrests and warrants. Some types of hearsay, such as official laboratory reports, may be introduced before a grand jury. A few jurisdictions have laws that permit the use of various declarations of persons since deceased. As previously mentioned, a written record of a "past recollection recorded" may sometimes be used where the witness has no present memory of the event.

C. HEARSAY ANALYZED

(11.12) *THE TWO-STEP RULE FOR DETERMINING HEARSAY*

There is a simple two-step rule that anyone can use to determine if evidence offered is hearsay. All you need to do is ask yourself two questions.

First, is the statement offered to prove the truth of its contents? If it is offered for some purpose other than to prove its truth, it is not hearsay. Remember the Napoleon illustration of the man on the street corner with his hand in his shirt, saying "I'm Napoleon." That statement was receivable, not to prove he was the Emperor, but to show that the speaker was insane.

Always do this *first*, and you will find that most conversations or writings offered are not hearsay, and the problem is eliminated.

Many attorneys and even some judges miss this first step. First, stop and say to yourself, "Is this offered to prove it is true or for some other purpose?"

So—should hearsay arise, Napoleonize.

Next, if it is offered to prove its truth, the statement is hearsay, but it still may be usable.

A hearsay objection?
Try all the exceptions.

So, secondly, you must ask yourself, "Does the statement fall within any of the exceptions to the hearsay rule?" Number the exceptions off mentally. Is it a confession, an admission, an excited utterance, a dying declaration, an explanatory statement, or some other exception? Now, you have the final answer.

Follow the two-step rule and you will always find the answer to the hearsay question.

(11.13) *SUMMARY*

Hearsay is an out-of-court statement offered to prove the truth of the matter contained in the statement. An oral or written statement offered for purposes other than its truth is not hearsay. Many written and oral statements are admitted as evidence, however, not to prove their truth, but to demonstrate motive, intent, bias, or other state of mind. They are not hearsay.

There is a two-step exercise in deciding hearsay. First, is the statement offered to prove its truth? If so, it is classed as hearsay. Second, if it is hearsay, does it fall within any of the exceptions?

Several recognized exceptions to the rule exist, even though they may actually be classified as hearsay. The best-known exception is a confession, which is an out-of-court statement received for its own truth. Admissions, even admissions by silence, fall in the same class. Statements of coconspirators made during and in furtherance of a conspiracy are usable against all conspirators as an exception to the hearsay ban.

Declarations made by a witness against his own pecuniary or penal interests are received in evidence as proof of the content of the statement itself. A dying declaration of a homicide victim is allowed, provided he knew that death was near and then subsequently died. By their very nature, these statements are considered reliable and hence received in evidence, though they are plainly hearsay.

Many utterances accompanying or near in time to when the crime was committed are accepted, even though they are offered to prove their truth. Among these are excited or spontaneous utterances, explanatory statements delineating ambiguous conduct, and verbal acts that in themselves constitute a crime. Contemporaneous complaints by the victim of a sex crime are recognized as valid proof of the matter contained in the complaint even though they are properly classed as hearsay.

Records that are regularly kept in the course of any business are generally accepted. These include, among others, business and police records. Prior testimony and prior statements of a witness can be used in some circumstances as direct proof of the matter in the statement. Minor varieties of other hearsay exceptions include records of family lineage, official records, vital statistics, and records of criminal convictions.

chapter 12

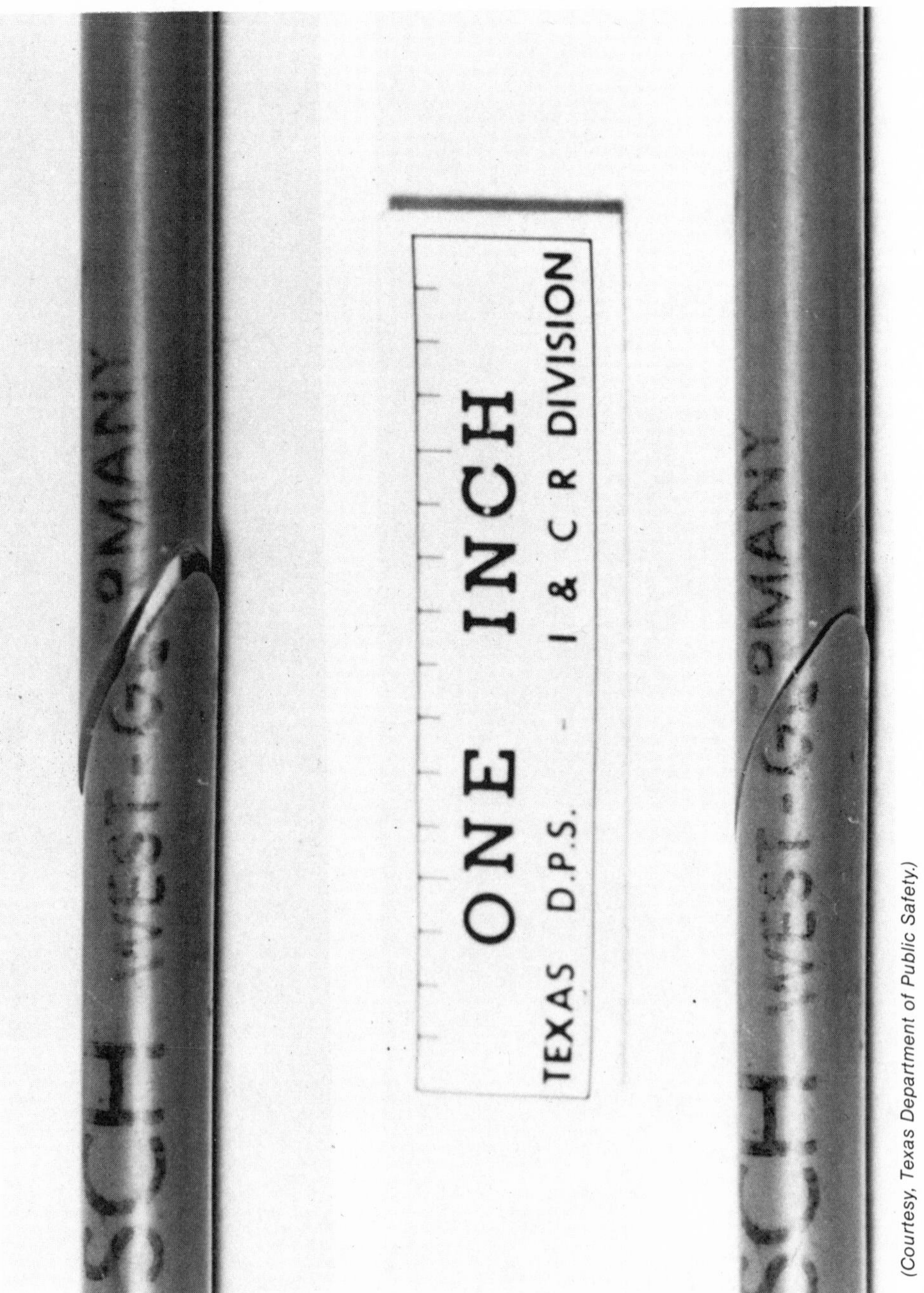

(Courtesy, Texas Department of Public Safety.)

Two ends of a catheter. End on top was discovered in an abortionist's office. End on the bottom was found with the victim of an illegal abortion.

BETTER THAN A THOUSAND WORDS

Documentary Evidence, Photographs, Demonstrations, and the Best Evidence Rule

(12.1) *DOCUMENTARY EVIDENCE IN GENERAL*

Legal evidence is not, of course, limited to the oral testimony of witnesses. Tangible objects that can express a fact are admissible under the classification of documentary evidence. Many documents are used as evidence in court. This broad category includes private writings, documents, official records, newspapers, maps, or any other object on which symbols have been placed with the intention of preserving a record of events or impressions.

Documentary evidence is subject to the same rules that govern oral testimony. It must be relevant and competent. The competence or reliability of documentary evidence presents problems that do not exist with oral testimony. As a result, the judge is often called upon to make a decision as to the reliability of the document that is being offered. One rule is that a document shall be considered reliable if it was made and preserved in such a way as to appear to state directly, accuately, and truthfully a fact material to the legal issue in question (*Curtis* v. *Bradley*, 65 Conn. 99, 31 Atl. 591 [1894]).

(12.2) *AUTHENTICATION OF DOCUMENTS*

Before a document can be admitted in evidence it must be authenticated. Often opposing counsel will concede its genuineness, or it may fall within one of the limited exceptions where authentication is not required. Otherwise, the trial judge must first be satisfied that the writing is genuine before he will admit it in evidence. If there had been an attesting witness, the old rule was that he had to be called to testify. Now attested documents can generally be admitted without this witness. A common method is to prove the document by handwriting testimony.

(12.3) *SPECIFIC KINDS OF RECORDS*

a. Church Records

Church records and baptismal, marriage, and other certificates are admissible as evidence if made by the clergyman, official, or other person authorized to make such records. Because these records are private, they do not fit within the range of public reports for which authentication is unnecessary. If the clergyman who made the record is still living at the time of the lawsuit, he will be required by some courts to authenticate the reliability of his records. Such records can only serve the limited purpose for which they were intended; they cannot be used for extraneous purposes. For example, in *State* v. *Larocca*, 157 La. 50, 101 So. 868 (1924), a priest was not allowed to testify concerning the age of a party when his information was based on the age he had been told to place on the party's baptismal certificate.

It is well established that entries in a family Bible or similar record can be entered in evidence when offered to prove the birth, death, marriage, or other fact of history there recorded.

b. Letters

Authentication is a vital element of a letter offered as documentary evidence. The fact that the letter purports by its signature to have been written by a particular party on a particular date is inconclusive in a determination of authenticity. When it is impossible to obtain evidence from the alleged author or from a witness, and handwriting comparisons fail to settle the issue, courts have allowed circumstantial or secondary evidence to complete the authentication. This type of evidence may include the style or tone of the letter if it is in any way distinctive or proof that only the alleged author could have had the knowledge required to write the particular letter.

Letters written between third persons are generally excluded from evidence on the basis of their being outside the scope of the trial (irrelevant) or violative of the hearsay evidence rule (incompetent). They may be admitted, however, if it can be shown that the person against whom the evidence is presented was in some way aware of the communications or if they are used to prove a collateral issue such as the person's state of mind or location at a particular time.

c. Telegraph Messages

These messages are subject to the same rules of evidence as all other types of documentary evidence but with an additional twist. A telegram may be accidentally or intentionally altered by telegraph operators at either end of the line. This means that telegrams are subject to the rule that prefers the original written message as evidence if it is still available. Should it not be available, the sender is faced with a major problem of authentication; he must prove that a telegram was sent in his name and that he authorized or caused the telegram to be sent in his name on a particular date.

d. Books

Books or other publications will not usually be received as documentary evidence, despite their usefulness as sources of information. This is in keeping with the general rule barring hearsay. There are several recognized exceptions to this general rule. If, for example, a particular book is the work of a deceased author who is unquestionably reliable, and if the book concerns general facts of history, the work will be admitted.

e. Newspaper and Magazine Articles

Newspaper articles or magazine accounts usually will not be admissible. The statements made in these publications were not made by a party under oath, and there is no opportunity to cross-examine the author. A newspaper account may be admissible if it concerns historical events of obscure or ancient origins that cannot appropriately be the subject of oral testimony. A newspaper account can also be accepted as evidence if it qualifies as an ancient document. In all cases, printed material—whether a newspaper, a magazine, or a book—must be adequately authenticated to the satisfaction of the trial judge. *Dallas County* v. *Commercial Union Assurance Co.,* 286 F. 2d 388 (5th Cir., 1961), involved a newspaper account of a fire in a clock tower, an issue relevant to the trial. The court admitted the account as evidence, not because it was fifty-eight years old and was an ancient document, but because it felt that the requirements of materiality, relevance, and reliability were all satisfied, and there was no other means of obtaining the information that was contained in the article.

f. Learned Treatise

The use of a learned treatise as documentary evidence has recently been redefined by the Federal Rules of Evidence. Most jurisdictions had refused to admit medical and scientific treatises as evidence of the theories and opinions they stated. Rule 803 (18) allows such evidence once its authoritativeness has been established before the trial judge. For the first time it may be used as substantive evidence in federal courts rather than merely as a means of impeaching the expert testimony offered by the opposing side.

g. Commercial and Scientific Publications

The rule against hearsay evidence is further relaxed regarding the use of commercial or scientific publications, which include market quotations, scientific treatises, histories, atlases, and similar reference publications. If it is established that the commercial world does indeed rely on these figures, the document will be admitted as evidence.

h. Official Records

Official records are an exception to the hearsay rule and will usually be admitted without proof by the person who actually made the entries. Many states have statutes dealing with records. Usually all that is needed is a certificate attached to the record certifying that it is a correct copy of an official record. The Federal Rules of Evidence (Sec. 803 [8]) even allow findings from criminal investigations to be used in some cases.

i. Records Concerning Death

Death certificates and autopsy reports are special types of documentary evidence, combining an investigating and a recording function. Either the original certificate or certified copies are admissible evidence of the facts contained in those reports. In addition, the records of the coroner and his staff or copies of those records are accepted as evidence. These reports are not conclusive evidence, however, and are subject to impeachment and contradiction.

(12.4) *TABLES*

Most charts, graphs, and tables constitute another form of documentary evidence. They must also be authenticated before they are received as competent evidence. Some tables, however, are used so frequently and unquestioningly that they have generally become admissible without further proof of authenticity. As an example, life insurance companies prepare mortality or life expectancy tables to establish the probable remaining life expectancy for a person at any given age. In all cases involving tables, the trial judge must be satisfied that the tables are authentic and accurate. If the court is not satisfied, it will be necessary to establish the authenticity of the table through the presentation of competent evidence.

(12.5) *VITAL STATISTICS*

Data relating to birth, marriage, death, or other vital statistics that are collected by a public official pursuant to a requirement of the law are admissible as evidence on judicial notice, and there is no requirement of authenticating such documents.

(12.6) *BUSINESS RECORDS*

Business records of all kinds are widely received as an exception to the hearsay rule (sec. 11.9). The general rule is that:

1. The record must be a writing or recording, not an oral one.
2. The entry must have been made in the regular course of business.
3. The offering party must be able to show that the custom of the business was to make a record at the time of the transaction or within a reasonable period thereafter.
4. The party offering the record must be connected with the business.
5. The record must be authenticated by showing that the entry was made in the customary place and the book in which it was kept was the actual one kept by the business.

The usual procedure is for the custodian of the records to bring the account book, checkbook, or whatever document is sought as evidence. He must then prove to the court's satisfaction that what he brought is the authentic record of business activities. If the court is so convinced, the business record is entered into evidence although no one has authenticated the making of the actual entry sought as evidence.

(12.7) *DEMONSTRATIONS IN GENERAL*

There are two general kinds of demonstrative evidence. The first could be a scale model, diagram, drawing, or photograph used to better show conditions or to illustrate issues. Another type is a reproduced demonstration done in court. For example, in a murder trial, if a woman defendant claims she is incapable of wielding the murder weapon, a baseball bat, the prosecution might introduce one in evidence as a sample of a typical bat.

Any demonstrative evidence must be authenticated by first establishing its reliability. Its use is within the discretion of the trial judge.

a. Photographs and Recordings in General

Photograph and sound recordings are routinely used once their reliability and accuracy has been established. A witness is required to testify first that the photograph fairly and accurately represents the conditions shown at a material time. It is not necessary that the photographer himself be a witness or that the authenticating witness be present when the picture was actually taken. Even if there has been a lapse of time between the incident in question and the making of the photograph, it can still be used if the jury is instructed on any differences in condition and is told the limited purposes for which the picture may be used.

Unduly gruesome or nude photographs may be excluded by the trial judge because they are inflammatory or might overly influence the jury. The decision is within the judge's discretion.

Colored photographs and slides are generally accepted on the commonsense basis that color film, though not completely accurate, is a more accurate representation than black and white.

Motion pictures are used, but authentication here is more complex. Motion pictures can be exaggerated by lens settings, interruptions, or editing, and evidence of any of these circumstances must first be shown. It is necessary to have someone available who was present at the making of the film to testify that the movie is an accurate portrayal of the events filmed.

b. Videotapes and Sound Recordings

There is an increase in the use of videotapes for television surveillances. At this point it appears that they will be subject to the same rules that apply to the admission of motion pictures. Once again there is a danger of tampering, but if the foundation of accuracy and relevancy is adequately established, there is no reason why these tapes should not be an acceptable form of demonstrative evidence.

It is generally accepted that sound recordings are admissible if they are appropriately authenticated. The process of authentication includes a demonstration that the recording device was capable of making an accurate recording, that the operator of the device was authentic and accurate, that there were no additions to or deletions from the recording, that the recording was properly preserved, and that voices or other sounds on the recording were properly identified by the offering party. At the preliminary hearing concerning admissibility, the judge may instruct the offering party to erase irrelevant or incompetent materials, which do not, of course, affect an otherwise admissible sound recording.

c. Models and Casts

A trial judge has the discretionary power to admit any model into evidence if he is satisfied that it is relevant to the issues in a trial and is an accurate replica or representation of the object in issue. If it is likely that a model will mislead or confuse a jury, it may be excluded from evidence.

Models often help the jury to understand the complex physical conditions or such things as the layout of a building or any other structure with which they could not be familiar but which they must understand in order to render a verdict in the case. Perhaps the most common types of models used are reproductions of the human body, its skeleton and organs, which are used to illustrate the expert testimony of a medical authority.

Another common type of demonstrative evidence is the plaster cast, which reproduces an impression made in mud, sand, or a similar substance. As an effective substitute for photography, the cast is often used by police to present a three-dimensional reproduction for the purpose of recreating a mark left at the scene of the crime. If a proper foundation of relevancy and accuracy is laid, judges generally admit casts in evidence.

d. Experiments

To the extent that experiments conducted by police are relevant to the issues of a trial they should be admissible as evidence. When these experiments are performed outside the courtroom, the party offering the evidence should show that the tests were made under circumstances similar to those existing at the time of the incident or crime. Among the experiments that are treated with great respect by the courts are ballistics tests, tests of various parts of motor vehicles such as brakes and headlights, tests of the sensory powers of a witness, and chemical tests for intoxication. This type of evidence can be very persuasive as well as being an important source of factual information. Since accuracy is the single most important test of admissibility, these experiments should be conducted by qualified experts whenever possible.

Courts do not generally favor proposals for the jury's participation in experiments that take place in the courtroom. Where test results are inconclusive or might be confusing to the jury, the trial judge should properly exclude them from evidence.

e. Diagrams, Drawings, and Graphs

Drawings and diagrams are often used in court in addition to photographs. They can be used even if not drawn strictly to scale. On the other hand, if the drawing is used as substantive evidence, such as proof of an exact location, then it must be done carefully to scale. Graphs are also commonly accepted.

(12.8) *BEST AND SECONDARY EVIDENCE RULE*

The *best evidence rule* is actually an expression of the legal system's preference for the strongest or most authentic evidence available. Although the rule generally applies only to documents in writing, the Federal Rules of Evidence (Sec. 1001) also make the rule applicable to recordings, photographs, X rays, and films.

The rule requires that the contents of any writing be proven by the contents of the writing itself or that failure to do so be adequately explained. If the trial court finds the explanation satisfactory, the judge has the discretionary power to admit secondary evidence of the writing, usually in the form of a carbon copy or other copy. When there are no secondary sources, oral testimony concerning the contents of the writing is admitted so long as the court is satisfied that no superior (that is, written) evidence is available.

In order to have secondary evidence of a writing admitted, the offering party must go through a three-part proof. Thus, he must prove:

1. that the original existed at one time;
2. that the original was genuine and represented the intent of the parties;
3. that there is an adequate explanation for the failure to produce the original.

a. Legal Documents and Public Records

If the evidence sought concerns a legal proceeding, the best available evidence is always the official record of the proceeding. It thus becomes necessary to produce the official transcript or record to establish any evidence made public at a trial. A witness is not allowed to give oral testimony concerning the outcome of a trial or testimony given at trial if an objection is made under the best evidence rule. Secondary evidence of legal proceedings is admissible only where the judicial records are no longer available or where the trial record is incomplete with respect to the issue at trial.

The best evidence rule also applies to records kept by public officials or agencies and to the proceedings of public bodies. Secondary evidence is only admissible when there is no available official record.

b. Photographic Copies, Duplicates, and Carbon Copies

It used to be that you could not use duplicates from an original photograph when the original was still available. Now, in the modern age of copy machines and general photography, copies will normally be given the same standing as the original.

There is a division of opinion concerning the application of the best evidence rule to carbon copies of the original document. Some jurisdictions treat carbon copies as the equivalent of duplicate originals even when there has been no formal execution of the copies. In such cases, the carbon copy must still be authenticated in some way as having been made at the same time as the original.

Where either the original document or the copy of the original has not been accounted for, the rule operates to exclude a copy made from a copy, unless it is the best evidence available.

(12.9) *FORM OF PROOF, ADVERSE PRODUCTION, AND COMPLEX DOCUMENTS*

The objective of the party seeking to have secondary evidence introduced is to convince the trial judge that he has exhausted all reasonable avenues of discovery and has been unable to locate the original writing. Any competent proof may be used to establish that the original has been lost, destroyed, or otherwise made unavailable. It is not necessary to offer positive proof of a writing's destruction. If the trial judge has any suspicion that the document is being improperly withheld, however, he may deny the admission of secondary evidence by invoking the best evidence rule.

It is not sufficient for the party seeking to produce secondary evidence of a document to indicate that the adverse party is in possession of the original. In order to fulfill the requirements of the best evidence rule, he must be able to show that he has given the opponent a request for production (notice), and there has been a failure to comply. The requirements of notice vary among jurisdictions but generally include a written request for production of the document and allowance of a reasonable period in which to produce it. If the document is clearly unavailable by reason of its remoteness, it is within the court's discretion to order admission of the secondary evidence. In addition, most jurisdictions do not require a defendant to produce a document that incriminates him.

In some complex cases involving a vast number of documents, the court may allow the use of an approximate summary. Here, the original documents must be submitted in advance to the adverse party so the accuracy of the summary can be tested on cross-examination.

(12.10) *SUMMARY*

Most of the underlying rules governing admissibility of documentary evidence do not differ in principle from those regulating testimonial evidence. Like hearsay, there are well-recognized rules governing particular types of documents such as church records, letters, books, and other publications.

Official records are usually admissible if made by a public servant who had firsthand knowledge of the information recorded. Photographs, motion pictures, and videotapes are also admissible if there are sufficient indicia of reliability. Like models, casts, and diagrams, they assist in the fact-finding process.

The best evidence rule serves to ensure that the most original record or copy will be the one received in evidence. Duplicates and copies of copies will not be excluded if originals are not available, but the rule requires parties to make an effort to locate documents that are more likely to be trustworthy.

chapter 13

(© Mary Murphy, Picture Group.)

PHYSICAL EVIDENCE TAGGED AND HELD IN POLICE CUSTODY

Physical and Scientific Evidence: Preservation and Custody

A. ROUTINE PHYSICAL EVIDENCE

(13.1) *IN GENERAL*

Any physical evidence that tends to prove or disprove the crime charged may be offered. If it is relevant and the proper foundation laid, it will be admitted as part of the proof. The range of objects and materials that may be offered in evidence is limitless. Relevancy is the key word.

(13.2) *ADMISSIBLE OBJECTS*

No rule excludes any particular object as evidence. As long as the evidence tends to prove the issue, it should be usable.

If, however, the exhibit is too gruesome or inflammatory, the court will exclude it on these grounds. In a homicide case arising out of an illegal abortion, for example, the dead fetus may have been preserved and offered in evidence. It would be excluded on these grounds, no matter how relevant it might be to the proof. If the exhibit can be misleading, such as an unfair or slanted photograph, it will be rejected if there is an objection.

(13.3) *FRUITS OF THE CRIME*

"Fruits of the crime," such as loot from a robbery or a burglary, are relevant and admissible in evidence. If it is impracticable to bring the actual objects into court, photographs of them can be used in evidence. A stolen car or truck, for example, would be returned to the owner and could be described by witnesses with the aid of photographs.

(13.4) *INSTRUMENTALITIES*

Anything used to commit a crime is relevant evidence. A murder weapon, a gun employed in a robbery, a burglar's tools, an acetylene torch used to open a safe, a gasoline can from an arson scene—all such objects may properly be offered in evidence in each particular case.

Pattern of wire screen installed as a protection against burglary.

(Courtesy, Columbus Police Department, Ohio.)

An imprint on shirt owned by a suspect.

(13.5) *MASKS AND CLOTHING*

Any type of mask used during the commission of a crime would be admitted in evidence. Police sometimes overlook clothing as evidence of a crime. Frequently the suspect's or victim's clothing may yield stains, foreign substances, powder burns, or wound marks that make the clothing very useful as evidence.

At one time a medical examiner in Maryland issued a death certificate stating that a man had died from natural causes. The deceased, a middle-aged man with a history of heart trouble, was found dead, lying across the bed in his motel room, clad in his underwear. The cause of death was determined to be heart disease. Because of an anonymous telephone tip suggesting murder, the medical examiner reopened the case. The examiner found a tiny hole in the front of the man's undershirt with a bloodstain on it. The autopsy revealed that he had been stabbed to death with one blow of an ice pick, which was apparently delivered by the other occupant of the room, his paramour. Thus, the overlooked undershirt was a prime bit of evidence in the prosecution's murder case.

(13.6) *CHANGES IN OBJECTS*

If an exhibit is to be admitted in evidence, it must reasonably be in the same condition at the trial as it was at the time of the crime. In the event it has been altered because of laboratory or scientific testing, expert witnesses can describe the changes, and the evidence will still be admitted even though it is in a different condition. Though some types of evidence deteriorate naturally, they still may be allowed in evidence if they remain usable and if the change in condition is not prejudicial in some way. If evidence is carelessly handled or damaged so that it has been changed materially, the court may exclude it.

(13.7) *EXHIBITION OF PERSONS*

As mentioned in chapter 6, the defendant can be ordered to present himself in a lineup. He can also be made to rise in court or otherwise exhibit himself or any part of his body if this is relevant to the proof. He may have, for example, been described as strong and husky. The court may thus allow him to remove his shirt and show that he really is of slight physique or that he has a physical impairment, such as a crippled arm. Exhibiting a part of the body is also left to the discretion of the judge. He will allow nothing of this nature if it is indecent or inflammatory in the court's judgment.

B. SCIENTIFIC EVIDENCE

(13.8) *IN GENERAL*

With the advance of science, scientific evidence allowed in court has changed. Pictures of bank robbers taken by hidden cameras or closed-circuit television, for example, are now used in evidence. Such proof was unknown years ago. Acceptance by the courts of new types of scientific evidence is slow and does not keep pace with the latest advances in science. Whenever a new type of scientific evidence is offered, considerable expert testimony must support it. The general rule on scientific evidence has always been that it will not be received until it has "general scientific acceptance" (*Frye* v. *U.S.*, 293 F. 1013 [CADC 1923]).

There is a modern tendency for courts to relax this, following the lead of Federal Rules of Evidence, Sec. 702, and to admit any scientific proof that will help the jury "understand the evidence or determine a fact" (*State* v. *Hall*, 28 Cr. L. 2105 [Iowa Sup. Ct.] 1980).

(13.9) *FIREARMS AND BALLISTICS*

Much valuable evidence can be obtained by firearms and ballistics tests, but they are not as completely perfect as popularly imagined.

In case of close-range firing, reliable tests exist to measure burning, powder marks, and other residues. Tissue may be burned or fabrics scorched. Carbon or powder particles may penetrate or adhere to the surface of the wound. Such proof is often crucial in determining whether a shooting was suicide, accidental, or homicide.

Firearms themselves may be identified through restoring obliterated serial numbers. Gun barrels leave distinguishing marks on bullets. Shell casings also receive individual markings that can often identify the weapon from which the shell was fired. Bullet or shell comparisons, however, are not always completely conclusive, depending on the fragment recovered at the time of the crime. Experts can often state only that the bullet could have come from the weapon in question. The evidence is still acceptable, although it is not conclusive proof of the connection between the projectile and the weapon.

(Courtesy of Media Services Subunit, Federal Bureau of Investigation.)

Comparison of cartridges by means of photomicrography.

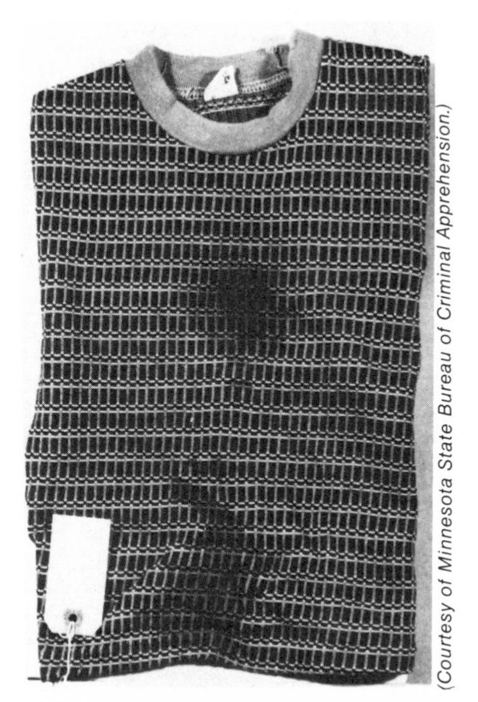
(Courtesy of Minnesota State Bureau of Criminal Apprehension.)

Shirt photographed to increase the details of the powder pattern.

Gunshot residue tests from a suspect's hands—the so-called paraffin tests—have been known for many years. Many experts now doubt their value, largely because similar residues may be found on an innocent person's skin (*see* Inbau, Moenssens, and Moses, *Scientific Evidence in Criminal Cases,* Sec. 4.12).

(13.10) *TOOL MARKS AND MICROGRAPHY*

Photographs taken through a microscope and then enlarged often provide strong circumstantial evidence for use in court. Pry marks from a forced entry may show identical markings with a tool when they are compared microscopically. Other examples include broken tools compared with a piece recovered at the scene of the crime, knife marks on bone, cut marks on wires, and crimp marks on detonators.

Microscopic examination of such evidence is often successful. The phrase "comparative micrography" is used to describe such examinations where a hard object is applied against a softer one.

(13.11) *FORENSIC PATHOLOGY*

The trained medical examiner can often supply the best evidence of the details of a suspected crime. In all suspicious or violent deaths, an autopsy is required. The pathologist determines the cause and the approximate time of death. Was it a drowning, or did death occur outside the water? The postmortem tells.

Bruises and wounds can be measured and photographed. Hairs, blood, bodily fluids, stomach and blood contents, and the condition of the body and wounds—all reveal a story to the trained examiner. In the case of sexual offenses, seminal and other stains may be analyzed. Blood alcohol is commonly tested where intoxication is involved. Evidence concerning poisons, drugs, and many other physical conditions is often given by pathologists.

(13.12) *TOXICOLOGY AND CHEMISTRY*

When poisoning is suspected, the pathologist performing the autopsy removes the bodily material such as blood, urine, stomach contents, or tissue from vital organs. He then turns the material over to a toxicologist (a specialist on poisons and their effect) for his examination. The toxicologist presents his findings in a report.

A chemical expert may be called in for laboratory tests in cases concerned with drug abuse or situations involving intoxication. These tests include the use of chemical reagents, crystalline comparisons, chromatography, and other methods of chemical testing. All methods have strengths and weaknesses, and an investigator or attorney should be aware of them as they relate to evidence involved in a criminal prosecution.

(13.13) *SEROLOGY*

A serologist is used to analyze bodily fluids such as blood, semen, saliva, and the like. Blood analysis is the most common.

Several tests are first conducted to definitely classify the specimen as blood. Lipstick, catsup, even iodine are some of the substances that resemble blood. Further tests indicate whether it is animal or human blood. Once it is found to be human, blood is divided into types, either A, B, AB, or O. The types can be readily determined. Approximately 40 percent of Americans are type A, 43 percent are type O, 14 percent are type B, and 3 percent are type AB. There are also other systems for classifying human blood.

Until recently, blood samples could not be identified with any particular person but could only show that the sample was of the same or different blood group as that of the individual involved. A new blood testing technique is now being developed. The test, electrophoresis, came to us from Scotland Yard. It involves a method of sorting out enzymes in the blood and can come much closer to identifying the individual from whom the sample came.

In a Florida murder case, Priscilla Bradford was accused of beating her husband to death. She claimed that the blood stain on her blouse came from herself and not from her murdered husband. Electrophoresis showed that she and her husband had three similar enzymes in their blood but that they differed in two. The differences in the enzymes showed that the blood on the blouse was his. The court accepted these test results. She was convicted and sentenced to thirty-six years in prison.

The Kansas Court of Appeals (*State* v. *Washington*, 28 Cr.L. 2449 [1981]) approved the use of the Multi-System blood analysis test in which three enzyme systems are tested from one blood sample at one time. A chemist was allowed to testify from these test results in a murder case, the court finding that this test now had general scientific approval.

Electrophoresis has great potential in homicide and rape cases. One enzyme will even show race. Test advances may eventually allow the expert to say "This blood came from that man."

People who have type A, B, or AB blood secrete the antigens characteristic of these blood groups in such bodily fluids as saliva, tears, semen, and perspiration. Blood-grouping tests from these bodily secretions can, therefore, be made for about 80 percent of the population.

In cases involving rape or perversion, serology tests are often made to determine the presence of semen and sperm cells. Seminal fluid is secreted by the glands along the seminal tract to which sperm is supplied from the testes. Sperm will not be present if the suspect has had a vasectomy or if too much time has elapsed between the crime and the taking of the sample. The specimen may be tested for acid phosphatase to reveal if it is human seminal fluid. Swabs may be taken from the vaginal or cervical area of the female. In cases of perversion, anal or oral swabs are used. Stains may be found on the clothing of the victim or suspect or at the scene of the crime.

The HLA (Human Leukocyte Antigen) test has been developed as a more scientific method of proving paternity than the use of blood types. Florida now admits the test results as evidence and can order the putative father to submit to it (*Simons* v. *Jorg,* 384 So. 2d 1362; *McQueen* v. *Stratton*, 389 So. 2d 1190 [Fla. 2d DCA 1980]). This test may have application in some criminal cases.

Saliva stains are not often thought of, and yet they may be found on cigarette butts, cigars, pipes, or other objects. As stated, they can often be used to classify blood types. Similar results can be obtained from perspiration stains, which normally remain on coats, hats, shirts, and dresses. Even fecal matter and vomitus yield test results to the serologist.

(13.14) *NARCOTICS AND DRUGS*

Because the use of narcotics and various drugs has become so widespread, law enforcement personnel continuously find themselves deeply involved in drug control.

It has even been a legal problem to devise a definition of the term "narcotic" that is specifically correct. Those who draft statutes have avoided the problem by simply listing a series of drugs that must be labeled "controlled substances."

a. Types of Drugs

Opiates are one of the general classes of drugs. Derived from the opium poppy, they include opium, codeine, morphine, heroin, and synthetics such as methadone and meperidine. All opiates are addictive and are labeled narcotics.

Marijuana, often listed as a narcotic, is correctly classified as a hallucinogen, as are mescaline and LSD. As the term indicates, users of hallucinogens perceive sights, sounds, and colors that are not real. Though none of these drugs are considered addictive, many are dangerous.

Cocaine is an alkaloid derived from cocoa leaves. A stimulant, it reduces inhibitions. Extended use may produce hallucinations. It is normally taken by sniffing or by injection.

Barbiturates are used as sedatives, hypnotics, and antispasmodics. Overuse produces symptoms similar to intoxication and can result in physical dependence.

Amphetamines are stimulants. Their use does not cause physical dependence.

b. Tests for Drugs

The police chemist is frequently called on to identify unknown materials in order to determine if they are drugs or narcotics. In cases of deaths and of traffic violations, tests of blood or urine are used to provide information concerning the use of drugs. These range from relatively simple physical and chemical tests to nuclear activation analysis.

Tests to determine addiction to narcotics are among those generally employed by police laboratories. Urinary analysis is the best-known method. Laboratory findings based on urinalysis are accepted as legal evidence. One problem with urinalysis is that police are often careless in obtaining and preserving the sample.

In the 1950s, the nalline test was developed to discover narcotic addiction or recent use by individuals. The test involves injecting a drug, nalorphine, into a subject and measuring the reaction of the pupil of his eye.

An early California case ruled on the admissibility of nalline test results for narcotics use (*People* v. *Williams*, 164 Cal. App. 2d 858 [1959]). Two suspects had been arrested as being drug users. Each admitted to having used drugs previous to that time but denied recent use. Both of them had old and new needle marks on their arms. The doctor who administered the test testified in court that the subjects were injected with nalline after having their pupils measured with a test card that contained a series of dots. Thirty minutes later their pupils were measured again. A comparison of the measurements showed that each one had dilated pupils. The appellate court approved the use of the test results in conjunction with the expert's opinion that both defendants were then under the influence of narcotics. While the nalline test itself has limitations, such as the possibility of inaccurate readings of the pupillometer, it is now generally received in court.

Courts now routinely allow witnesses to testify concerning needle marks ("tracks") on a suspect's arm and to give an opinion as to whether they are recent or old. Such evidence has been received as proof in possession of heroin cases.

A wide variety of scientific tests for narcotics and drugs are accepted by modern courts, providing there is proper identification of the sample, its custody, and the qualification of the expert witness.

(13.15) *FINGERPRINTS*

The skin of a person's fingers, palms, toes, and feet contains a series of friction ridges, which are nature's method of giving man traction. These ridges form patterns that remain the same from birth to death. All friction skin has perspiration pores, and body oils leave a pattern wherever the skin ridges touch a smooth surface. Impressions accidentally left on such a surface are called latent prints. Though they are normally invisible, they can be made visible by means of powders, vapors, or chemicals. They can be lifted by the use of a transparent adhesive tape or other means and kept as a permanent record. The latent prints once brought to life can be photographed and then compared with known fingerprints.

All fingerprints can be classified under an accepted formula that makes it possible for them to be filed and retrieved. Identifying the unknown latent print with the known one is entirely different from classifying it. There can be an untold number of prints in the same general class, but there is only one print of a particular individual.

To identify the particular print, the expert looks for four elements. The standard rule is that there must be at least eight identical ridge comparisons, though more concordances are generally desired. The latent print at the scene of the crime is usually used to identify the defendant and to place him at the scene.

Thus, fingerprint evidence has two uses: to prove the identity of the accused or of the victim or to provide evidence that the defendant committed the crime.

Testimony regarding fingerprints must come from an expert trained and experienced in the science of classifying and identifying them. This type of evidence is so widely accepted that the defense now has little room for attacking the technician's testimony. There are, in fact, a number of cases in which a conviction has been won and sustained even though it is based mainly on fingerprints.

People v. *Rodis*, 145 Cal. App. 2d 44 (1956), concerned the burglary of a drugstore in California. The burglar entered the store through a rear window that was nine feet from the ground. A screen was removed, and the defendant's fingerprint was found on the outside of the window. At the trial the only evidence against the defendant was this fingerprint. Contrary evidence was provided by his family who testified that he was at home the night of the burglary. The defendant himself took the stand

and denied ever having been in the store. In spite of the evidence provided by the defense, the defendant was convicted on the strength of the fingerprint evidence. The appellate court affirmed the conviction, pointing out that the fingerprint was found on the outside of the window, nine feet from the ground. Thus it would have been necessary for a person to use a ladder or a platform to remove the screen. All of these facts militated against an innocent placement of the fingerprint.

There is, however, a generally accepted rule regarding fingerprint evidence. It holds that in cases where the only evidence of guilt consists of fingerprints found at the scene, the evidence, to be legally sufficient, must be coupled with proof of other circumstances tending reasonably to exclude the idea that the fingerprint was left at a different time. Unless these circumstances are present, the courts will not sustain a conviction based only on fingerprint evidence. This was demonstrated in *Barum* v. *U.S.*, 380 F. 2d 590 (1967), and 380 U.S. 2d 595 (1967), plus *Fladung* v. *State*, 4 Md. App. 664 (1968).

It is often important to know when a latent print was made, but it is doubtful if such proof can be obtained from fingerprint evidence. The courts sometimes make unusual decisions on this point, as illustrated by the two *Barum* cases cited above. In one of these, Barum was convicted of stealing from a private home a valuable coin collection contained in two empty jars. His fingerprints were found on the jars, but the government's witness admitted that the prints could have been on the jars "for a period of . . . years." The appellate court reversed the conviction. It held that there was insufficient evidence to convict and said that the prosecution should have produced evidence to show that the prints "were placed on the jars at the time of the crime." Barum's other burglary conviction resulted from fingerprints found on three objects in a house, a tea canister, a metal cash box, and a glass tabletop. The appellate court upheld this conviction on the theory that Barum could have had no previous access to these articles.

In presenting fingerprint evidence, the prosecution must demonstrate the qualifications of its expert and his method of gathering the evidence and its custody, the means of expert examination, and his opinion. The defense may counterattack by attempting to show errors made by the technician and irregularities owing to dirt, variations in finger pressure, scars, and excess use of ink. If the fingerprints were incident to an unlawful arrest, the defense can have them excluded from evidence (*Davis* v. *Mississippi*, 394 U.S. 721 [1969]).

(13.16) *QUESTIONED DOCUMENTS*

The modern specialist who examines documents has come a long way from the so-called "handwriting expert" of previous years. Aided by present-day scientific developments, he is able to do many more things than analyze handwriting. It is true that a questioned document often involves handwriting comparisons, and the expert is called in solely to perform this function. He might, for example, identify the author of a written extortion or ransom note, a forgery, or a letter. He is often asked to do more than this. Has the original document been changed? Were words inserted? Have pages been added? Is the entire paper a fake? These and many similar questions are often submitted to the examiner of questioned documents for his analysis and for his subsequent court testimony.

During the last hundred years, the science of document examination has grown and become more sophisticated. There were initially many so-called experts whose court testimony was based more on self-confidence than on expertise. While there is no recognized professional course of study for a document examiner, the individual must have a technical background and much experience in his field. Those prerequisites will qualify him as an "expert." Though document examiners sometimes vary in their opinions, this does not occur often. When they do disagree, it is usually because they did not have the same materials or they worked under different conditions.

What is a questioned document? It may be a letter, a check, a contract, or a will. It may, in fact, be any material that contains a mark or signature. Criminal cases often involve a variety of things, from the psychopath's scrawled message in lipstick on a mirror to hotel registers, drivers' licenses, and passports. Whenever a document or any part of it is questioned or its authorship is in doubt, the examiner is called in to analyze it and to give his opinion.

The document itself must be treated with great care by the field investigator. Handling is avoided whenever possible so that fingerprints will not be added or minute changes made. The document will usually be picked up with tweezers, placed in a plastic envelope, and sealed. The investigator's mark will then be put on the outside of the container, not on the item itself.

If handwriting is involved, the examiner must have as many genuine exemplars as possible. The defendant can be ordered to furnish these specimens. The expert prefers examples of the suspect's handwriting that use the same words as those appearing in the questioned document. Similarities as well as differences are important in arriving at an opinion on handwriting.

A typewritten document can often be traced to a particular machine. The document examiner keeps a file of typed samples from various kinds of typewriters. This often allows him to determine immediately the make or model of the typewriter involved. Because each machine develops its own particular characteristics due to type wear and varying impressions, the expert can go on to make a precise identification of the typewriter used. It is even possible to identify typewriters with revolving elements, although this type of machine does cause added problems for the expert examiner. The trial of Alger Hiss was one of the most widely publicized cases in which the conviction was largely based on typewriter evidence.

In the field of altered documents,the skilled examiner can often show the most dramatic results. By using infrared or ultraviolet light and other methods, he may be able photographically to reproduce charred documents, disclose words previously removed by chemicals, or even reproduce the original writing from indentations transferred to paper that lay underneath.

When materials are properly handled in the field, and when the modern qualified document examiner is provided adequate handwriting exemplars, he can often be the strongest witness the state can produce.

(13.17) *MICROANALYSIS*

The term "microanalysis" generally refers to analysis of minute particles of evidence and not just to evidentiary testing by microscope. Microscopes of various kinds are used by technicians in this process.

Examination of small particles of hair, paint, fibers, soil, and glass frequently yields significant results. Paint smears from burglaries or chips from an automobile accident, for example, can often be analyzed and classified by such testing. Paint may be many layers, and the number and kinds of layers can reveal matching characteristics.

Glass fragments from car headlights, broken windows, eyeglasses, and the like may be important evidence. Particles may be found in a suspect's clothing or matched with those in a suspected vehicle. Various techniques of microanalysis can also reveal the chemical or physical characteristics of glass for scientific comparison.

One can test hair to discover whether it is human or animal. It is possible to identify hair from different areas of the body. Racial differences and sometimes sex can be determined by the examination of human hair.

Fibers are of varied types, from synthetic to animal, and the examiner can usually classify them and make accurate comparisons. Even in very small quantities, fibers yield information that can be useful. Those obtained from clothing, for example, may match those from insulation where burglars forced an entry through a wall or ceiling. Tools, clothing, and fired bullets may have fibers connected to them. Threads found on a murder or rape victim may help identify the suspect.

Soil may be either left or removed from the location where the crime occurred. Proper preservation by the investigator enables laboratory technicians to obtain useful evidence from soil, but comparisons are very difficult.

(13.18) *NEUTRON ACTIVATION ANALYSIS*

One by-product of atomic science, which has been employed since 1964, is neutron activation analysis of evidence in criminal cases. This process involves bombarding the evidence with a stream of nuclear particles from a nuclear reactor that is used for research. This produces radioactivity in the bombarded material. The radioactive material "decays," and in so doing it gives off gamma rays. The rays are counted and their intensity measured. This information is then compared with known data to give an analysis of the quantity of the elements present in the evidentiary sample. Gunshot residue, soils, paint, grease, drugs, and a variety of other substances can be tested for by this method. It is obvious, however, that the facilities for this type of testing are limited.

U.S. v. *Stifel*, 433 F. 2d 431, cert. den. 401 U.S. 994 (1970), is the leading case supporting evidence obtained by neutron activation analysis. Orville Stifel was convicted of murdering Dan Ronec, in his parents' home, by sending a bomb through the mail. The package was in the form of a mailing tube that exploded when Ronec unscrewed the top. The evidence against Stifel was circumstantial, the alleged motive being jealousy over a woman. Stifel had worked for a large soap company and had access to its mailing tubes and labels. The government used neutron activation analysis on these, and its expert testified that the mailing label and tube fragments were the same "elemental composition" as those of the company. The metal cap and the tape "were the same manufacture" and were produced on the same day as the ones made for the company. The court admitted the evidence resulting from the neutron activation analysis, pointing out that no appeals court had refused it and that its scientific basis had been widely accepted by a variety of state decisions.

There appears to be no serious court opposition to the use of this new method. While its access to the police is necessarily somewhat limited, the results can be spectacular.

(13.19) *POLYGRAPH*

This is a widely used device for testing a person's truthfulness. Developed a number of years ago, it operates on the theory that lying produces tension even in a hardened criminal. This in turn affects bodily reactions such as blood pressure and respiration. These reactions are measured by the machine as the subject is being questioned, and they are recorded on a continuous graph. By reading the graph, a well-trained operator can determine the speaker's truthfulness with great accuracy.

Police forces everywhere have used the polygraph for a number of years in criminal investigations. Was the woman raped, or did she consent? Did the witness see the shooting, or is he purposely accusing an innocent man? Prosecutors and police need to know the truthfulness of witnesses and complainants, and the polygraph has been a useful aid in determining this.

An accused sometimes submits to a test voluntarily. If the machine indicates his protestations of innocence are true, the prosecution is ordinarily dropped. If it shows that he is lying, a confession may follow. Even where there is no confession, and the machine points to guilt, the police at least know that they are on firm ground in making the charge against him.

If a suspect refuses to be tested, the prosecution usually feels that he is guilty. An innocent person has nothing to fear, and the device should show his innocence.

It occasionally happens that both the defense and the prosecution stipulate that a polygraph test be given and the test results used in evidence. Without such a stipulation, most courts will refuse to admit polygraph evidence. They feel that the machine is being used as a substitute for the court's and the jury's determination of truthfulness.

New York's highest court excluded polygraph evidence in *People* v.

Leone, N.Y. 2d 511 (1969). Oklahoma also refused to admit it in *Fulton* v. *State*, 541 P. 2d 871 (Okla. Cr. App. 1975), even though both sides had agreed by stipulation that the results could be used.

Ballard v. *Supreme Court*, 64 Cal. 2d 159 (1966), illustrates the narrow view that courts can take regarding polygraph tests. Walter Ballard, a physician, was charged with raping a woman patient. He was alleged to have given her a drug to prevent her resistance and then to have had sexual intercourse with her. The police physician examined her and found semen on her clothing. Later the police put a microphone in her purse and had her see the doctor in his office while they recorded their conversation outside. They also did the same thing by having her call the doctor on the telephone. The police subsequently gave her a polygraph test. When the doctor was arrested, he demanded the results of the test in order to prepare for trial. The court refused his request, saying that polygraph test results could not be used in court, and, therefore, the evidence was inadmissible. It did, however, allow him to be given the questions asked and her replies to them.

As has been said, most courts have consistently refused to allow such test results to be used. At present, however, there are a few indications that polygraph test results will be allowed under prescribed restrictions. One such indication came in *State* v. *Dorsey*, 532 P. 2d 912 (N.M. App. 1975), aff'd 539 P. 2d 204 (N.M., 1975). In that case the defendant was accused of attacking another person with a knife. He claimed self-defense, saying that he did not pull his knife before leaving his car and that the alleged victim struck the first blow. A polygraph test indicated that the defendant was telling the truth. He offered the test result to support his statement. The prosecution objected, and the trial court excluded the evidence. The appeals court held that this was in error. It ruled that even though there had been an objection, the use of the polygraph was now a scientifically approved test, and, within the reasoning of *Chambers* v. *Mississippi*, supra, it should have been admitted.

An Ohio court decided that a robbery suspect was constitutionally entitled to have a pretrial polygraph test. The case against him rested on a brief personal observation of the identifying witness. The court held that polygraph evidence was proven to be effective and that in circumstances such as these a defendant was entitled to take the test at his own request (*State* v. *Sims*, 21 Cr. L. 2191 [Cuyahoga Cty. Common Pleas Ct. 1977]). Similar results came in a New York trial court, *People* v. *Daniels*, 26 Cr. L. 2385 [1979]).

It is inevitable that the use of the polygraph will be approved more extensively in court decisions, but its acceptance is extremely slow.

(13.20) *VOICEPRINTS*

Another scientific device now coming into wider use is the voiceprint, which reproduces a person's voice spectrographically. The test is based on the fact that no two people have the same voice characteristics. This is because the vocal cavities and organs of articulation—lips, tongue, teeth, and so on—vary from individual to individual.

The voice spectrograph electronically analyzes the complex speech sounds, disburses them into their various parts, and reproduces them on current-sensitive paper. This visual result is the voiceprint. When certain cue words are compared with previously recorded voiceprints of the same words, identification of the voice becomes possible. The prints lend themselves to computerized classification so that a central file can be compiled. This file makes it possible, for example, to compare a kidnapper's or a blackmailer's telephone call with voiceprints of known criminals with similar backgrounds.

Scientific opinion regarding voiceprints is presently divided, despite their very high degree of accuracy. Both federal and state courts are also divided. At this point some courts in Massachusetts, California, New York, and Minnesota have accepted voice spectrographs as positive identification evidence in criminal cases; a few federal courts have as well. (*See People* v. *Rogers*, 385 NYS 2d 228 [Kings City. Sup. Ct. 1976] and cases cited therein.)

Commonwealth v. *Lykus*, 327 N.E. 2d 671 (Mass., 1975), involved the kidnapping and murder of a young boy. The police taped the kidnapper's ransom calls. A specified amount of money was dropped, and, after three attempts, the suspect collected it. When it was traced to him, he admitted that he had picked up the money. He stated, however, that he had been hired to do it for $500 by a man who was involved in drug traffic, and he claimed that he had left the money where this person had instructed him to do so. The boy was found shot to death in a wooded area. At the trial, six witnesses identified the defendant's voice, but one could not. A voiceprint expert testified that the defendant was the one who made the calls. He based his statement on the tapes and voice exemplars. The defendant was found guilty and appealed. The appellate court approved the use of the voiceprint evidence and upheld the conviction.

The latest device designed to evaluate the voice electronically is the psychological stress evaluator. This machine is similar to that of the polygraph in that it measures certain stress-related parts of speech. Involuntary indications of stress made by the voice are traced on a graph, and the results are interpreted. Unlike a polygraph, the machine does not have to be attached to the subject. (*State* v. *Thompson*, 381 So. 2d 823 [La. Sup. Ct. 1980].) It is necessary only to make a recording of the questions and answers. The recording of the interview is later fed through the evaluator, and the voice reactions are charted. The psychological stress evaluator is presently being used as an investigative tool in law enforcement agencies and in the business world, but it has not yet received court approval.

(13.21) *NARCOANALYSIS AND HYPNOSIS*

Scopolamine, sodium pentothal, and the like, often labeled truth serums, are, at times, used as an interrogation or diagnostic tool. The technique is known as narcoanalysis and is based on the theory that this type of drug will break down the subject's mental resistance so that he will respond truthfully to questioning. Suspects may consent to such a test in order to clear themselves, or both counsels may stipulate that the test be given.

Courts consistently reject the introduction of any statement, by either a defendant or a witness, made under the influence of these drugs. They hold that the validity of the test has not been scientifically proven. Cases illustrative of this rejection by the courts are *People* v. *McCracken*, 39 Cal. 2d 336 (1952); *People* v. *Harper*, 111 Ill. App. 2d 204 (1969).

Statements made while the subject is under hypnosis are viewed by the courts in the same way as those made while an individual is undergoing narcoanalysis. A hypnotized person is, of course, powerfully subject to suggestion. Stage performers for many years have used posthypnotic suggestions to induce subjects to perform actions after the hypnotic trance is over. Yet in spite of the court's rejection of these tests and the widespread nonprofessional use of hypnosis, both hypnosis and narcoanalysis have legitimate investigative and diagnostic applications.

The human mind is a strange and largely unknown mechanism. Even the process of memory is not fully understood. People remember by different means; some remember consciously less than others. Also, many tend to erase unpleasant or horrible experiences from their minds. What of the rape victim who cannot recall the events of the assault? Narcoanalysis or hypnotism may actually allow her to remember.

Courts in Florida and New York have allowed in-court identifications where the witness originally was unable to identify the suspect but had had his memory revived by hypnosis (*Clark* v. *State*, 379 So. 2d 372 [1st. DCA-Fla. 1980]; *State* v. *Hurd*, 414 A. 2d 291 [N.J. Super. Ct. 1980]). A Minnesota court has refused similar testimony saying that hypnosis has not yet been accepted by the scientific community (*State* v. *Mack*, 292 N.W. 2d 764 [Minn. Sup. Ct. 1980]).

Narcoanalysis is a recognized method used by psychiatrists to diagnose mental illness, but the information the patient gives the psychiatrist when drugs are administered for the purpose of diagnosis cannot be admitted as proof of the truth of what was said. An example of this occurred in a murder case in New York (*People* v. *Esposito*, 287 N.Y. 389 [1942]). In response to the defendant's request for a sanity test, one examining psychiatrist used a drug injection as a method of diagnosis to determine whether the defendant was insane or malingering. The trial judge allowed the doctor to describe this method of testing and to give his resulting opinion on the sanity of the subject. The physician was not, however, allowed to relate any admissions or drug-induced statements that the defendant made. The appellate court approved this decision and affirmed the conviction.

A more difficult problem exists when a statement is given after the truth serum treatment is completed. A similar situation can occur where the defendant is an addict and he has been given medication to ease his withdrawal symptoms, and then confesses. At the time of trial, he may claim that his confession was drug induced and thus involuntary.

In *People* v. *Townsend*, 11 Ill. 2d 30 (1957), the defendant, Townsend, was convicted of a mugging murder in which $4.80 was involved. While he was being interrogated at the time of his arrest, he complained of stomach pains. A doctor was called in and found that the suspect was an addict suffering withdrawal symptoms. He administered phenobarbital and other drugs to relieve him. The defendant later gave a detailed statement confessing to the murder. He was subsequently sentenced to death. On appeal, Townsend claimed that his confession was drug induced and thus involuntary. The Illinois court affirmed his conviction, saying that the fact that he was given beneficial drugs to ease his pain was not proof that he was drugged for the purpose of securing a confession.

Six years later Townsend took his case to the U.S. Supreme Court via habeas corpus (*Townsend* v. *Sain*, 372 U.S. 293 [1963]). It found that one of the drugs given Townsend for treatment of his pains was hyocine, which is the same as scopolamine—a truth serum. For this reason, the court found that there was a real possibility that Townsend's later confession was drug induced, not voluntary. Thus, they remanded the case to the district court for a complete hearing on the subject.

In at least one reported incident—in a murder trial in Ohio—hypnosis was allowed in the courtroom (*State* v. *Nebb*, no. 39, 450 [Ohio Cm. Pl. 5/28/62]). The jury was excused, and, by agreement of attorneys, the defendant was hypnotized in the presence of the judge. The prosecution then questioned him. As a result of the questioning, the prosecutor reduced the charge to manslaughter.

Witnesses have been allowed to testify concerning their recollections, even though their present memory was acquired through hypnotism. This was the case in *Harding* v. *State*, 5 Md. App. 230, cert. den. 395 U.S. 949 (1969), and *Cornell* v. *Superior Court*, 52 Cal. 2d 99 (1959).

Thus, while both narcoanalysis and hypnosis are recognized scientific tools for investigation and treatment, their results are narrowly circumscribed in the courts.

(13.22) *MISCELLANEOUS*

Fluorescein powders have long been in use. Though invisible to the naked eye, they produce a fluorescent glow when excited by an ultraviolet lamp. They are frequently used to catch sneak thieves, such as dishonest employees.

In a highly publicized case in suburban Chicago, police suspected a dentist of performing indecent acts upon his femal patients after administering gas. One woman volunteered for "dental treatment" and was gassed. Her private parts had been lightly covered with gynecological jelly mixed with fluorescein paste. When the dentist was later confronted, his face and sexual organs fluoresced.

At least one case (*Brock* v. *U.S.*, 223 F. 2d 681, 685 [5th Cir. 1955]) has held that the use of ultraviolet lamps on a suspect's outer clothing or hands is not a search within the meaning of the Fourth Amendment. Thus, a search warrant is unnecessary.

A variety of other things provide scientific proof in criminal cases. Dentistry, for example, is increasingly used as a method of identifying unknown bodies. This method is highly reliable because it is unlikely that any two people exist with the same dental history. In addition, dentists' records are carefully kept and so provide good scientific evidence.

Bite-mark identification was used in the Bundy murder case in

Florida where an expert testified that in his opinion the defendant had made the bite marks found on the buttock of a murdered coed. Other state decisions that have admitted bite-mark evidence are *People* v. *Milone*, 356 N.E. 2d 1350 (2nd DCA Ill. 1976); *State* v. *Routh*, 568 P 2d 704 (Or. App. 1977); *State* v. *Sager*, 27 Cr. L. 2289 (Ct. App. Mo. 1980). Anthropologists and others may be able to supply information on sex, race, and other characteristics from human remains found many years after death.

As science progresses, new fields of scientific evidence in criminal cases will continue to develop.

It is necessary to insert a word of caution concerning scientific proof that depends on scientific measuring instruments. There are no American court decisions holding that evidence of measurements by mechanical means or scientific instruments are presumed to be correct. Seldom does the defense raise the objection that there has been no proof of the accuracy of the scientific measuring device used by the expert witness. The legal question is open, however, and anyone offering scientific proof should be aware that the problem exists (21 ALR 2d 1200).

C. PRESERVATION AND CUSTODY OF EVIDENCE

(13.23) *IN GENERAL*

Evidence is of no value to the prosecutor unless it can be used in court. The police must, therefore, exercise care in collecting, identifying, and preserving any physical evidence connected with a crime. Unless properly connected with the crime and sufficiently authenticated at the trial, the evidence cannot be used.

(13.24) *COLLECTION*

Evidence at the scene of the crime cannot be collected too carefully. Photographing the weapon at the scene of a murder or the tool marks of forced entry where a burglary occurred should, for example, be routinely done. The evidence itself must be kept free of contamination, fingerprints, or damage so that its original condition remains unchanged. If the item is numbered, the numbers should be written down for the police records. Exhibits should be carefully placed in separate evidence envelopes, preferably of clear plastic, and should be tagged immediately.

(13.25) *MARKING*

Where possible, evidence should be marked by the officer who first recovers it. His initials may be put on the exhibit. The butt plate from a rifle, for example, can be removed and the initials scratched on the stock before replacing the plate. If the object itself cannot be marked, the envelope or other containers should be labeled with the investigator's initials. Where glass or tube containers are used, it is a sound practice to seal them with tape and then sealing wax, with the officer's fingerprint placed on the warm wax.

(13.26) *PRESERVATION*

All evidence should be placed in a locked cabinet. Valuable and dangerous items should be kept in a fireproof locked vault or safe. Laboratory technicians ought to preserve by chemical or other methods anything that might decompose, such as bodily tissue. Any article taken into custody or removed should be logged in and out in an evidence register. The 3M Company markets a specially developed tape that is transparent except for the word "Evidence," which is in red letters. The tape is designed to be affixed over initials or a signature. It destroys itself in a noticeable manner whenever it is tampered with.

(13.27) *TESTING*

Testing, whether done by the laboratory or by a firearms expert, may consume part or all of an exhibit. This is acceptable, and the expert witness can easily explain it in court. Any material remaining after the tests are made must be returned to police custody for later use at the trial.

(13.28) *CHAIN OF CUSTODY*

The general rule of "chain of custody" (which is more accurately termed "chain of identification") applies to evidence that has undergone expert analysis, such as a blood sample or material from bodily specimens. The side offering the evidence must show that the technician received the same sample that was originally taken from the person involved or from the place in question. It must also lay a foundation by testimony from every person who had the object in his custody, beginning with the officer who originally took it through the technician who examined it. If one person who had it in his custody cannot be found to testify to this, the court will usually rule that the chain has been broken and that the object will not be admitted into evidence. It is obviously impossible to follow the chain of custody rule exactly. If, for example, a specimen is mailed to a laboratory, every postman and clerk who handled it cannot be produced in court. Proof of mailing and the laboratory receipt of the package will suffice. What is required is proof that the exhibit now in court is the same one that was tested. It is extremely important for police authorities to keep the chain of custody unbroken and to maintain an exact record of everyone who had any object in his possession.

This rule usually applies only to exhibits that are part of an expert's testimony. If the knife found at the scene of a murder is proved by a witness to be in the same condition as when found, it generally is admissible in evidence without the various police evidence custodians having to testify that it was in their possession.

(13.29) *COURTROOM AUTHENTICATION*

There is a standard way of introducing an exhibit. First, it is marked for identification. Next counsel says: "I show you Exhibit 2 for identification. What is it?" The witness identifies the object and describes finding it. He is then asked: "Is it in the same condition now as when you originally found it?" If he answers in the affirmative, the exhibit is sufficiently authenticated to be offered in evidence.

(13.30) *DESTRUCTION OF EVIDENCE*

Evidence must be preserved during the time of trial and any appeals, including postconviction attacks through habeas corpus. Once the process has ended, the evidence can be safely returned to its rightful owner. In some cases, the defendant, through his attorney, will acknowledge the existence of an item, its value, and the description of it. This enables the owner to obtain his property much sooner, and thus prevent a hardship. Police often receive a court order allowing the destruction of evidence from closed cases some time before they actually dispose of it. Because of growing police corruption arising from narcotics, some jurisdictions provide for analysis of the evidence and a court-ordered destruction of the drugs even before the trial (*see* N.Y. CPL, Article 715 [1973]).

Destruction of evidence can create problems. In *Brady* v. *Maryland*, 373 U.S. 83 (1963), the police secretly videotaped a jail-house visit two people made to an accused murderer. The district attorney viewed the tape to see if it contained anything that would be helpful to the defense. Finding nothing, he erased the tape. One of the visitors was later a prosecution witness at the trial. Brady was found guilty and appealed. During the second trial, the defendant argued that the destruction of the tape violated his right to impeach the witness. Though the court affirmed the conviction, it warned that if the police destroy evidence as being nonmaterial without first notifying the defendant, the burden will be on the prosecution to show that this destruction did not prejudice the defense.

In the past, police in California encountered a problem concerning destruction of evidence because they routinely destroyed breathalizer ampules that had been used to detect the presence of alcohol in those accused of driving while intoxicated. Thus, a defendant contesting the result could not retest the ampule. The court ruled, therefore, that they should not be destroyed (*People* v. *Hitch*, 527 P. 2d 361 [Cal. 1974]).

A safe rule to follow before destroying evidence is this: Notify the defendant and seek court approval where it is appropriate.

(13.31) *SUMMARY*

Physical evidence relevant to the crime can be used if properly taken and preserved. Fruits of the crime, burglar's tools, clothing, even the defendant's person, may be relevant evidence.

Much scientific proof, such as fingerprints, ballistics tests, and chemical analysis, is available. Tests for narcotics are now commonplace. Document examiners using modern methods can give detached proof of forgeries, handwriting comparisons, and even individual typewriter identification.

Microanalysis of soil samples, paint chips, or fibers often can supply dramatic evidence against a defendant. Neutron activation analysis is a more recent method of identifying the elements present in evidentiary samples. It has been used to identify the place and even the date of manufacture of items. Courts are now recognizing the validity of neutron activation analysis.

Polygraph and voiceprint analysis are both widely used investigative tools. Courts still reject polygraph results, but are beginning to allow voiceprint evidence in court.

Narcoanalysis and hypnosis are medically approved diagnostic tools, but any courtroom use is narrowly circumscribed.

Proper care must always be taken in the collection and custody of both physical and scientific evidence. Evidence collected at the scene must be properly labeled and preserved. The chain of custody of any bodily sample used in a laboratory test must be carefully recorded and then testified to in court.

Any after-trial destruction of evidence should normally be done under court order.

chapter 14

Special Problems of Proof

A. CONSPIRACY AND ACTING IN CONCERT

(14.1) *CONSPIRACY IN GENERAL*

Conspiracy (an agreement among conspirators) is a common-law crime that has been codified in each jurisdiction. The agreement itself is punished, not the purpose of the conspiracy. To prove the offense, the prosecution must show an agreement by two or more people to perform an unlawful act or else to perform a lawful act by unlawful means. An example of the latter would include the operation of a legitimate business using illicit methods. Although it is not a necessary element of the common-law offense, statutory conspiracies also require proof of an overt act in furtherance of the conspiratorial purpose. This act need not be a crime, but it must further the unlawful aims of the conspirators.

Conspiracy laws are useful in prosecuting organized crime and corruption cases in which it would be difficult to prove a multitude of well-concealed crimes. Further, it is unnecessary to prove that each conspirator was an equal partner in the arrangement.

Because it is the act of agreement that constitutes the crime, not the overt acts in furtherance of the conspiracy, the conscious and continuous union of minds to engage in unlawful activity forms the bases of prosecution. No particular words or "forms of agreement" are necessary to form a conspiracy. Since it is unlikely, without testimony from a coconspirator, that the agreement can be reconstructed in court, the conspiracy may be proved by the conduct of its participants. It is not sufficient to show that a particular defendant had knowledge of the agreement; he must actually have agreed to be a part of the conspiracy, either by word or deed.

(14.2) *PARTIES TO A CONSPIRACY*

Not all conspirators are equal partners. Some might receive large profits while others suffer losses. It is unnecessary to allege or to prove that each coconspirator knew the identities of all other conspirators. Many defendants do not, in fact, know the size of the conspiracy or the number of participants. It is only necessary to prove that the particular defendant knew that he was joining an organization that had an unlawful purpose or used unlawful means to accomplish a lawful purpose.

One unusual aspect of conspiracy prosecutions is that a person who joins a conspiracy with full knowledge of its prior acts of misconduct becomes fully liable for such acts. For example, a person joins a narcotics conspiracy knowing that the organization has committed murder. When he is prosecuted for membership in the conspiracy, proof of the murder may be admitted in his trial. It must be remembered, however, that he will be tried for conspiracy, not murder. On the other hand, it is also possible to try a defendant for conspiracy to commit a substantive crime when he has been acquitted of the substantive crime itself. Once a conspirator severs his relationship with a group, he is no longer liable for future conspiratorial acts, even though he might have formed the illegal combine himself.

A party to a conspiracy need not be acquainted with the intimate details of the plan. It is not necessary for him to know the identities of the victims or even how many victims will be involved. Liability attaches to insignificant participation as well as to leadership roles. Punishment might differ, of course, but, again, it is the act of agreement and not its purposes that the law punishes.

(14.3) *KNOWLEDGE AND INTENT*

The prosecution must allege and prove that each conspirator knew that he was engaging in criminal activity. Even when it is unnecessary to show criminal knowledge in the prosecution of the substantive offense, knowledge is a necessary element of proof.

It is also necessary to prove that each defendant had criminal intent. The courts have held that if two persons are tried for conspiracy, and criminal intent can only be proved against one of them, he may use this as a defense, but the one whose intent was evident cannot. It may be necessary in some federal crimes to show an "antifederal" intent in addition to a "guilty mind," that is, an intent to violate a law that is federal in nature. A conspiracy may be prosecuted either in a federal court, state courts, or both.

(14.4) *ACTING IN CONCERT*

Two or more persons may act together for a criminal purpose and still not be coconspirators. A burglar may act in concert with a fence, a bet taker with a layoff operator, a policy wheel operator with a numbers printer, or a car thief with the owner of a paint and body shop. Such arrangements take on the character of a conspiracy only when there is a conscious agreement, knowledge, intent, and an overt act.

The distinction has given rise to the so-called Wharton rule, named after the famous author of a treatise on criminal law. It states: "If only a minimum number of parties logically necessary to commit the substantive offense are involved, conspiracy indictments will not lie." This is because no greater danger to the public is posed if the exact number of people necessary to commit the crime are involved. Thus, it would be improper to prosecute a "conspiracy" to commit adultery, incest, bigamy, sodomy, a simple bribery, or other substantive offenses requiring at least but not more than two people. When, however, two individuals agree to bribe a third, the minimum number of actors is exceeded, and prosecution would be proper.

It has been held that a person can conspire with a corporation, and each can be prosecuted. If, however, the corporate soul is the same mind as one of the conspirators, the corporate entity cannot be counted as another "person."

(14.5) *THE OVERT ACT REQUIREMENT*

In common law a conspiracy was indictable as soon as the unlawful agreement was formed. The statutory versions require proof of an overt act. Though the act is usually a crime, it may be a misdemeanor or even noncriminal behavior in furtherance of the conspiracy, such as the purchase of equipment. The act must occur after the agreement was entered into and before it was terminated. The statute of limitations runs from the time the act took place, since it is a necessary element of the offense. In most jurisdictions, however, continued overt acts prolong the statute of limitations.

(14.6) *PROBLEMS OF PROOF*

Unlike prosecutions for other crimes, at a conspiracy trial circumstantial evidence may be admitted with wide latitude. Inferential evidence may be needed, since the underlying agreement could be impossible to prove otherwise. It is possible for the words, deeds, books, and records of one conspirator to be admitted into evidence against the penal interests of all other conspirators. Some jurisdictions allow hearsay evidence against alleged conspirators. Finally, one conspirator may testify against the interests of all other conspirators, including those he has not met.

B. ACCOMPLICES

(14.7) *WHAT IS AN ACCOMPLICE?*

To understand the role the accomplice plays in the law of evidence, it is necessary to know how the law defines an accomplice. Courts differ on the definition. The term can be broadly defined as any person who participates in a crime whether as a principal, aider and abettor, or accessory before the fact. The more established rule is to treat as accomplices all persons who could be indicted or charged either as a principal or accessory for the same offense that the defendant is charged with.

The mere fact that a person was present or acquiesed in the commission of a crime is not sufficient to make him an accomplice. Knowledge that a crime is about to be committed or the failure to report a crime is also insufficient to make the person an accomplice.

Either the judge or the jury determines whether or not an individual is an accomplice. It need not be established beyond a reasonable doubt that a witness is an accomplice, but if the testimony of the individual raises a strong presumption to that effect, it has been considered sufficient to justify the application of the special rules of accomplice testimony.

Whether a person is an accomplice also depends on his legal capacity to commit a crime. A child or adult who is not of sound mind (non compos mentis) cannot be either a principal or an accessory to a crime.

(14.8) *CREDIBILITY*

The testimony of an accomplice has questionable reliability. First, he was a participant in the crime itself. As such, he may have an interest in the outcome, hope of leniency, or even be hostile. Historically, accomplice testimony has always been received with caution. Judges normally instruct juries about this, and the jury must decide whether or not the accomplice is to be believed.

At common law there could not be a conviction based only on the uncorroborated testimony of an accomplice. Many states follow this same rule. Other jurisdictions do not follow the accomplice corroboration rule, and conviction can stand solely on the accomplice's word. Jurisdictions that do follow the corroboration rule still require it even if the accomplice himself is acquitted.

Where accomplice testimony must be corroborated, it is not necessary that every fact be confirmed. The prosecution must develop enough outside proof to establish a connection between the accused and the crime that indirectly corroborates the accomplice's testimony. The testimony of one accomplice, however, cannot be used to corroborate the testimony of another.

When an accomplice confesses and is willing to testify against the accused, the defense cannot prevent this and can only cross-examine him. As pointed out (sec.11.3 [c]), the accomplice's actual *confession* cannot be used against the accused, but his direct trial testimony can. The prosecution will often give one accomplice immunity in order to convict another defendant, or they may agree to a light sentence for the accomplice. There is nothing illegal about this so long as the jury is told.

If the accomplice himself has been convicted, he can then be compelled by subpoena to testify against the other parties accused. Having once been convicted, the accomplice has lost his right against self-incrimination.

An accomplice is not the same as an accessory. An accessory before the fact is one who assists in some way before the crime is committed. Many states have abolished the difference, and accessories before the fact are charged the same as principals. Accessories after the fact are those who aid the felon after the crime is completed. An accessory after the fact is seen as committing a separate offense from that committed by the principal.

C. CORROBORATION

(14.9) *CORROBORATING EVIDENCE*

Corroborating evidence supplements and supports previously offered evidence. It must, however, come from a separate source. On some occasions it is offered to support a witness who has been conclusively impeached. If the witness has not been contradicted, evidence to corroborate his story would be kept out as being irrelevant.

Similarly, prior consistent statements of a witness cannot be used to corroborate his present testimony. Exceptions to this may be past identifications or when the witness is attacked on the grounds he has recently fabricated his story or has a self-interest in the outcome. In this type of situation, prior consistent statements may be used as corroboration.

Sex crimes may be treated differently in some jurisdictions. At common law, a rape or other sex crime conviction could be had simply on the testimony of the victim. Many states have restricted this by court decision or statute and require corroboration of the victim's story if there is a sex offense charged. Where corroboration is required in sex cases, the supporting evidence need not go to each of the elements of the crime but only to the sex act itself.

Corroborating evidence is also required to support a confession. If a confession is all the state has, there can be no conviction. Mentally ill people, for example, have been known to confess to crimes that were never committed. So before the prosecution can introduce a confession in evidence, they must produce independent proof to support the facts—enough so that a jury can at least infer the truth of the confession.

Evidence corroborating a confession does not have to prove the entire crime; it must only be enough to support the confession. For example, a statement by the accused that he murdered his wife is not enough to convict him. Discovery of her body would supply enough corroboration to support the truth of the confession and make a conviction valid.

D. GRAND JURIES AND SUPPRESSION HEARINGS

(14.10) *GRAND JURIES*

The grand jury is part of our legal inheritance from England. The term "grand jury" comes about because it is composed of a larger number of people than the traditional jury of twelve persons. It is used today as an accusatory body, charging suspects with serious crimes.

Some states use grand juries sparingly, filing written prosecutor's informations instead. Others use grand jury indictments as a pretrial requisite in all felony cases.

The grand jury ordinarily hears only evidence presented by the prosecution, and generally only enough proof is presented to justify an indictment. The grand jury, like a trial court, must base its finding on legal proof. With minor exceptions, it must follow the same rules of evidence as every other court. There is an increasing trend to relax strict evidence rules in grand jury proceedings, and many states allow the use of hearsay in the form of official laboratory reports and the like.

The grand jury occasionally hears tainted evidence, such as a confession that is subsequently ruled to be invalid or evidence from a search and seizure that is later suppressed. The fact that a grand jury has heard illegal evidence will not in and of itself invalidate the indictment. If, after excluding the illegal evidence, the court finds that the grand jury heard sufficient legal proof to sustain the charge, the indictment will stand (*U.S.* v. *Calandra*, 94 S. Ct. 613 [1974]).

(14.11) *SUPPRESSION HEARINGS*

Pretrial suppression hearings are generally held whenever there is a possibility of invoking the exclusionary rule. Here, the defendant may seek to suppress a confession that he claims is involuntary or was taken in violation of *Miranda*. Very commonly, evidence seized from an alleged illegal search and seizure is sought to be eliminated in the same way.

The legality of evidence is often contested on the following grounds: (1) defective search warrants, (2) searches beyond the scope of warrants, (3) improper execution of search warrants, (4) warrantless entrance of premises, (5) extension of arrest searches, (6) no probable cause, and (7) defective consent.

Intangible evidence will also be suppressed if it has been seized illegally. Unauthorized wiretaps, illegal electronic surveillances, or conversations overheard through trespass are prime examples.

Physical evidence of all kinds is subject to suppression motion. This can include such things as fingerprints, blood or urine samples, fingernail scrapings, or hair samples claimed to have been taken illegally. Eyewitness identification from suggestive lineups or otherwise done unconstitutionally can be excluded.

Any derivative evidence coming as a result of a prior improper act is also tainted and is inadmissible under the "Poisoned Tree Doctrine." For example, if a confession is taken without complying with *Miranda*, and the police are able to locate a murder weapon because of what was told them in the confession, the weapon itself can be surpressed.

The defendant may or may not testify at the suppression hearing. He can testify there and still not take the stand at his actual trial. His testimony at the suppression hearing cannot be used directly against him at the trial stage (*Simmons* v. *U.S.*, 390 U.S. 377 [1968]). This does not mean that the defendant can perjure himself at the time of trial. Also, it may be possible to use his suppression hearing testimony to impeach his testimony at the trial should there be a material contradiction between the two.

Suppression hearings are heard by a judge without a jury, and they are less formal and more flexible than jury trials. Hearsay and otherwise inadmissible evidence may be introduced to demonstrate the existence of probable cause. This takes three common forms: (1) statements from confidential informants, (2) surveillance reports, and (3) defendant's arrest records.

Each state is free to set its own rules on the conduct of suppression hearings. Although the state cannot appeal an acquittal (this would be double jeopardy), it can appeal from an adverse ruling granting suppression of evidence. The defendant has not been "put in jeopardy" at this pretrial stage, and if a state were not able to appeal from suppression hearings, prosecutions could be permanently lost because of erroneous pretrial suppression rulings.

(14.12) *SUMMARY*

A conspiracy is a separate offense, which is the conscious agreement of two or more persons to commit one or more offenses, coupled with an overt act in furtherance of the aims of the conspiracy. Equal participation in the scheme or the equal sharing of benefits is not necessary. A coconspirator may not even know the identity of all other participants. Often there are several conspiracies in simultaneous existence, and only a few of the participants may be active in multiple conspiracies.

Accomplices may be either active or passive participants in a crime. An accomplice does not need to be present during the commission of the offense; knowledge and assent are sufficient. Prosecutors frequently offer accomplices immunity from prosecution in return for their testimony against the principal offender.

Corroborating evidence supplements and supports previously offered evidence. Proof of uncontradicted testimony may be rejected as cumulative. On the other hand, certain kinds of testimony require corroboration. A confession is not admissible against the accused unless the crime itself is proved. Sexual offenses, by judicial decision and often by statute, require corroboration.

The grand jury originated in England. It is made up of twelve to twenty-three persons who inquire into serious offenses and either indict accused people or dismiss the charges against them. Some jurisdictions use grand juries sparingly, substituting prosecutor's informations instead of grand jury indictments. Only the state's proof is heard before grand juries. Evidence is still required to be in legal form, but there is some relaxation of evidentiary rule.

Suppression hearings are usually pretrial proceedings seeking to suppress illegal evidence, improper confessions, or invalid identifications. Such matters as defective search warrants, illegal arrests, lack of *Miranda* warnings, and the like can be inquired into.

APPENDIX

(© Jack Spratt, Picture Group.)

FINAL EXAM

Rules of Evidence for United States Courts and Magistrates

Article I. General Provisions

Rule 101. Scope

These rules govern proceedings in the courts of the United States and before United States magistrates, to the extent and with the exceptions stated in Rule 1101.

Rule 102. Purpose and Construction

These rules shall be construed to secure fairness in administration, elimination of unjustifiable expense and delay, and promotion of growth and development of the law of evidence to the end that the truth may be ascertained and proceedings justly determined.

Rule 103. Rulings on Evidence

(a) Effect of erroneous ruling. Error may not be predicated upon a ruling which admits or excludes evidence unless a substantial right of the party is affected, and

(1) Objection. In case the ruling is one admitting evidence a timely objection or motion to strike appears of record, stating the specific ground of objection, if the specific ground was not apparent from the context; or

(2) Offer of proof. In case the ruling is one excluding evidence, the substance of the evidence was made known to the judge by offer or was apparent from the context within which questions were asked.

(b) Record of offer and ruling. The court may add any other or further statement which shows the character of the evidence, the form in which it was offered, the objection made, and the ruling thereon. It may direct the making of an offer in question and answer form.

(c) Hearing of jury. In jury cases, proceedings shall be conducted, to the extent practicable, so as to prevent inadmissible evidence from being suggested to the jury by any means, such as making statements or offers of proof or asking questions in the hearing of the jury.

(d) Plain error. Nothing in this rule precludes taking notice of plain errors affecting substantial rights although they were not brought to the attention of the court.

Rule 104. Preliminary Questions

(a) Questions of admissibility generally. Preliminary questions concerning the qualification of a person to be a witness, the existence of a privilege, or the admissiblity of evidence shall be determined by the court, subject to the provisions of subdivision (b). In making its determination it is not bound by the rules of evidence except those with respect to privileges.

(b) Relevancy conditioned on fact. When the relevancy of evidence depends upon the fulfillment of a condition of fact, the judge shall admit it upon, or subject to the introduction of evidence sufficient to support a finding of the fulfillment of the condition.

(c) Hearing of jury. Hearings on the admissibility of confessions shall in all cases be conducted out of the hearing of the jury. Hearings on other preliminary matters shall be so conducted when the interest of justice require or, when an accused is a witness, if he so requests.

(d) Testimony by accused. The accused does not, by testifying upon a preliminary matter, subject himself to cross-examination as to other issues in the case.

(e) Weight and credibility. This rule does not limit the right of a party to introduce before the jury evidence relevant to weight or credibility.

Rule 105. Limited Admissibility

When evidence which is admissible as to one party or for one purpose but not admissible as to another party or for another purpose is admitted, the court, upon request, shall restrict the evidence to its proper scope and instruct the jury accordingly.

Rule 106. Remainder of or Related Writings or Recorded Statements

When a writing or recorded statement or part thereof is introduced by a party, an adverse party may require him at that time to introduce any other part or any other writing or recorded statement which ought in fairness to be considered contemporaneously with it.

Article II. Judicial Notice

Rule 201. Judicial Notice of Adjudicative Facts

(a) Scope of rule. This rule governs only judicial notice of adjudicative facts.

(b) Kinds of facts. A judicially noticed fact must be one not subject to reasonable dispute in that it is either (1) generally known within the territorial jurisdiction of the trial court or (2) capable of accurate and ready determination by resort to sources whose accuracy cannot reasonably be questioned.

(c) When discretionary. A court may take judicial notice, whether requested or not.

(d) When mandatory. A court shall take judicial notice if requested by a party and supplied with the necessary information.

(e) Opportunity to be heard. A party is entitled upon timely request to an opportunity to be heard as to the propriety of taking judicial notice and the tenor of the matter noticed. In the absence of prior notification, the request may be made after judicial notice has been taken.

(f) Time of taking notice. Judicial notice may be taken at any stage of the proceeding.

(g) Instructing jury. In a civil action or proceeding, the court shall instruct the jury to accept as conclusive any fact judicially noticed. In a criminal case, the court shall instruct the jury that it may, but is not required to, accept as conclusive any fact judicially noticed.

Article IV. Relevancy and Its Limits

Rule 401. Definition of "Relevant Evidence"

"Relevant evidence" means evidence having any tendency to make the existence of any fact that is of consequence to the determination of the action more probable or less probable than it would be without the evidence.

Rule 402. Relevant Evidence Generally Admissible; Irrelevant Evidence Inadmissible

All relevant evidence is admissible, except as otherwise provided by the Constitution of the United States, by Act of Congress, by these rules, or by other rules prescribed by the Supreme Court pursuant to statutory authority. Evidence which is not relevant is not admissible.

Rule 403. Exclusion of Relevant Evidence on Grounds of Prejudice, Confusion, or Waste of Time

Although relevant, evidence may be excluded if its probative value is substantially outweighed by the danger of unfair prejudice, confusion of the issues, or misleading the jury, or by considerations of undue delay, waste of time, or needless presentation of cumulative evidence.

Rule 404. Character Evidence Not Admissible to Prove Conduct; Exceptions; Other Crimes

(a) Character evidence generally. Evidence of a person's character or a trait of his character is not admissible for the purpose of proving that he acted in conformity therewith on a particular occasion, except:

(1) Character of accused. Evidence of a pertinent trait of his character offered by an accused, or by the prosecution to rebut the same;

(2) Character of victim. Evidence of a pertinent trait of character of the victim of the crime offered by an accused, or by the prosecution to rebut the same, or evidence of a character trait of peacefulness of the victim offered by the prosecution in a homicide case to rebut evidence that the victim was the first aggressor;

(3) Character of witness. Evidence of the character of a witness, as provided in Rules 607, 608, and 609.

(b) Other crimes, wrongs, or acts. Evidence of other crimes, wrongs, or acts is not admissible to prove the character of a person in order to show that he acted in conformity therewith. It may, however, be admissible for other purposes, such as proof of motive, opportunity, intent, preparation, plan, knowledge, identity, or absence of mistake or accident.

Rule 405. Methods of Proving Character

(a) Reputation or opinion. In all cases in which evidence of character or a trait of character of a person is admissible, proof may be made by testimony as to reputation or by testimony in the form of an opinion.

On cross-examination, inquiry is allowable into relevant specific instances of conduct.

(b) Specific instances of conduct. In cases in which character or a trait of character of a person is an essential element of a charge, claim, or defense, proof may also be made of specific instances of his conduct.

Rule 406. Habit; Routine Practice

Evidence of the habit of a person or of the routine practice of an organization, whether corroborated or not and regardless of the presence of eyewitnesses, is relevant to prove that the conduct of the person or organization on a particular occasion was in conformity with the habit or routine practice.

Rule 407. Subsequent Remedial Measures

When, after an event, measures are taken which if taken previously, would have made the event less likely to occur, evidence of the subsequent measures is not admissible to prove negligence or culpable conduct in connection with the event. This rule does not require the exclusion of evidence of subsequent measures when offered for another purpose, such as proving ownership, control, or feasibility of precautionary measures, if controverted, or impeachment.

Rule 410. Offer to Plead Guilty; Nolo Contendere; Withdrawn Plea of Guilty

Except as otherwise provided by Act of Congress, evidence of a plea of guilty, later withdrawn, or a plea of nolo contendere, or of an offer to plead guilty or nolo contendere to the crime charged or any other crime, or of statments made in connection with any of the foregoing pleas or offers, is not admissible in any civil or criminal action, case, or proceeding against the person who made the plea or offer. This rule shall not apply to the introduction of voluntary and reliable statements made in court on the record in connection with any of the foregoing pleas or offers where offered for impeachment purposes or in a subsequent prosecution of the declarant for perjury or false statement.

This rule shall not take effect until August 1, 1976, and shall be superseded by any amendment to the Federal Rules of Criminal Procedure which is inconsistent with this rule, and which takes effect after the date of the enactment of the Act establishing these Federal Rules of Evidence.

Proposed Amendment

The amendment of this rule transmitted by the United States Supreme Court to the Congress on Apr. 30, 1979 to become effective Aug. 1, 1979, was postponed by Pub.L. 95–42, July 31, 1979, 93 Stat. 326, until December 1, 1980 or until and then only to the extent approved by Act of Congress, whichever is earlier.

As thus amended this rule will read as follows:

Except as otherwise provided in this rule, evidence of the following is not, in any civil or criminal proceeding, admissible against the defendant who made the plea or was a participant in the plea discussions:

(1) a plea of guilty which was later withdrawn;

(2) a plea of nolo contendere;

(3) any statement made in the course of any proceedings under Rule 11 of the Federal Rules of Criminal Procedure or comparable state procedure regarding either of the foregoing pleas; or

(4) any statement made in the course of plea discussions with an attorney for the prosecuting authority which do not result in a plea of guilty or which result in a plea of guilty later withdrawn.

However, such a statement is admissible (i) in any proceeding wherein another statement made in the course of the same plea or plea discussions has been introduced and the statement ought in fairness be considered contemporaneously with it, or (ii) in a criminal proceeding for perjury or false statement if the statement was made by the defendant under oath, on the record and in the presence of counsel.

Rule 412. Rape Cases; Relevance of Victim's Past Behavior

(a) Notwithstanding any other provision of law, in a criminal case in which a person is accused of rape or of assault with intent to commit rape, reputation or opinion evidence of the past sexual behavior of an alleged victim of such rape or assault is not admissible.

(b) Notwithstanding any other provision of law, in a criminal case in which a person is accused of rape or of assault with intent to commit rape, evidence of a victim's past sexual behavior other than reputation or opinion evidence is also not admissible, unless such evidence other than reputation or opinion evidence is—

(1) admitted in accordance with subdivisions (c)(1) and (c)(2) and is constitutionally required to be admitted; or

(2) admitted in accordance with subdivision (c) and is evidence of—

(A) past sexual behavior with persons other than the accused, offered by the accused upon the issue of whether the accused was or was not, with respect to the alleged victim, the source of semen or injury; or

(B) past sexual behavior with the accused and is offered by the accused upon the issue of whether the alleged victim consented to the sexual behavior with respect to which rape or assault is alleged.

(c)(1) If the person accused of committing rape or assault with intent to commit rape intends to offer under subdivision (b) evidence of specific instances of the alleged victim's past sexual behavior, the accused shall make a written motion to offer such evidence not later than fifteen days before the date on which the trial in which such evidence is to be offered is scheduled to begin, except that the court may allow the motion to be made at a later date, including during trial, if the court determines either that the evidence is newly discovered and could not have been obtained earlier through the exercise of due diligence or that the issue to which such evidence relates has newly arisen in the case. Any motion made under this paragraph shall be served on all other parties and on the alleged victim.

(2) The motion described in paragraph (1) shall be accompanied by a written offer of proof. If the court determines that the offer of proof contains evidence described in subdivision (b), the court shall order a hearing in chambers to determine if such evidence is admissible. At such hearing the parties may call witnesses, including the alleged victim, and offer relevant evidence. Notwithstanding subdivision (b) of rule 104, if the relevancy of the evidence which the accused seeks to offer in the trial depends upon the fulfillment of a condition of fact, the court, at the hearing in chambers or at a subsequent hearing in chambers scheduled for such purpose, shall accept evidence on the issue of whether such condition of fact is fulfilled and shall determine such issue.

(3) If the court determines on the basis of the hearing described in paragraph (2) that the evidence which the accused seeks to offer is relevant and that the probative value of such evidence outweighs the danger of unfair prejudice, such evidence shall be admissible in the trial to the extent an order made by the court specifies evidence which may be offered and areas with respect to which the alleged victim may be examined or cross-examined.

(d) For purposes of this rule, the term "past sexual behavior" means sexual behavior other than the sexual behavior with respect to which rape or assault with intent to commit rape is alleged.

Added Pub.L. 95-540, § 2(a), Oct. 28, 1978, 92 Stat. 2046.

Article V. Privileges

Rule 501. General Rule

Except as otherwise required by the Constitution of the United States or provided by Act of Congress or in rules prescribed by the Supreme Court pursuant to statutory authority, the privilege of a witness, person, government, State, or political subdivision thereof shall be governed by the principles of the common law as they may be interpreted by the courts of the United States in the light of reason and experience. However, in civil actions and proceedings, with respect to an element of a claim or defense as to which State law supplies the rule of decision, the privilege of a witness, person, government, State, or political subdivision thereof shall be determined in accordance with State law.

Article VI. Witnesses

Rule 601. General Rule of Competency

Every person is competent to be a witness except as otherwise provided in these rules. However, in civil actions and proceedings, with respect to an element of a claim or defense as to which State law supplies the rule of decision, the competency of a witness shall be determined in accordance with State law.

Rule 602. Lack of Personal Knowledge

A witness may not testify to a matter unless evidence is introduced sufficient to support a finding that he has personal knowledge of the matter. Evidence to prove personal knowledge may, but need not, consist of the testimony of the witness himself. This rule is subject to the provisions of Rule 703, relating to opinion testimony by expert witnesses.

Rule 603. Oath or Affirmation

Before testifying, every witness shall be required to declare that he will testify truthfully, by oath or affirmation administered in a form calculated to awaken his conscience and impress his mind with his duty to do so.

Rule 604. Interpreters

An interpreter is subject to the provisions of these rules relating to qualification as an expert and the administration of an oath or affirmation that he will make a true translation.

Rule 605. Competency of Judge as Witness

The judge presiding at the trial may not testify in that trial as a witness. No objection need be made in order to preserve the point.

Rule 606. Competency of Juror as Witness

(a) At the trial. A member of the jury may not testify as a witness before that jury in the trial of the case in which he is sitting as a juror. If he is called so to testify, the opposing party shall be afforded an opportunity to object out of the presence of the jury.

(b) Inquiry into validity of verdict or indictment. Upon an inquiry into the validity of a verdict or indictment, a juror may not testify as to any matter or statement occurring during the course of the jury's deliberations or to the effect of anything upon his or any other juror's mind or emotions as influencing him to assent to or dissent from the verdict or indictment or concerning his mental processes in connection therewith, except that a juror may testify on the question whether extraneous prejudicial information was improperly brought to the jury's attention or whether any outside influence was improperly brought to bear upon any juror. Nor may his affidavit or evidence of any statement by him concerning a matter about what he would be precluded from testifying be received for these purposes.

Rule 607. Who May Impeach

The credibility of a witness may be attacked by any party, including the party calling him.

Rule 608. Evidence of Character and Conduct Witness

(a) Opinion and reputation evidence of character. The credibility of a witness may be attacked or supported by evidence in the form of opinion or reputation, but subject to these limitations: (1) the evidence may refer only to character for truthfulness or untruthfulness, and (2) evidence of truthful character is admissible only after the character of the witness for truthfulness has been attacked by opinion or reputation evidence or otherwise.

(b) Specific instances of conduct. Specific instances of the conduct of a witness, for the purpose of attacking or supporting his credibility, other than conviction of crime as provided in Rule 609, may not be proved by

extrinsic evidence. They may, however, in the discretion of the court, if probative of truthfulness or untruthfulness, be inquired into on cross-examination of the witness (1) concerning the character for truthfulness or untruthfulness of another witness as to which character the witness being cross-examined has testified.

The giving of testimony, whether by an accused or by any other witness, does not operate as a waiver of his privilege against self-incrimination when examined with respect to matters which relate only to credibility.

Rule 609. Impeachment by Evidence of Conviction of Crime

(a) General rule. For the purpose of attacking the credibility of a witness, evidence that he has been convicted of a crime shall be admitted if elicited from him or established by public record during cross-examination but only if the crime (1) was punishable by death or imprisonment in excess of one year under the law under which he was convicted, and the court determines that the probative value of admitting this evidence outweighs its prejudicial effect to the defendant, or (2) involved dishonesty or false statement, regardless of the punishment.

(b) Time limit. Evidence of a conviction under this rule is not admissible if a period of more than ten years has elapsed since the date of the conviction or of the release of the witness from the confinement imposed for that conviction, whichever is the later date, unless the court determines, in the interests of justice, that the probative value of the conviction supported by specific facts and circumstances substantially outweighs its prejudicial effect. However, evidence of a conviction more than 10 years old as calculated herein, is not admissible unless the proponent gives to the adverse party sufficient advance written notice of intent to use such evidence to provide the adverse party with a fair opportunity to contest the use of such evidence.

(c) Effect of pardon, annulment, or certificate of rehabilitation. Evidence of a conviction is not admissible under this rule if (1) the conviction has been the subject of a pardon, annulment, certificate of rehabilitation, or other equivalent procedure based on a finding of the rehabilitation of the person convicted, and that person has not been convicted of a subsequent crime which was punishable by death or imprisonment in excess of one year, or (2) the conviction has been the subject of a pardon, annulment, or other equivalent procedure based on a finding of innocence.

(d) Juvenile adjudications. Evidence of juvenile adjudications is gen-

erally not admissible under this rule. The court may, however, in a criminal case allow evidence of a juvenile adjudication of a witness other than the accused if conviction of the offense would be admissible to attack the credibility of an adult and the court is satisfied that admission in evidence is necessary for a fair determination of the issue of guilt or innocence.

(e) Pendency of appeal. The pendency of an appeal therefrom does not render evidence of a conviction inadmissible. Evidence of the pendency of an appeal is admissible.

Rule 610. Religious Beliefs or Opinions

Evidence of the beliefs or opinions of a witness on matters of religion is not admissible for the purpose of showing that by reason of their nature his credibility is impaired or enhanced.

Rule 611. Mode and Order of Interrogation and Presentation

(a) Control by court. The court shall exercise reasonable control over the mode and order of interrogating witnesses and presenting evidence so as to (1) make the interrogation and presentation effective for the ascertainment of the truth, (2) avoid needless consumption of time, and (3) protect witnesses from harassment or undue embarrassment.

(b) Scope of cross-examination. Cross-examination should be limited to the subject matter of the direct examination and matters affecting the credibility of the witness. The court may, in the exercise of discretion, permit inquiry into additional matters as if on direct examination.

(c) Leading questions. Leading questions should not be used on the direct examination of a witness except as may be necessary to develop his testimony. Ordinarily leading questions should be permitted on cross-examination. When a party calls a hostile witness, an adverse party, or a witness identified with an adverse party, interrogation may be by leading questions.

Rule 612. Writing Used to Refresh Memory

Except as otherwise provided in criminal proceedings by section 3500 of title 18, United States Code, if a witness uses a writing to refresh his memory for the purpose of testifying, either—

(1) while testifying, or

(2) before testifying, if the court in its discretion determines it is necessary in the interests of justice,

an adverse party is entitled to have the writing produced at the hearing, to inspect it, to cross-examine the witness thereon, and to introduce in evidence those portions which relate to the testimony of the witness. If it is claimed that the writing contains matters not related to the subject matter of the testimony the court shall examine the writing in camera, excise any portions not so related, and order delivery of the remainder to the party entitled thereto. Any portion withheld over objections shall be preserved and made available to the appellate court in the event of an appeal. If a writing is not produced or delivered pursuant to order under this rule, the court shall make any order justice requires, except that in criminal cases when the prosecution elects not to comply, the order shall be one striking the testimony or, if the court in its discretion determines that the interests of justice so require, declaring a mistrial.

Rule 613. Prior Statements of Witnesses

(a) Examining witness concerning prior statement. In examining a witness concerning a prior statement made by him, whether written or not, the statement need not be shown nor its contents disclosed to him at that time, but on request the same shall be shown or disclosed to opposing counsel.

(b) Extrinsic evidence of prior inconsistent statement of witness. Extrinsic evidence of a prior inconsistent statement by a witness is not admissible unless the witness is afforded an opportunity to explain or deny the same and the opposite party is afforded an opportunity to interrogate him thereon, or the interests of justice otherwise require. This provision does not apply to admissions of a party-opponent as defined in Rule 801 (d)(2).

Rule 614. Calling and Interrogation of Witnesses by Court

(a) Calling by court. The court may, on its own motion or at the suggestion of a party, call witnesses, and all parties are entitled to cross-examine witnesses thus called.

(b) Interrogation by court. The court may interrogate witnesses, whether called by itself or by a party.

(c) Objections. Objections to the calling of witnesses by the court or to interrogation by it may be made at the time or at the next available opportunity when the jury is not present.

Rule 615. Exclusion of Witnesses

At the request of a party the court shall order witnesses excluded so that they cannot hear the testimony of other witnesses, and it may make the order of its own motion. This rule does not authorize exclusion of (1) a party who is a natural person, or (2) an officer or employee of a party which is not a natural person designated as its representative by its attorney, or (3) a person whose presence is shown by a party to be essential to the presentation of his cause.

Article VII. Opinions and Expert Testimony

Rule 701. Opinion Testimony by Lay Witnesses

If the witness is not testifying as an expert, his testimony in the form of opinions or inferences is limited to those opinions or inferences which are (a) rationally based on the perception of the witness and (b) helpful to a clear understanding of his testimony or the determination of a fact in issue.

Rule 702. Testimony by Experts

If scientific, technical, or other specialized knowledge will assist the trier of fact to understand the evidence or to determine a fact in issue, a witness qualified as an expert by knowledge, skill, experience, training, or education, may testify thereto in the form of an opinion or otherwise.

Rule 703. Bases of Opinion Testimony by Experts

The facts or data in the particular case upon which an expert bases an opinion or inference may be those perceived by or made known to him at or before the hearing. If of a type reasonably relied upon by experts in the particular field in forming opinions or inferences upon the subject, the facts or data need not be admissible in evidence.

Rule 704. Opinion on Ultimate Issue

Testimony in the form of an opinion or inference otherwise admissible is not objectionable because it embraces an ultimate issue to be decided by the trier of fact.

Rule 705. Disclosure of Facts or Data Underlying Expert Opinion

The expert may testify in terms of opinion or inference and give his reasons therefor without prior disclosure of the underlying facts or data, unless the judge requires otherwise. The expert may in any event be required to disclose the underlying facts or data on cross-examination.

Rule 706. Court Appointed Experts

(a) Appointment. The court may on its own motion or on the motion of any party enter an order to show cause why expert witnesses should not be appointed, and may request the parties to submit nominations. The court may appoint any expert witnesses agreed upon by the parties, and may appoint witnesses of its own selection. An expert witness shall not be appointed by the court unless he consents to act. A witness so appointed shall be informed of his duties by the court in writing, a copy of which shall be filed with the clerk, or at a conference in which the parties shall have opportunity to participate. A witness so appointed shall advise the parties of his findings, if any; his deposition may be taken by any party; and he may be called to testify by the court or any party. He shall be subject to cross-examination by each party, including a party calling him as a witness.

(b) Compensation. Expert witnesses so appointed are entitled to reasonable compensation in whatever sum the court may allow. The compensation thus fixed is payable from funds which may be provided by law in criminal cases and civil actions and proceedings involving just compensation under the Fifth Amendment. In other civil actions and proceedings the compensation shall be paid by the parties in such proportion and at such time as the court directs, and thereafter charged in like manner as other costs.

(c) Disclosure of appointment. In the exercise of its discretion, the court may authorize disclosure to the jury of the fact that the court appointed the expert witness.

(d) Parties' experts of own selection. Nothing in this rule limits the parties in calling expert witnesses of their own selection.

Article VIII. Hearsay

Rule 801. Definitions

The following definitions apply under this Article:

(a) Statement. A "statement" is (1) an oral or written assertion or (2) nonverbal conduct of a person, if it is intended by him as an assertion.

(b) Declarant. A "declarant" is a person who makes a statement.

(c) Hearsay. "Hearsay" is a statement, other than one made by the declarant while testifying at the trial or hearing, offered in evidence to prove the truth of the matter asserted.

(d) Statements which are not hearsay. A statement is not hearsay if—

(1) Prior statement by witness. The declarant testifies at the trial or hearing and is subject to cross-examination concerning the statement, and the statement is (A) inconsistent with his testimony, and was given under oath subject to the penalty of perjury at a trial, hearing, or other proceeding, or in a deposition, or (B) consistent with his testimony and is offered to rebut an express or implied charge against him of recent fabrication or improper influence or motive, or

(2) Admission by party-opponent. The statement is offered against a party and is (A) his own statement, in either his individual or a representative capacity or (B) a statement of which he has manifested his adoption or belief in its truth, or (C) a statement by a person authorized by him to make a statement concerning the subject, or (D) a statement by his agent or servant concerning a matter within the scope of his agency or employment, made during the existence of the relationship, or (E) a statement by a co-conspirator of a party during the course and in furtherance of the conspiracy.

Rule 802. Hearsay Rule

Hearsay is not admissible except as provided by these rules or by other rules prescribed by the Supreme Court pursuant to statutory authority or by Act of Congress.

Rule 803. Hearsay Exceptions: Availability of Declarant Immaterial

The following are not excluded by the hearsay rule, even though the declarant is available as a witness:

(1) Present sense impression. A statement describing or explaining an event or condition made while the declarant was perceiving the event or condition, or immediately thereafter.

(2) Excited utterance. A statement relating to a startling event or condition made while the declarant was under the stress of excitement caused by the event or condition.

(3) Then existing mental, emotional, or physical condition. A statement of the declarant's then existing state of mind, emotion, sensation, or physical condition (such as intent, plan, motive, design, mental feeling, pain, and bodily health), but not including a statement of memory or belief to prove the fact remembered or believed unless it relates to the execution, revocation, identification, or terms of declarant's will.

(4) Statements for purposes of medical diagnosis or treatment. Statements made for purposes of medical diagnosis or treatment and describing medical history, or past or present symptoms, pain, or sensations, or the

inception or general character of the cause or external source thereof insofar as reasonable pertinent to diagnosis or treatment.

(5) Recorded recollection. A memorandum or record concerning a matter about which a witness once had knowledge but now has insufficient recollection to enable him to testify fully and accurately, shown to have been made or adopted by the witness when the mater was fresh in his memory and to reflect that knowledge correctly. If admitted, the memorandum or record may be read into evidence but may not itself be received as an exhibit unless offered by an adverse party.

(6) Records of regularly conducted activity. A memorandum, report, record, or data compilation, in any form, of acts, events, conditions, opinions, or diagnoses, made at or near the time by, or from information transmitted by, a person with knowledge, if kept in the course of a regularly conducted business activity, and if it was the regular practice of that business activity to make the memorandum, report, record, or data compilation, all as shown by the testimony of the custodian or other qualified witness, unless the source of information or the method or circumstances of preparation indicate lack of trustworthiness. The term "business" as used in this paragraph includes business, institution, association, profession, occupation, and calling of every kind, whether or not conducted for profit.

(7) Absence of entry in records kept in accordance with the provisions of paragraph (6). Evidence that a matter is not included in the memoranda, reports, records, or data compilations, in any form, kept in accordance with the provisions of paragraph (6), to prove the nonoccurrence or nonexistence of the matter, if the matter was of a kind of which a memorandum, report, record, or data compilation was regularly made and preserved, unless the sources of information or other circumstances indicate lack of trustworthiness.

(8) Public records and reports. Records, reports, statements, or data compilations, in any form, of public officers or agencies, setting forth (A) the activities of the office or agency, or (B) matters observed pursuant to duty imposed by law as to which matters there was a duty to report, excluding, however, in criminal cases matters observed by police officers and other law enforcement personnel, or (C) in civil actions and proceedings and against the Government in criminal cases, factual findings resulting from an investigation made pursuant to authority granted by law, unless the sources of information or other circumstances indicate lack of trustworthiness.

(9) Records of vital statistics. Records or data compilations, in any form, of births, fetal deaths, deaths, or marriages, if the report thereof was made to a public office pursuant to requirements of law.

(10) Absence of public record or entry. To prove the absence of a record, report, statement, or data compilation, in any form, or the nonoccurrence or nonexistence of a matter of which a record, report, statement, or data compilation, in any form, was regularly made and preserved by a public office or agency, evidence in the form of a certification in accordance with Rule 902, or testimony, that diligent search failed to disclose the record, report, statement, or data compilation, or entry.

(11) Records of religious organizations. Statements of births, marriages, divorces, deaths, legitimacy, ancestry, relationship by blood or marriage, or other similar facts of personal or family history, contained in a regularly kept record of a religious organization.

(12) Marriage, baptismal, and similar certificates. Statements of fact contained in a certificate that the maker performed a marriage or other ceremony or administered a sacrament, made by a clergyman, public official, or other person authorized by the rules or practices of a religious organization or by law to perform the act certified, and purporting to have been issued at the time of the act or within a reasonable time thereafter.

(13) Family records. Statements of fact concerning personal or family history contained in family Bibles, genealogies, charts, engravings on rings, inscription on family portraits, engravings on urns, crypts, or tombstones, or the like.

(14) Records of documents affecting an interest in property. The record of a document purporting to establish or affect an interest in property, as proof of the content of the original recorded document and its execution and delivery by each person by whom it purports to have been executed, if the record is a record of a public office and an applicable statute authorized the recording of documents of that kind in that office.

(15) Statements in documents affecting an interest in property. A statement contained in a document purporting to establish or affect an interest in property if the matter stated was relevant to the purpose of the document, unless dealings with the property since the document was made have been inconsistent with the truth of the statement or the purport of the document.

(16) Statements in ancient documents. Statements in a document in existence 20 years or more whose authenticity is established.

(17) Market reports, commercial publications. Market quotations, tabulations, lists, directories, or other published compilations, generally used and relied upon by the public or by persons in particular occupations.

(18) Learned treatises. To the extent called to the attention of an expert witness upon cross-examination or relied upon by him in direct examination, statements contained in published treatises, periodicals, or pamphlets on a subject of history, medicine, or other science or art, established as a reliable authority by the testimony or admission of the witness or by other expert testimony or by judicial notice. If admitted, the statements may be read into evidence but may not be received as exhibits.

(19) Reputation concerning personal or family history. Reputation among members of his family by blood, adoption, or marriage, or among his associates, or in the community, concerning a person's birth, adoption, marriage, divorce, death, legitimacy, relationship by blood, adoption, or marriage, ancestry, or other similar fact of his personal or family history.

(20) Reputation concerning boundaries or general history. Reputation in a community, arising before the controversy, as to boundaries of or customs affecting lands in the community, and reputation as to events of general history important to the community or state or nation in which located.

(21) Reputation as to character. Reputation of a person's character among his associates or in the community.

(22) Judgment of previous conviction. Evidence of a final judgment, entered after a trial or upon a plea of guilty (but not upon a plea of *nolo contendere*), adjudging a person guilty of a crime punishable by death or imprisonment in excess of one year, to prove any fact essential to sustain the judgment, but not including,when offered by the government in a criminal prosecution for purposes other than impeachment, judgments against persons other than the accused. The pendency of an appeal may be shown but does not affect admissibility.

(23) Judgment as to personal, family or general history, or boundaries. Judgments as proof of matters personal, family or general history, or boundaries, essential to the judgment, if the same would be provable by evidence of reputation.

(24) Other exceptions. A statement not specifically covered by any of the foregoing exceptions but having equivalent circumstantial

guarantees of trustworthiness, if the court determines that (A) the statement is offered as evidence of a material fact; (B) the statement is more probative on the point for which it is offered than any other evidence which the proponent can procure through reasonable efforts; and (C) the general purposes of these rules and the interests of justice will best be served by admission of the statement into evidence. However, a statement may not be admitted under this exception unless the proponent of it makes known to the adverse party sufficiently in advance of the trial or hearing to provide the adverse party with a fair opportunity to prepare to meet it, his intention to offer the statement and the particulars of it, including the name and address of the declarant.

Rule 804. Hearsay Exceptions: Declarant Unavailable

(a) Definition of unavailability. "Unavailability as a witness" includes situations in which the declarant:

(1) Is exempted by ruling of the court on the ground of privilege from testifying concerning the subject matter of his statement; or

(2) Persists in refusing to testify concerning the subject matter of his statement despite an order of the court to do so; or

(3) Testifies to a lack of memory of the subject matter of his statement; or

(4) Is unable to be present or to testify at the hearing because of death or then existing physical or mental illness or infirmity; or

(5) Is absent from the hearing and the proponent of his statement has been unable to procure his attendance (or in the case of a hearsay exception under subdivision (b)(2), (3), or (4), his attendance or testimony) by process or other reasonable means.

A declarant is not unavailable as a witness if his exemption, refusal, claim of lack of memory, inability, or absence is due to the procurement or wrongdoing of the proponent of his statement for the purpose of preventing the witness from attending or testifying.

(b)Hearsay exceptions. The following are not excluded by the hearsay rule if the declarant is unavailable as a witness:

(1) Former testimony. Testimony given as a witness at another hearing of the same or a different proceeding, or in a deposition taken in compliance with law in the course of the same or another proceeding, if the party against whom the testimony is now offered, or, in a civil action or proceeding, a predecessor in interest, had an opportunity and similar motive to develop the testimony by direct, cross, or redirect examination.

(2) Statement under belief of impending death. In a prosecution for homicide or in a civil action or proceeding, a statement made by a declarant while believing that his death was imminent, concerning the cause or circumstances of what he believed to be his impending death.

(3) Statement against interest. A statement which was at the time of its making so far contrary to the declarant's pecuniary or proprietary interest, or so far tended to subject him to civil or criminal liability, or to render invalid a claim by him against another, that a reasonable man in his position would not have made the statement unless he believed it to be true. A statement tending to expose the declarant to criminal liability and offered to exculpate the accused is not admissible unless corroborating circumstances clearly indicate the trustworthiness of the statement.

(4) Statement of personal or family history. (A) A statement concerning the declarant's own birth, adoption, marriage, divorce, legitimacy, relationship by blood, adoption, or marriage, ancestry, or other similar fact of personal or family history, even though declarant had no means of acquiring personal knowledge of the matter stated; or (B) a statement concerning the foregoing matters, and death also, of another person, if the declarant was related to the other by blood, adoption, or marriage or was so intimately associated with the other's family as to be likely to have accurate information concerning the matter declared.

(5) Other exceptions. A statement not specifically covered by any of the foregoing exceptions but having equivalent circumstantial guarantees of trustworthiness, if the court determines that (A) the statement is offered as evidence of a material fact; (B) the statement is more probative on the point for which it is offered than any other evidence which the proponent can procure through reasonable efforts; and (C) the general purposes of these rules and the interests of justice will best be served by admission of the statement into evidence. However, a statement may not be admitted under this exception unless the proponent of it makes known to the adverse party sufficiently in advance of the trial or hearing to provide the adverse party with a fair opportunity to prepare to meet it, his intention to offer the statement and the particulars of it, including the name and address of the declarant.

Rule 805. Hearsay within Hearsay

Hearsay included within hearsay is not excluded under the hearsay rule if each part of the combined statements conforms with an exception to the hearsay rule provided in these rules.

Rule 806. Attacking and Supporting Credibility of Declarant

When a hearsay statement, or a statement defined in Rule 801 (d)(2), (C), (D), or (E), has been admitted in evidence, the credibility of the declarant may be attacked, and if attacked may be supported, by any evidence which would be admissible for those purposes if declarant had testified as a witness. Evidence of a statement or conduct by the declarant at any time, inconsistent with his hearsay statement, is not subject to any requirement that he may have been afforded an opportunity to deny or explain. If the party against whom a hearsay statement has been admitted calls the declarant as a witness, the party is entitled to examine him on the statement as if under cross-examination.

Article IX. Authentication and Identification

Rule 901. Requirement of Authentication or Identification

(a) General provision. The requirement of authentication or identification as a condition precedent to admissibility is satisfied by evidence sufficient to support a finding that the matter in question is what its proponent claims.

(b) Illustrations. By way of illustration only, and not by way of limitation, the following are examples of authentication or identification conforming with the requirements of this rule:

(1) Testimony of witness with knowledge. Testimony that a matter is what it is claimed to be.

(2) Nonexpert opinion on handwriting. Nonexpert opinion as to the genuineness of handwriting, based upon familiarity not acquired for purposes of the litigation.

(3) Comparison by trier or expert witness. Comparison by the trier of fact or by expert witnesses with specimens which have been authenticated.

(4) Distinctive characteristics and the like. Appearance, contents, substance, internal patterns, or other distinctive characteristics, taken in conjunction with circumstances.

(5) Voice identification. Identification of a voice, whether heard firsthand or through mechanical or electronic transmission or recording, by opinion based upon hearing the voice at any time under circumstances connecting it with the alleged speaker.

(6) Telephone conversations. Telephone conversations, by evidence that a call was made to the number assigned at the time by the telephone

company to a particular person or business, if (A) in the case of a person, circumstances, including self-identification, show the person answering to be the one called, or (B) in the case of a business, the call was made to a place of business and the conversation related to business reasonably transacted over the telephone.

(7) Public records or reports. Evidence that a writing authorized by law to be recorded or filed and in fact recorded or filed in a public office, or a purported public record, report, statement, or data compilation, in any form, is from the public office where items of this nature are kept.

(8) Ancient documents or data compilations. Evidence that a document or data compilation, in any form, (A) is in such condition as to create no suspicion concerning its authenticity, (B) was in a place where it, if authentic, would likely be, and (C) has been in existence 20 years or more at the time it is offered.

(9) Process or system. Evidence describing a process or system used to produce a result and showing that the process or system produces an accurate result.

(10) Methods provided by statute or rule. Any method of authentication or identification provided by Act of Congress or by other rules prescribed by the Supreme Court pursuant to statutory authority.

Rule 902. Self-Authentication

Extrinsic evidence of authenticity as a condition precedent to admissibility is not required with respect to the following:

(1) Domestic public documents under seal. A document bearing a seal purporting to be that of the United States, or of any state, district, commonwealth, territory, or insular possession thereof, or the Panama Canal Zone, or the Trust Territory of the Pacific Islands, or of a political subdivision, department, officer, or agency thereof, and a signature purporting to be an attestation or execution.

(2) Domestic public documents not under seal. A document purporting to bear the signature in his official capacity of an officer or employee or any entity included in paragraph (1) hereof, having no seal, if a public officer having a seal and having official duties in the district or political subdivision of the officer or employee certifies under seal that the signer has the official capacity and that the signature is genuine.

(3) Foreign public documents. A document purporting to be executed or attested in his official capacity by a person authorized by the laws of a foreign country to make the execution or attestation, and

accompanied by a final certification as to the genuineness of the signature and official position (A) of the executing or attesting person, or (B) of any foreign official whose certificate of genuineness of signature and official position relates to the execution or attestation or is in a chain of certificates of genuiness of signature and official position relating to the execution or attestation. A final certification may be made by a secretary of embassy or legation, consul general, consul, vice consul, or consular agent of the United States, or a diplomatic or consular official of the foreign country assigned or accredited to the United States. If reasonable opportunity has been given to all parties to investigate the authenticity and accuracy of official documents, the court may, for good cause shown, order that they be treated as presumptively authentic without final certification or permit them to be evidenced by an attested summary with or without final certification.

(4) Certified copies of public records. A copy of an official record or report or entry therein, or of a document authorized by law to be recorded or filed and actually recorded or filed in a public office, including data compilations in any form, certified as correct by the custodian or other person authorized to make the certification, by certificate complying with paragraph (1), (2) or (3) of this Rule or complying with any Act of Congress or rule prescribed by the Supreme Court pursuant to statutory authority.

(5) Official publications. Books, pamphlets, or other publications purporting to be issued by public authority.

(6) Newspapers and periodicals. Printed materials purporting to be newspapers or periodicals.

(7) Trade inscriptions and the like. Inscriptions, signs, tags, or labels purporting to have been affixed in the course of business and indicating ownership, control, or origin.

(8) Acknowledged documents. Documents accompanied by a certificate of acknowledgment executed in the manner provided by law by a notary public or other officer authorized by law to take acknowledgments.

(9) Commercial paper and related documents. Commerical paper, signatures thereon, and documents relating thereto to the extent provided by general commercial law.

(10) Presumptions under acts of Congress. Any signature, document, or other matter declared by Act of Congress to be presumptively or prima facie genuine or authentic.

Rule 903. Subscribing Witness' Testimony Unnecessary

The testimony of a subscribing witness is not necessary to authenticate a writing unless required by the laws of the jurisdiction whose laws govern the validity of the writing.

Article X. Contents of Writings, Recordings, and Photographs

Rule 1001. Definitions

For purposes of this article the following definitions are applicable.

(1) Writings and recordings. "Writings" and "recordings" consist of letters, words, or numbers, or their equivalent, set down by handwriting, typewriting, printing, photostating, photographing, magnetic impulse, mechanical or electronic recording, or other form of data compilation.

(2) Photographs. "Photographs" include still photographs, X-ray films, and motion pictures.

(3) Original. An "original" of a writing or recording is the writing or recording itself or any counterpart intended to have the same effect by a person executing or issuing it. An "original" of a photograph includes the negative or any print therefrom. If data are stored in a computer or similar device, any printout or other output readable by sight, shown to reflect the data accurately, is an "original."

(4) Duplicate. A "duplicate" is a counterpart produced by the same impression as the original, or from the same matrix, or by means of photography, including enlargements and miniatures, or by mechanical or electronic re-recording, or by chemical reproduction, or by other equivalent techniques which accurately reproduce the original.

Rule 1002. Requirement of Original

To prove the content of a writing, recording, or photograph, the original writing, recording, or photograph is required, except as otherwise provided in these rules or by Act of Congress.

Rule 1003. Admissibility of Duplicates

A duplicate is admissible to the same extent as an original unless (1) a genuine question is raised as to the authenticity of the original or (2) in the circumstances it would be unfair to admit the duplicate in lieu of the original.

Rule 1004. Admissibility of Other Evidence of Contents

The original is not required, and other evidence of the contents of a writing, recording, or photograph is admissible if—

(1) Originals lost or destroyed. All originals are lost or have been destroyed, unless the proponent lost or destroyed them in bad faith; or

(2) Original not obtainable. No original can be obtained by any available judicial process or procedure; or

(3) Original in possession of opponent. At a time when an original was under the control of the party against whom offered, he was put on notice, by the pleadings or otherwise, that the contents would be a subject of proof at the hearing, and he does not produce the original at the hearing; or

(4) Collateral matters. The writing, recording, or photograph is not closely related to a controlling issue.

Rule 1005. Public Records

The contents of an official record, or of a document authorized to be recorded or filed and actually recorded or filed, including data compilations in any form, if otherwise admissible, may be proved by copy, certified as correct in accordance with Rule 902 or testified to be correct by a witness who has compared it with the original. If a copy which complies with the foregoing cannot be obtained by the exercise of reasonable diligence, then other evidence of the contents may be given.

Rule 1006. Summaries

The contents of voluminous writings, recordings, or photographs which cannot conveniently be examined in court may be presented in the form of a chart, summary, or calculation. The originals, or duplicates, shall be made available for examination or copying, or both, by other parties at reasonable time and place. The court may order that they be produced in court.

Rule 1007. Testimony or Written Admission of Party

Contents of writings, recordings, or photographs may be proved by the testimony or deposition of the party against whom offered or by his written admission, without accounting for the nonproduction of the original.

Rule 1008. Functions of Court and Jury

When the admissibility of other evidence of contents of writings, recordings, or photographs under these rules depends upon the fulfillment of a condition of fact, the question whether the condition has been fulfilled is ordinarily for the court to determine in accordance with the provisions of Rule 104. However, when an issue is raised (a) whether the asserted writing ever existed, or (b) whether another writing, recording, or photograph produced at the trial is the original, or (c) whether other evidence of contents correctly reflects the contents, the issue is for the trier of fact to determine as in the case of other issues of fact.

Article XI. Miscellaneous Rules

Rule 1101. Applicability of Rules

(a) Courts and magistrates. These rules apply to the United States district courts, the District Court of Guam, the District Court of the Virgin Islands, the District Court for the District of the Canal Zone, the United States courts of appeals, the Court of Claims, and to United States magistrates, in the actions, cases, and proceedings and to the extent hereinafter set forth. The terms "judge" and "court" in these rules include United States magistrates, referees in bankruptcy, and commissioners of the Court of Claims.

(b) Proceedings generally. These rules apply generally to civil actions and proceedings, including admiralty and maritime cases, to criminal cases and proceedings, to contempt proceedings except those in which the court may act summarily, and to proceedings and cases under the Bankruptcy Act.

(c) Rule of privilege. The rule with respect to privileges applies at all stages of all actions, cases, and proceedings.

(d) Rules inapplicable. The rules (other than with respect to privileges) do not apply in the following situations:

(1) Preliminary questions of fact. The determination of questions of fact preliminary to admissibility of evidence when the issue is to be determined by the court under Rule 104.

(2) Grand jury. Proceedings before grand juries.

(3) Miscellaneous proceedings. Proceedings for extradition or rendition; preliminary examinations in criminal cases; sentencing, or granting or revoking probation; issuance of warrants for arrest, criminal sum-

monses, and search warrants; and proceedings with respect to release on bail or otherwise.

(e) Rules applicable in part. In the following proceedings these rules apply to the extent that matters of evidence are not provided for in the statutes which govern procedure therein or in other rules prescribed by the Supreme Court pursuant to statutory authority; the trial of minor and petty offenses by United States magistrates; review of agency actions when the facts are subject to trial de novo under section 706(2)(F) of title 5, United States Code; review of orders of the Secretary of Agriculture under section 2 of the Act entitled "An Act to authorize association of producers of agricultural products" approved February 18, 1922 (7 U.S.C. 292), and under sections 6 and 7(c) of the Perishable Agricultural Commodities Act, 1930 (7 U.S.C. 499f, 499g(c)); naturalization and revocation of naturalization under sections 310–318 of the Immigration and Nationality Act (8 U.S.C. 1421–1429); prize proceedings in admiralty under sections 7651–7681 of title 10, United States Code; review of orders of the Secretary of the Interior under section 2 of the Act entitled "An Act authorizing associations of producers of aquatic products" approved June 25, 1931 (15 U.S.C. 522); review of orders of petroleum control boards under section 5 of the Act entitled "An Act to regulate interstate and foreign commerce in petroleum and its products by prohibiting the shipment in such commerce of petroleum and its products produced in violation of State law, and for other purposes," approved February 22, 1935 (15 U.S.C. 715d); actions for fines, penalties, or forfeitures under part V of title IV of the Tariff Act of 1930 (19 U.S.C. 1581–1624), or under the Anti-Smuggling Act (19 U.S.C. 1701–1711); criminal libel for condemnation, exclusion of imports, or other proceedings under the Federal Food, Drug, and Cosmetic Act (21 U.S.C. 301–392); disputes between seamen under sections 4079, 4080, and 4081 of the Revised Statutes (22 U.S.C. 256–258); habeas corpus under sections 2241–2254 of title 28, United States Code; motions to vacate, set aside or correct sentence under section 2255 of title 28, United States Code; actions for penalties for refusal to transport destitute seamen under section 4578 of the Revised Statutes (46 U.S.C. 679); actions against the United States under the Act entitled "An Act authorizing suits against the United States in admiralty for damage caused by and salvage service rendered to public vessels belonging to the United States, and for other purposes," approved March 3, 1925 (46 U.S.C. 781–790), as implemented by section 7730 of title 10, United States Code.

Rule 1102. Amendments

Amendments to the Federal Rules of Evidence may be made as provided in section 2076 of title 28 of the United States Code.

Rule 1103. Title

These rules may be known and cited as the Federal Rules of Evidence.

Effective date: July 1, 1975

Glossary

Abandoned property. Property that has been abandoned and belongs to no one. The voluntary relinquishment of possession, right, and claim to something, accompanied by an apparent intention of not reclaiming it.

Accessory. A person who has aided, abetted, or assisted the principal offender, or who has counseled and encouraged the perpetration of a crime.

Accessory after the fact. A person who has knowledge of the crime and assists the perpetrator in avoiding arrest or in an escape.

Accessory before the fact. A person who has aided or encouraged the offense before its commission, but who did not, either actually or constructively, physically participate in its commission.

Accomplice. A person who knowingly, voluntarily, and with the common intent with the principal offender unites in the commission of a crime. The cooperation must be real, not apparent; mere presence coupled with knowledge that a crime is about to be committed, without some contribution, does not raise the liability of an accomplice.

Acquittal. A verdict of not guilty. The certification by a court or jury of the innocence of a defendant during or after trial.

Adjudicate. To hear, try, and determine the claims of litigants before the court.

Admissibility. Determination of whether testimony, exhibits, or evidence will be allowed in trial.

Advocacy. The act of defending, assisting, or pleading for another; to defend by argument.

Advocate. One who renders legal advice and pleads the cause of another before a court or tribunal; one who speaks in favor of another. A lawyer.

Affidavit. A voluntary, sworn written statement.

Alibi. A plea by a suspect of having been elsewhere at the time of the commission of the crime.

Ancient document rule. A document is "ancient" if it is twenty or more years old, and the proof of its age suffices as authentication. An ancient document, if relevant to the inquiry and free from suspicion, can be admissible in evidence without the ordinary requirements of proof of execution.

Answer. Defendant's written response to a civil complaint, containing his admission or denial of each of the allegations in the complaint. *Cf.* Plea.

Arm's reach doctrine. Officers can only search without a warrant the arrestee and the area immediately around him where the arrestee can reach or jump over to. This curtailment of the scope of searches evident to a legal arrest was ruled by the Supreme Court in *Chimel* v. *California*, 395 U.S. 752 (1969).

Arrest. To take a person into custody for the purpose of answering to the court. To consummate an arrest an officer must have the authority to make an arrest and an intention to arrest the suspect. There must be some restraint of the suspect, either physical or mental, and the suspect must understand that he is arrested.

Authenticating witness. One who establishes that a writing or document is what it purports to be and that it was made by the party to whom it was attributed.

Authentication. A legal process of proof that is designed to establish the genuineness, not the truth, of the contents of a writing or document.

Bail. To procure the release of a defendant from legal custody by guaranteeing his future appearance in court and compelling him to remain within jurisdiction of the court. Cash or other security may be required.

Ballistics. The identification of the firing characteristics of a firearm or cartridge; the scientific examination of evidence found at crime scenes and connected with firearms; firearms, spent bullets, empty cartridge or shell cases, cartridges, and shells.

Bench. The presiding judge (and his position at the front of the courtroom).

Best evidence rule. The contents of any writing must be proven by the writing itself or the failure to do so must be adequately explained. In addition to documents in writing, the rule is also applicable to recordings, X rays, photographs, and films.

Bill of particulars. A written statement of the facts upon which a charge is brought, that is more specific than the complaint of information, and is produced on the demand of a defendant.

Burden of proof. The duty of establishing the truth of the issue at trial by such a quantum of evidence as the law requires.

Circumstantial evidence. Facts and circumstances concerning a transaction from which the jury may infer other connected facts that reasonably follow according to common human experience.

Citation. Reference to an authority for a point of law, as a case by title, volume, and page of the report or reports in which the opinion appears and the year it was decided.

Citizen's arrest. Citizens are authorized to make arrests in felonies or breach of the peace without a warrant, when the offense is committed in their presence.

Complaint. The pleading that initiates a criminal proceeding; sometimes called a criminal affidavit.

Consensual search. The party in possession of what is to be searched validly consents to a search by police. The suspect voluntarily, without coercion or deceit, relinquishes the right under the Fourth and Fourteenth Amendments to demand a search warrant.

Conspiracy. An agreement between two or more people to commit a criminal act, coupled with an overt act in furtherance.

Contraband. Things that are illegally possessed and that cannot be lawfully owned.

Corpus delicti. Body of crime.

Corroborating evidence. Evidence that supports and supplements previously offered evidence. It is directed at the same issue as the initial evidence, but it comes from a separate source and is designed to enhance the credibility of the prior testimony.

Criminal act. Any act or omission that is punishable as a crime.
Criminal intent. A guilty or evil state of mind to do an act prohibited as a crime by law.
Cross-examination. The interrogation of a witness by counsel for the opposing party by questions to test the truthfulness and accuracy of his testimony.
Curtilage. The area immediately surrounding a person's home and all attached structures that has the same constitutional protections as the home.
Declarant. A person who makes a statement.
Declarations against interest. Out-of-court statements by a person that are in conflict with his pecuniary interests.
Declarations against penal interest. Out-of-court statements by a person that are in conflict with his innocence.
Demonstrative evidence. A model, an illustration, a chart, or an experiment offered as proof; real evidence.
Deposition. The testimony of a witness, compelled by subpoena, at a proceeding where counsel, but not the judge, attend. It is a pretrial discovery device.
Detention. A stop of a suspect by an officer; a temporary curtailment of personal freedoms. An officer may detain a suspicious individual to ask him questions about his conduct.
Direct evidence. Evidence that comes from any of the witness's five senses and is in itself proof or disproof of a fact in issue.
Discovery. The compelled disclosure of facts, statements, or the production of documents, through subpoena duces tecum, interrogatories, or deposition, prior to trial.
Documentary evidence. Tangible objects that can express a fact or that tend to clarify the truth or untruth of the issues in question. Broad category includes private writings, documents, official records, newspapers, maps, or any other objects on which symbols have been placed with the intention of preserving a record of events or impressions.
Double jeopardy. Being tried more than once for the same crime.
Duress. An affirmative defense by a suspect that he was forced or coerced to commit a crime.
Dying declaration. A statement made by a homicide victim about to die without any hope of recovery concerning the facts and circumstances under which the fatal injury was inflicted. This declaration

is offered in evidence at the trial of the person charged with having caused the speaker's death.

Entrapment. The procurement of a person to commit a crime that he did not contemplate or would not have committed, for the sole purpose of prosecuting that person.

Evidence. Anything offered in court to prove the truth or falsity of a fact in issue.

Exclusionary rule. A rule of evidence that suppresses and rejects otherwise admissible evidence because it was obtained in violation of the Fourth or Fifth Amendment; applies to direct and derivative evidence, seized as a result of an illegal arrest or search.

Exemplar. A sample of handwriting; a specimen; a model.

Exigent circumstances. An emergency situation. If a true emergency exists, or is reasonably believed to exist, police officers may enter the premises without a warrant. In most jurisdictions anything seen inside in plain view may be seized without a warrant.

Expert witness. A person who must appear to the trial judge to have such knowledge, skill, or experience within the particular subject of inquiry that his opinion will be of some aid to the trier of fact in arriving at the true facts.

Facts. Findings as to what particular occurrences did or did not take place, which must be proved by evidence.

Forensic. Pertaining to or belonging to the courts of justice.

Forensic science. The use of scientific knowledge to investigate and solve crimes.

Foundation. The preliminary basis required for the admission of certain evidence.

Fresh pursuit. See Hot pursuit doctrine.

Frisk. A limited form of searching; a pat-down of a person's outer clothing for a weapon.

Fruit of the crime. An object directly obtained by criminal means.

Fruit of the Poisoned Tree doctrine. The application of the exclusionary rule to evidence *derived* from an illegal search.

Grand jury. An accusatory body that inquires into felonies committed within a particular district.

Guilty. A defendant's plea in a criminal prosecution; admission of having committed the crime with which he is charged.

Habeas corpus. A writ seeking to bring a person already in custody before a court or judge to challenge the lawfulness of the imprisonment.

Hearsay. An out-of-court statement offered to prove the truth of the matter contained in the statement. It is only hearsay if it is offered to prove that the statement itself is true.

Hot pursuit doctrine. An officer who chases a fugitive, or is in fresh pursuit, does not need a search warrant to continue his chase into homes or offices, and anything found in the course of the pursuit and incident to it is an admissible item.

Impeachment. The act of discrediting a person or a thing. Questioning the credibility of a witness.

In camera. In judicial chambers. A hearing in which all but counsel are excluded from the courtroom.

Indictment. A written accusation, provided by a grand jury, charging a person with the commission of a crime.

Information. An affidavit, filed by the prosecutor, that initiates a criminal proceeding.

Informer's privilege. Right of the police *not* to disclose the identity of informants to protect them from retaliation and to maintain a confidential source of information about crime.

Inquest. An examination into the cause and circumstances of a violent or suspicious death.

Instructions to jury. A final charge given to the jury by the trial judge. An explanation of the law of the case being tried to furnish guidance to the jury in their deliberations.

Instrumentality. A thing used to facilitate a crime such as a tool or weapon.

Intent. The mental purpose to do a specific thing.

Interrogation. Any questioning likely or expected to yield incriminating statements.

Inventory. A check of the contents of an impounded vehicle by officers pursuant to departmental regulations or standing custom. It is conducted for the pupose of safeguarding any valuables found in the vehicle, and it protects the officers' liability from mysterious disappearance of the valuables.

Judicial notice. The recognition by the court that a given fact is true without requiring formal proof. The fact must be one that is certain and indisputable, or the fact must be one of common everyday knowledge in that jurisdiction, which everyone of average intelligence and knowledge can be presumed to know.

Juvenile. A child up to the age of eighteen who is tried in a special court on the issues of neglect and delinquency.

Latent (fingerprint). Present but not visible. A latent fingerprint must be searched for and developed by evidence technicians with special skill and equipment and preserved as evidence.

Lay witness. A nonexpert person who must be able to base his testimony upon his ability to observe, recollect, and explain to others. He may testify only to facts that he has acquired through his own senses.

Leading question. A question that suggests the desired answer to the witness.

Mens rea. An evil intent; criminal state of mind.

Modus operandi (MO). Method of operation; the characteristics of a particular criminal conduct or technique.

Motion. An application made to a court or judge to obtain an order.

Motion to suppress. A motion made by the defendant prior to the actual start of his trial to exclude evidence under the theory that it has been "tainted" by being seized or obtained in violation of the Fourth or Fifth Amendment.

Motive. The moving power, the reason for doing something.

Nolle prosequi. A formal entry on the record by the prosecutor that he will no longer prosecute the case.

Nolo contendere. A plea of "no contest," having the same effect as a plea of guilty.

Objection. A protest against a determination by the court, especially a ruling upon the admissibility of evidence.

Open field doctrine. Officers may enter private outdoor property to look for evidence without a warrant or other justification, and anything seen in the course of their expedition falls within the plain view rule.

Peace officer. A public officer such as a policeman, sheriff, deputy sheriff, marshal, constable, or state investigator; a "sworn" officer.

Per se. By or through itself.

Physical evidence. Items, things, and traces found at a crime scene; suspects or other persons or places concerned with a criminal investigation.

Plain view rule. Readily observable things seen by an officer (in a place where he has a right to be) that are not the product of a search and are not subject to exclusion from evidence.

Plea. In criminal cases, the official answer to the charge brought against him. The usual pleas are guilty, not guilty, and nolo contendere.

Plea bargaining. The process whereby a defendant and the state bargain a plea of guilty for a reduced sentence. The "agreement" is supervised by the court prior to approval.

Preliminary hearing. A judicial examination of witnesses to determine whether or not a crime has been committed and if the evidence presented against the accused is sufficient to warrant bail or commitment pending trial.

Presumption. The drawing of a particular inference of one fact from the existence of a related known or proven fact.

Prima facie. First view. Evidence in a criminal case that on its surface is sufficient to prove the charge.

Privileged communication. A communication between persons in a confidential relationship, such as husband and wife, attorney and client, confessor and penitent, or doctor and patient. Under public policy, the court will not allow such information to be disclosed or inquired into.

Probable cause. A conclusion of law that an offense probably was committed and the suspect probably is guilty thereof.

Public place. A place exposed to the public where people gather together and pass to and fro and where whatever occurs would be seen by a number of persons.

Punitive damages. Damages awarded by a jury to "teach and punish" the civil defendant. In most jurisdictions, neither cities nor insurance companies will indemnify an officer for punitive damages, and they cannot be discharged through the bankruptcy courts.

Real evidence. Tangible objects presented in the courtroom for the trier of fact to view. Something directly connected with the incident out of which the cause of action arose.

Relevancy. Relevant evidence is that evidence which "advances the inquiry"; that is, it proves something.

Res gestae. Exclamations and statements made by the participants, victims, or spectators of a crime immediately before, during, or after the commission of the crime, where such statements were made as a reaction to or inspired by the occasion and where there was no opportunity for the declarant to deliberate or fabricate a false statement.

Return (search warrant). A statement in writing of police action taken while executing a search warrant, including a description of the place searched and an inventory of property seized.

Rules of evidence. The laws that determine what evidence may be used to prove facts. These laws are not concerned with what the outcome will be once the facts are finally decided (as most laws are), but instead are only concerned with the admissibility of various evidence that is offered to prove facts.

Rules of law. Once the facts are determined from evidence presented, certain rules are then applied to those facts that determine the outcome of the case.

Search. The seeking of something not in plain sight in places where the object (or person) sought might be concealed.

Search warrant. A legal process, issued by a judge upon a supporting affidavit, that authorizes a peace officer to search a person or place for evidence of an offense, contraband, instrumentalities, and fruits of crime.

Secondary evidence. See Circumstantial evidence.

Stare decisis. To abide by or adhere to decided cases. Policy of courts to stand by precedent and not to disturb a settled point.

Statement. Oral, written, or even nonverbal conduct that conveys a message.

Stipulation. The admittance of proof by agreement of the opposing attorneys.

Stop and frisk. The right of a police officer to detain suspicious individuals temporarily and to frisk (pat-down search) those who appear dangerous. Upheld by the landmark case *Terry* v. *Ohio,* 392 U.S. 1 (1968).

Subpoena. A process to cause a witness to appear and give testimony, commanding him to lay aside all pretenses and excuses, and appear before a court or magistrate therein named at a time therein mentioned to testify.

Subpoena duces tecum. A process by which the court, at the request of a party, commands a witness who has in his possession or control some document or paper that is pertinent to the issues of a pending controversy to produce it at the trial.

Suppression hearing. A formal motion by a defendant's lawyer to suppress and reject either tangible or intangible evidence that was allegedly illegally obtained.

Testimony. Spoken evidence given by a competent witness under oath or affirmation, as distinguished from evidence derived from writings and other sources.

Tort. A civil wrong committed to the person or property of another and resulting in some damage or injury.

Venue. A neighborhood, place, or county in which an injury is declared to have been done or fact declared to have happened. Also, the county (or geographical division) in which an action or prosecution is brought for trial and which is to furnish the panel of jurors. In a criminal case the defendant has a constitutional right, which he can waive, to be tried in the district in which the crime was committed.

Verbal act. An action by words. A statement that shows the motive, character, and object of an act.

Vital statistics. Data relating primarily to health, such as the registration of births, marriages, and deaths, which have been compiled under public authority.

Voir dire. The examination of prospective jurors or witnesses before the trial begins to determine if they have the necessary qualifications to be fair and impartial.

Voluntary statement. A statement that is free of duress and coercion but is usually elicited by questioning.

Volunteered statement. An utterance made without elicitation, frequently a spontaneous statement.

Weight of evidence. The believability of evidence. Evidence may be technically legal and, thus, admissible in court, but the question remains as to whether or not it should be given any value or weight.

Witness. One who, being present, personally sees or perceives a thing; a beholder, spectator, or eyewitness.

Index

Chapter Exercises

Chapter 1

INTRODUCTION TO EVIDENCE

Instructor ____________________ **Student** ______________________

Completion Questions

1. The burden of proving duress rests on the ______.
2. A written agreement by attorneys regarding evidence in a trial is known as a _________.
3. Entrapment is an _________ defense.
4. The literal meaning of prima facie is ________.
5. The Federal Rules of Evidence are found in Public Law number _____.
6. The spoken words of a witness in court is called ________.
7. A 1965 Supreme Court case barring references to the accused's silence during a trial is ________________.
8. Adherence to legal precedence is called __________.
9. There are two general classes of evidence, _____________________.
10. Under common law, children under ____ years of age were presumed to be incapable of committing a crime.

Multiple-Choice Questions

11. Anything offered in court to prove a case is called
    a. prosecution evidence.
    b. direct proof.
    c. admissible evidence.
    d. none of the above.
12. Printed court reports are available to
    a. judges only.
    b. anyone.
    c. attorneys only.

13. Corpus delicti was involved in the following case:
    a. *Reynolds* v. *U.S.*
    b. *Leland* v. *Oregon.*
    c. *People* v. *Laietta.*
    d. none of the above.
14. An affirmative defense is
    a. judicial notice.
    b. res gestae.
    c. consent of the victim.
    d. appellate consent.

Chapter 2

ADMISSIBILITY OF EVIDENCE

Instructor ______________________ **Student** ______________________

Completion Questions

1. Courts generally will not take judicial notice of ______ laws.
2. Evidence of one's reputation in the community is called _______ _______.
3. An accused need not testify because of the ____ Amendment to the Constitution.
4. Indirect proof of a fact is called ____________ evidence.
5. The five exceptions allowing prosecution evidence of other crimes committed by the accused as direct proof of the offense in question are: ____.
6. If the defense offers evidence of good character, the state in rebuttal may offer evidence of ___ character.
7. The official acts of government officials are presumed to be ___.
8. There is a legal presumption ______ suicide.
9. The reason for committing a crime is called ______.
10. Any properly addressed letter that was mailed is presumed to have been ________.

Multiple-Choice Questions

11. Identity may be proven by
    a. other crimes.
    b. material evidence.
    c. relevant evidence.
    d. all of the above.

12. Examples of official presumptions are
    a. possession of fruits of crime.
    b. legitimacy.
    c. sanity.
    d. all of the above.
    e. none of the above.
13. A presumption indicating guilt is
    a. defendant's failure to testify.
    b. lack of corpus delicti.
    c. possession of fruits of crime.
14. Statutory presumptions are
    a. unknown.
    b. always rebuttable.
    c. part of the common law.
    d. none of the above.
15. Judicial notice can be taken of
    a. treaties.
    b. universal known facts.
    c. scientific phenomena.
    d. all of the above.

Chapter 3

DETENTION AND ARREST IN GENERAL

Instructor ____________________ **Student** ____________________

Underline the Correct Answer

1. A case involving the right of police to enter a private home to make an arrest is (*People* v. *Leib, Riddick* v. *New York*).
2. Police who have (suspicion, reasonable suspicion) may make a valid stop.
3. The (Fifth, Fourth) Amendment of the United States Constitution requires that all warrants be based on probable cause.
4. The right to stop (does, does not) give a right to frisk.
5. The landmark federal case on stop and frisk was (*Miranda* v. *Arizona, Terry* v. *Ohio*).
6. Police may not use deadly force to arrest a fleeing suspect if the offense was a (misdemeanor, federal crime).
7. Police have a wider latitude to search in a case of (arrest, stop and frisk).
8. In determining probable cause for an arrest, the police can use (inadmissible, only admissible) evidence.
9. Entrapment is a recognized legal defense (in federal cases only, in most jurisdictions).

Completion Questions

10. In order to frisk a stopped suspect, the officer must ________________ that the suspect is armed.
11. The two types of damages recoverable in false arrest suits are ________________________.
12. The four parts to an arrest are ____________________________ __________.

13. A widely adopted statute allowing officers to pursue fleeing suspects across state lines is known as the ______________________.
14. A federal case involving search of parolees was ________________.
15. *People* v. *Molineaux* involved the use of evidence of __________ in a criminal case.

Chapter 4

SEARCH AND SEIZURE GENERALLY

Instructor ____________________ **Student** ______________________

Completion Questions

1. The immediate area surrounding a home and structures is called _______.
2. A landmark California case on shocking searches is ________ ________.
3. Probable cause is never required for official ____________.
4. If there is a valid consent to a search, no _______ is required.
5. Two exceptional situations making a search warrant unnecessary are ____ ______________________________.

Underline the Correct Answer

6. The courts (agree, are split) on the wife's right to allow a police search of the home.
7. *Delaware* v. *Prouse* involved search of (homes, automobiles).
8. *Chimel* v. *California* involved searches of (abandoned property, the arm's reach area near an arrestee).
9. The use of spotlights (does, does not) make a police observation illegal.
10. The case of *Rakas* v. *Illinois* (did, did not) involve the necessity of having "standing" to move to suppress evidence.

Multiple-Choice Questions

11. Police standing across the street looked through an open window and saw illegal drugs inside a private home. The observation
    a. was an illegal interference into curtilage.
    b. was illegal since it was warrantless.
    c. all of the above.
    d. none of the above.

12. Landlords can consent to search of a tenant's property
    a. when the tenant is behind in his rent.
    b. whenever the tenant is absent.
    c. when requested by an authorized police officer.
    d. all of the above.
    e. none of the above.
13. *Jones* v. *U.S.* was overruled by
    a. *Miranda* v. *Arizona.*
    b. *Rakas* v. *Illinois, Rawlings* v. *Kentucky, U.S.* v. *Salvucci.*
    c. *Chimel* v. *California.*
14. *Carroll* v. *U.S.* involved
    a. border searches.
    b. automobile searches.
    c. curtilage.
15. Abandoned property
    a. can be held as evidence only if it is contraband.
    b. can be held as evidence only if directly connected to crime.
    c. is always open to police as evidence.

Chapter 5

ARREST AND SEARCH WARRANTS

Instructor ____________________ **Student** ____________________

Completion Questions

1. Title III of the Omnibus Crime and Safe Streets Act of 1968 regulates the issuance of __________ warrants.
2. A leading case involving disclosures by an informant is __________.
3. Both search and arrest warrants must be based on __________.
4. Use of a pen register was approved by the Supreme Court decision of __________.
5. Particular descriptions of the place to be searched and the objects sought is required by the ______ Amendment.

Underline the Correct Answer

6. It (is, is not) important that the affidavit for a search warrant list the parts of the building to be searched.
7. Common hallways in multiunit dwellings (may, may not) be searched without a warrant.
8. A name (is, is not) sufficient description for an arrest warrant.
9. The standards for a warrantless arrest (are, are not) the same as for an issuance of an arrest warrant.
10. An anonymous informer (can, cannot) be the legal basis for the issuance of a warrant.

Multiple-Choice Questions

11. Search warrants
    a. are wholly statutory.
    b. are always required for a legal search.
    c. can be secured for any offence.
    d. can be issued only by a police officer.
12. Informants can be classed as
    a. police.
    b. confidential.
    c. good citizen.
    d. named.
    e. all of the above.
13. Deceptive police practices are
    a. acceptable for surveillance.
    b. invalid if used to supply motive.
    c. invalid if used to supply criminal opportunity.
14. *Payton* v. *New York* involved
    a. the Fourth Amendment.
    b. routine felony arrest.
    c. warrentless entry into a suspect's home.
    d. all of the above.
15. Fluorescein powder may be used
    a. only by court order.
    b. only after a warrant is issued.
    c. without court approval.

Chapter 6

INTERROGATIONS, CONFESSIONS, AND NONTESTIMONIAL EVIDENCE

Instructor ____________________ **Student** ____________________

Underline the Correct Answer

1. Before (1974, 1964) the only legality test for confessions was voluntariness.
2. Courts (agree, disagree) on the amount of force that may be used to take a blood sample.
3. *Miranda* v. *Arizona* (did, did not) require warnings to a suspect in custody before any interrogation.
4. Seminal stains from a suspect's clothing can be taken by (force, only by court order).
5. If the detention is illegal, a confession (may, may not) be suppressed if the proper legal warnings were given.

Completion Questions

6. The cases of *Wade, Gilbert* and *Stovall* all involved the use of police ______.
7. Blood tests and fingernail scrapings are classed as ____________ evidence.
8. A suspect ___ a constitutional right to refuse to appear in a lineup.
9. The "focus test" involved in police questioning was applied in the leading federal case of ________________.
10. Suppression of a confession following an illegal temporary detention came from the 1979 New York case of ___________________.

Chapter 7

DISCOVERY

Instructor ____________________ **Student** ____________________

True-False Questions
(Write "true" or "false" in the space provided.)

____ 1. Work product of prosecuting attorneys is subject to discovery.

____ 2. Pretrial criminal discovery was not accepted under criminal law.

____ 3. The only remedy for refusal to allow court-ordered pretrial discovery is contempt of court.

____ 4. Discovery and depositions are not the same.

____ 5. Courts will seldom give the defendant pretrial discovery of laboratory reports if they were made by police laboratories.

____ 6. Fingerprinting of any felony defendant can be constitutionally required by court order.

____ 7. Tape recordings are not made available to the defense; only the written transcript is available before trial.

____ 8. Grand jury secrecy is frowned on as being unconstitutional.

____ 9. Pretrial criminal discovery is a constitutional right.

____ 10. *Jencks* v. *U.S.* is a leading case in broadening pretrial criminal discovery.

Chapter 8

PRIVILEGED COMMUNICATIONS

Instructor ____________________ **Student** ______________________

Completion Questions

1. The federal rule is that only the ________ spouse can waive the marital privilege.
2. The legal privilege can be waived only by the _____.
3. Hospital records in general are part of the _______ privilege.
4. The divinity privilege was ________ in the common law.

Underline the Correct Answer

5. The marital privilege was (a part of, unknown to) the common law.
6. The rule of privileged communications is based in (trial strategy, public policy).
7. In general, marital privilege (does, does not) apply to communications made before the marriage.
8. In a spouse abuse case, the injured spouse (may, may not) testify against the other.
9. Only the (patient, doctor) can waive the medical privilege.
10. (Any information, only confidential information) the client gives his lawyer for consultation purposes is protected by the legal privilege.

Multiple-Choice Questions

11. The privileged communication rule applies to
    - a. accountants.
    - b. nuns.
    - c. court-appointed medical examination.
    - d. none of the above.

12. The divinity privilege
    a. applies when the penitent has died.
    b. does not protect observations the clergyman has made.
    c. does not cover every communication with a priest.
    d. only two of the above.
    e. all of the above.
13. Executive privilege
    a. was claimed by President Nixon.
    b. is in various degrees.
    c. can prevent discovery.
    d. all of the above.
14. The duty to preserve the identity of police informants was decided in the case of
    a. *Mulberry* v. *State.*
    b. *McRay* v. *U.S.*
    c. *Knight* v. *Arizona.*
15. The medical privilege applies to
    a. psychiatrists.
    b. a doctor retained to observe the patient only.
    c. criminal cases in every state.

Chapter 9

QUESTIONS, ANSWERS, IMPEACHMENT AND CROSS-EXAMINATION OF WITNESSES

Instructor ____________________ **Student** ____________________

True-False Questions
(Write "true" or "false" in the space provided.)

____ 1. Testimony may be given by physical exhibits or questions and answers.
____ 2. *Parol* evidence is "word of mouth" proof.
____ 3. The relationship of a witness to the accused will not bar his testimony.
____ 4. An insane witness cannot testify.
____ 5. If opposing counsel does not object, any evidence may be used.
____ 6. Evidence showing bias of a witness will seldom be allowed in evidence over objection.
____ 7. The Federal Rules of Evidence restrict the use of criminal records to impeach a witness.
____ 8. There are statutes in some jurisdictions that forbid cross-examination of rape victims about past personal moral history.
____ 9. Expert opinion evidence is binding on the jury.
____ 10. A witness whose religion will not allow him to take an oath cannot testify.

Multiple-Choice Questions

12. Children under seven cannot testify in a criminal case
    a. because under common law they are incapable of committing a crime.
    b. unless the jury is satisfied that they understand the oath.
    c. unless the trial judge allows it.
13. A subpoena duces tecum can force the production of incriminating papers from
    a. a misdemeanor defendant.
    b. a noninvolved third party.
    c. a witness.
14. Self-serving declarations of the accused
    a. can never be offered by the defendant.
    b. are freely admitted as defense evidence.
    c. have been allowed by some courts.
15. Witnesses can be impeached by
    a. unsworn prior inconsistent statements.
    b. poor reputation for veracity.
    c. evidence of personal interest in the case.
    d. two of the above.
    e. all of the above.

Chapter 10

OPINION EVIDENCE

Instructor ____________________ **Student** ____________________

Underline the Correct Answer

1. The opinion of expert witnesses is often obtained by (leading, hypothetical) questions.
2. Character evidence is first introduced in a trial by the (defendant, prosecutor).
3. The skilled witness is a (lay, expert) witness.
4. *People* v. *Clay* was a California case involving (modus operandi, character evidence).
5. (Hypothetical, direct) questions cannot be used with a lay witness.

6. A lay witness (can, cannot) give his personal opinion as to insanity of another person.
7. An expert (can, cannot) give the jury his opinion as to the guilt or innocence of the defendant.
8. The (jury, court) must be satisfied that the expert witness is qualified before he can testify.
9. A lay witness can base his opinion only on (personal observations, scientific facts).
10. A lay witness (can, cannot) testify as to speed by making an estimate.

Multiple-Choice Questions

11. Scientific books
    - a. can never themselves be used as evidence.
    - b. can only be used on direct examination.
    - c. can often be used to cross-examine lay witnesses.
    - d. two of the above.
    - e. none of the above.

12. Opinion evidence on speed can be
    a. given by lay witnesses.
    b. given by expert witnesses.
    c. given by skilled witnesses.
    d. all of the above.
    e. none of the above.
13. In the field of scientific evidence
    a. polygraph evidence is seldom allowed.
    b. polygraph evidence is generally admissible.
    c. voiceprint evidence is never admissible.
    d. none of the above.
14. A case involved in skilled-witness evidence was
    a. *People* v. *Cole.*
    b. *Norton* v. *California.*
    c. *Byrd* v. *State.*
    d. none of the above.
15. Laypeople are considered capable of testifying about
    a. x-rays.
    b. cause of death.
    c. fingerprints.
    d. two of the above.
    e. none of the above

Chapter 11

HEARSAY EVIDENCE

Instructor ______________________ **Student** ______________________

True-False Questions
(Write "true" or "false" in the space provided.)

____ 1. Hearsay is any out of court statement offered by a witness.

____ 2. *California* v. *Green* involved the use of an earlier statement made by a witness.

____ 3. *Chambers* v. *Mississippi* involved the use of a declaration against interest.

____ 4. A written statement can never be classed as hearsay.

____ 5. A spontaneous statement given under stress of the event may be admissible as an exception to the hearsay rule.

____ 6. Only business records involving finances can be admitted as an exception to the hearsay rule.

____ 7. The excited utterance of a spectator cannot be admitted as a hearsay exception because it was not said by a party to the crime.

____ 8. A confession of one conspirator is admissible against the other because both were involved in the crime.

____ 9. *U.S.* v. *Dovico* and *Commonwealth* v. *Colon* both involved a declaration against penal interest.

____ 10. The complaint of a sex victim may in some cases be admitted as an exception to the hearsay rule.

Multiple-Choice Questions

11. A case illustrating dying declarations was
    a. *Corgell* v. *Reed.*
    b. *Salvatore* v. *State.*
    c. *Mix* v. *Florida.*
    d. none of the above.
12. Past recollection recorded is a
    a. federal rule only.
    b. phrase related to stare decisis.
    c. hearsay exception.
13. A sex victim's complaint is a valid hearsay exception if it is
    a. voluntary.
    b. an actual complaint.
    c. given at the first opportunity.
    d. all of the above.
14. Declarations against interest were involved in
    a. *U.S.* v. *Register.*
    b. *U.S.* v. *Seyfried.*
    c. *Chambers* v. *Mississippi.*
    d. all of the above.
15. Hearsay is
    a. an out-of-court statement.
    b. made only in the defendant's presence.
    c. offered to prove its truth.
    d. two of the above.

Chapter 12

DOCUMENTARY EVIDENCE, PHOTOGRAPHS, DEMONSTRATIONS, AND THE BEST EVIDENCE RULE

Instructor ____________________ **Student** ____________________

True-False Questions
(Write "true" or "false" in the space provided.)

___ 1. In order to have secondary evidence of a writing admitted, the party must go through a four-part proof.

___ 2. The judge must admit into evidence any model that is accurate.

___ 3. Market quotations from financial publications may be admitted in evidence.

___ 4. An oral business record is admissible in evidence as an exception to the hearsay rule.

___ 5. *State* v. *Larocca* involved the use of church records.

___ 6. Opposing counsel must authenticate a written record before it can be admitted in evidence.

___ 7. In complex cases, the court may allow the use of a summary of documents.

___ 8. The best evidence rule does not apply to public officials or public agencies.

___ 9. Colored photographs of body wounds are inadmissible in evidence.

___ 10. Demonstrative evidence use is always within the discretion of the judge.

Multiple-Choice Questions

11. Life insurance mortality tables
    - a. must always be authenticated.
    - b. are accepted without authentication.
    - c. are admissible when notarized.
12. A case involving use of a newspaper article was
    - a. *State* v. *Simon.*
    - b. *State* v. *Newsweek.*
    - c. *People* v. *Larson.*
    - d. none of the above.
13. A learned treatise may be used in evidence
    - a. under the Federal Rules of Evidence.
    - b. under the rule of caveat secundis.
    - c. as an affirmative defense.
14. In order to use secondary evidence a party must
    - a. invoke the rule of documentum secondum.
    - b. prove the existence of moribundum documentium.
    - c. exhibit the original to the judge.
    - d. two of the above.
    - e. none of the above.
15. Death certificates are
    - a. conclusive evidence.
    - b. nonrebuttable.
    - c. admitted as proof of the facts therein.
    - d. two of the above.

Chapter 13

PHYSICAL AND SCIENTIFIC EVIDENCE: PRESERVATION AND CUSTODY

Instructor ____________________ **Student** ____________________

Completion Questions

1. Comparative micrography is microscopic examination in which a hard object is applied against a ________.
2. *Barnum* v. *U.S.* involved __________ evidence.
3. Analysis of minute particles of evidence is called __________.
4. Anything used to commit a crime is ______ evidence.
5. A new type of scientific evidence will not be admitted in court until it has ______________ acceptance.
6. Analysis of bodily fluids is known as ______.
7. Marijuana is correctly classified scientifically as a __________.
8. A leading case involving neutron activation analysis is __________.
9. *Ballard* v. *Supreme Court* involved the admission of ________ evidence.
10. ________________ was a federal case involving the destruction of a videotaped conversation.

Multiple-Choice Questions

11. Voiceprint evidence was involved in
    a. *State* v. *Dorsey.*
    b. *People* v. *Rodes.*
    c. *Fladung* v. *State.*
    d. none of the above.

12. The nalline test for narcotics was involved in
    a. *People* v. *Williams.*
    b. *Davis* v. *Mississippi.*
    c. none of the above.
13. The HLA test involves
    a. fingerprints.
    b. ballistics.
    c. blood.
    d. narcotics.
14. Amphetamines are
    a. stimulants.
    b. narcotics.
    c. hallucinogens.
15. The use of hypnosis evidence was involved in
    a. *State* v. *Thompson.*
    b. *People* v. *Townsend.*
    c. *Townsend* v. *Gain.*
    d. *State* v. *Mack.*

Chapter 14

SPECIAL PROBLEMS OF PROOF

Instructor ____________________ **Student** ____________________

Multiple-Choice Questions

1. Conspirators are
   a. only those knowing all details of the plan.
   b. only those involved from the beginning of the plan.
   c. only those who are equal partners.
   d. none of the above.
2. Corroborating evidence is
   a. prior consistent identification evidence.
   b. always necessary.
   c. never required to support a confession.
3. Any two persons acting together for a criminal purpose are always
   a. conspirators.
   b. both guilty of a criminal act.
   c. none of the above.
4. An accomplice's confession
   a. may be used against a codefendant.
   b. may not be used against a codefendant.
   c. is subject to the rule of lex urbana.
5. Felonies
   a. must be prosecuted by indictment.
   b. do not need to be presented to grand juries in some states.
   c. are never considered by federal grand juries.
6. The use of a defendant's suppression hearing testimony at his later trial was involved in
   a. *Simmons* v. *U.S.*
   b. *Miranda* v. *Arizona.*
   c. *U.S.* v. *Calnitra.*

7. An accessory is
    a. the same as an accomplice.
    b. not the same as an accomplice.
    c. one who assists before or after the criminal act.
    d. two of the above.
8. A grand jury
    a. must base its finding on legal proof.
    b. was unknown in England.
    c. is composed of more than twelve members.
    d. all of the above.
9. Suppression hearings are
    a. pretrial hearings.
    b. often used to contest searches.
    c. often used to contest warrantless entries into premises.
    d. all of the above.
10. Evidence in conspiracy trials
    a. often is given a wider latitude.
    b. includes hearsay in some jurisdictions.
    c. may include the records of one conspirator being used as evidence against the others.
    d. two of the above.
    e. all of the above.